Cecilia Vicuña
Brain Forest Quipu

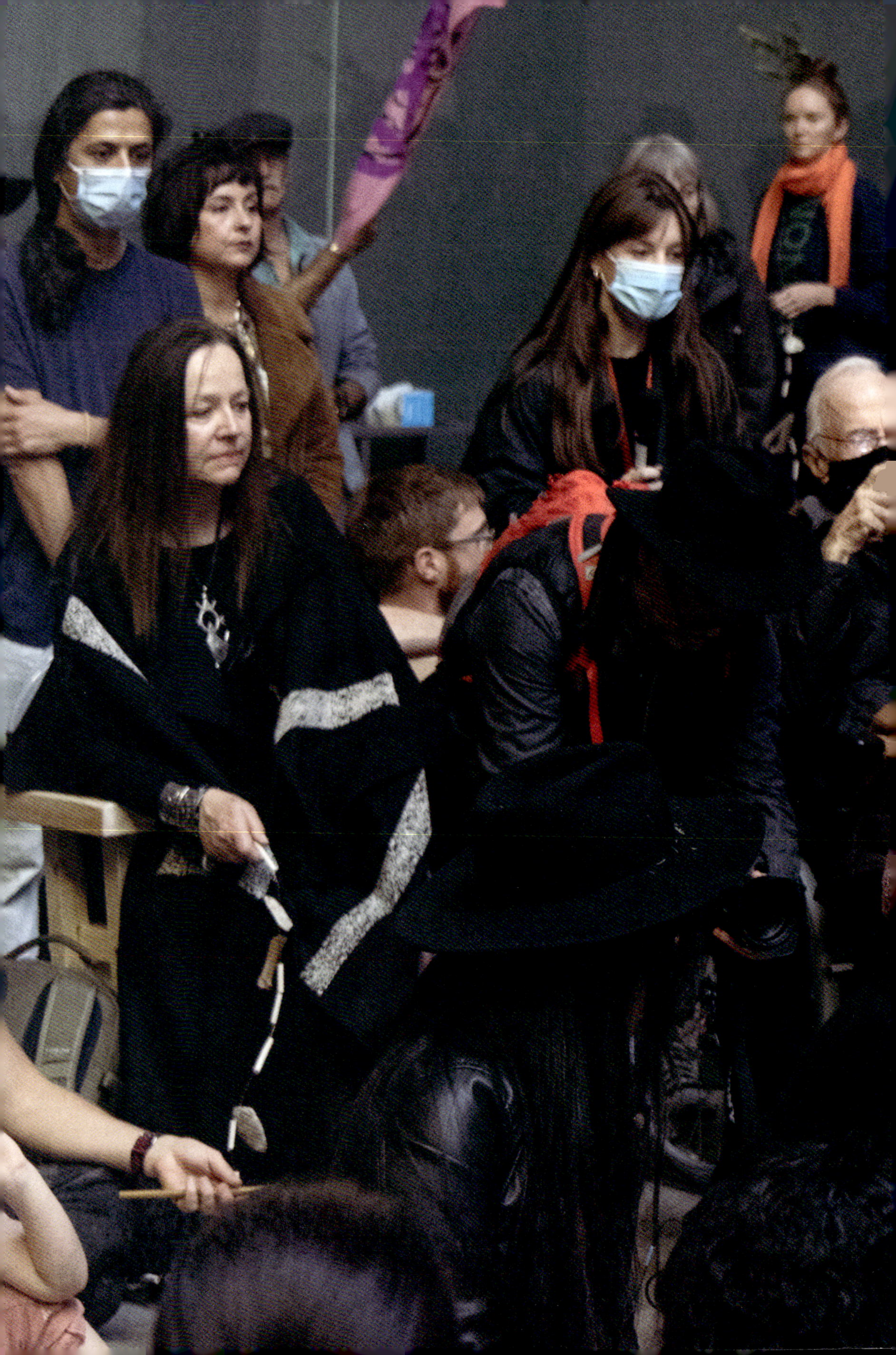

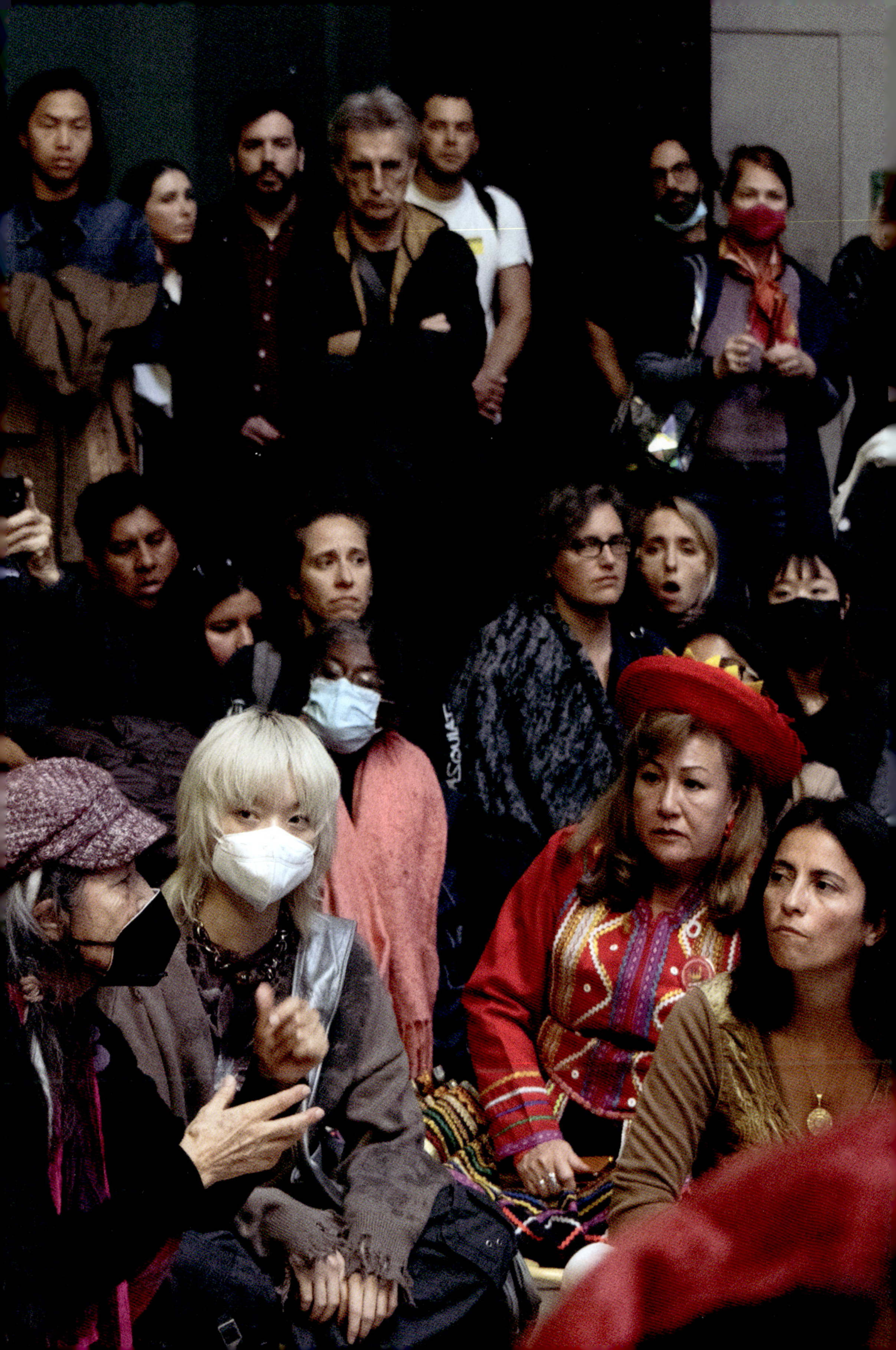

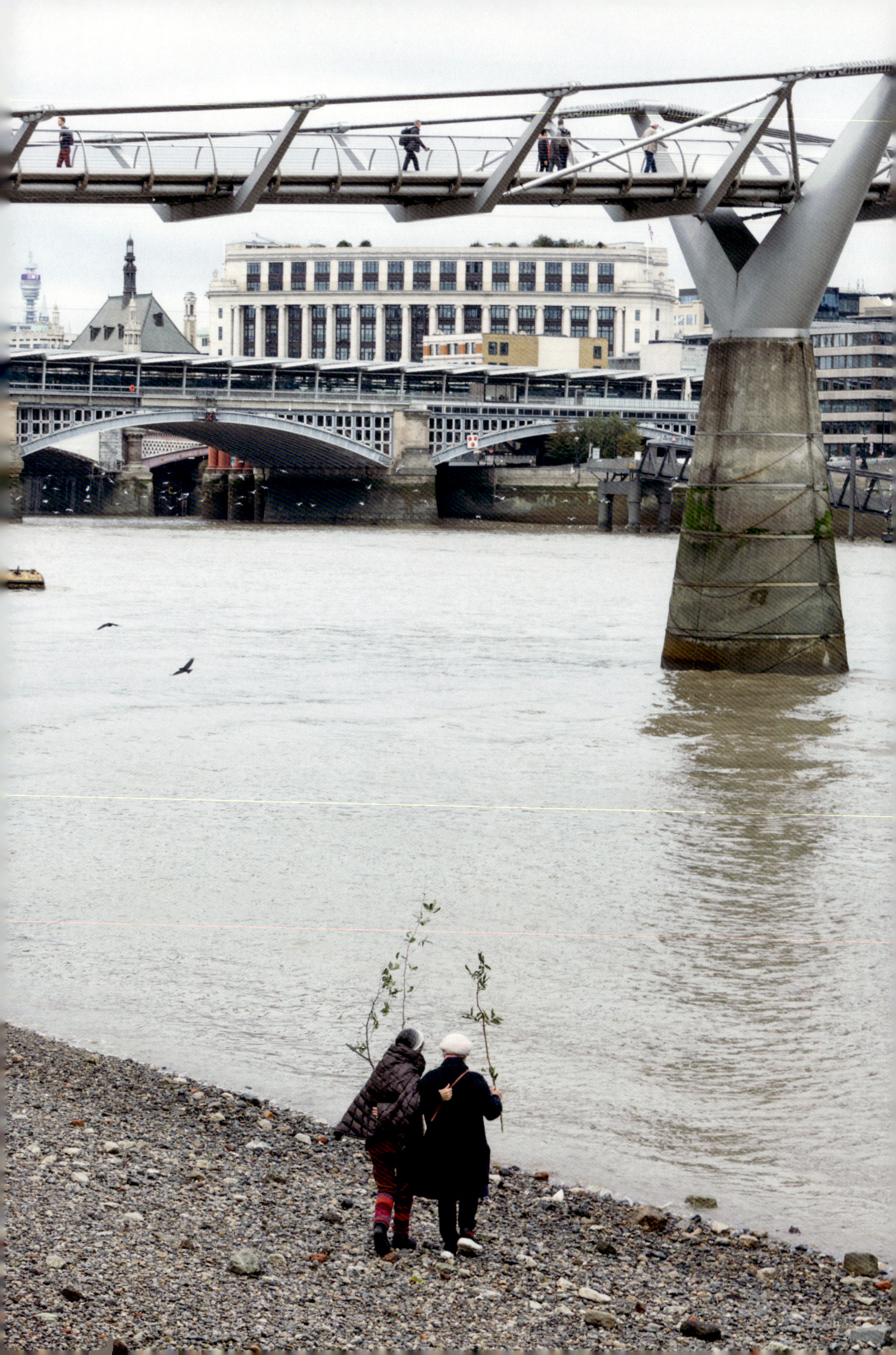

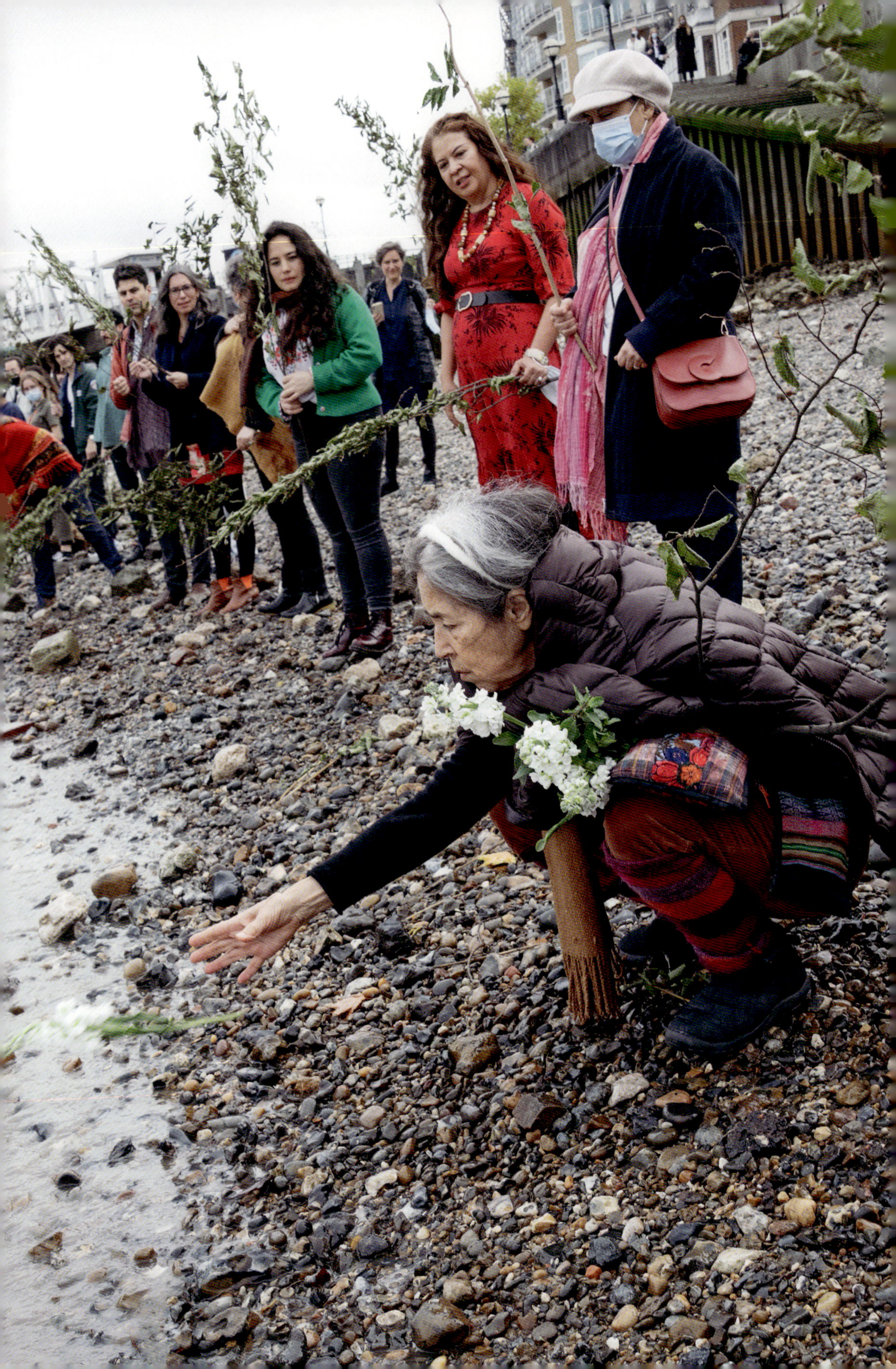

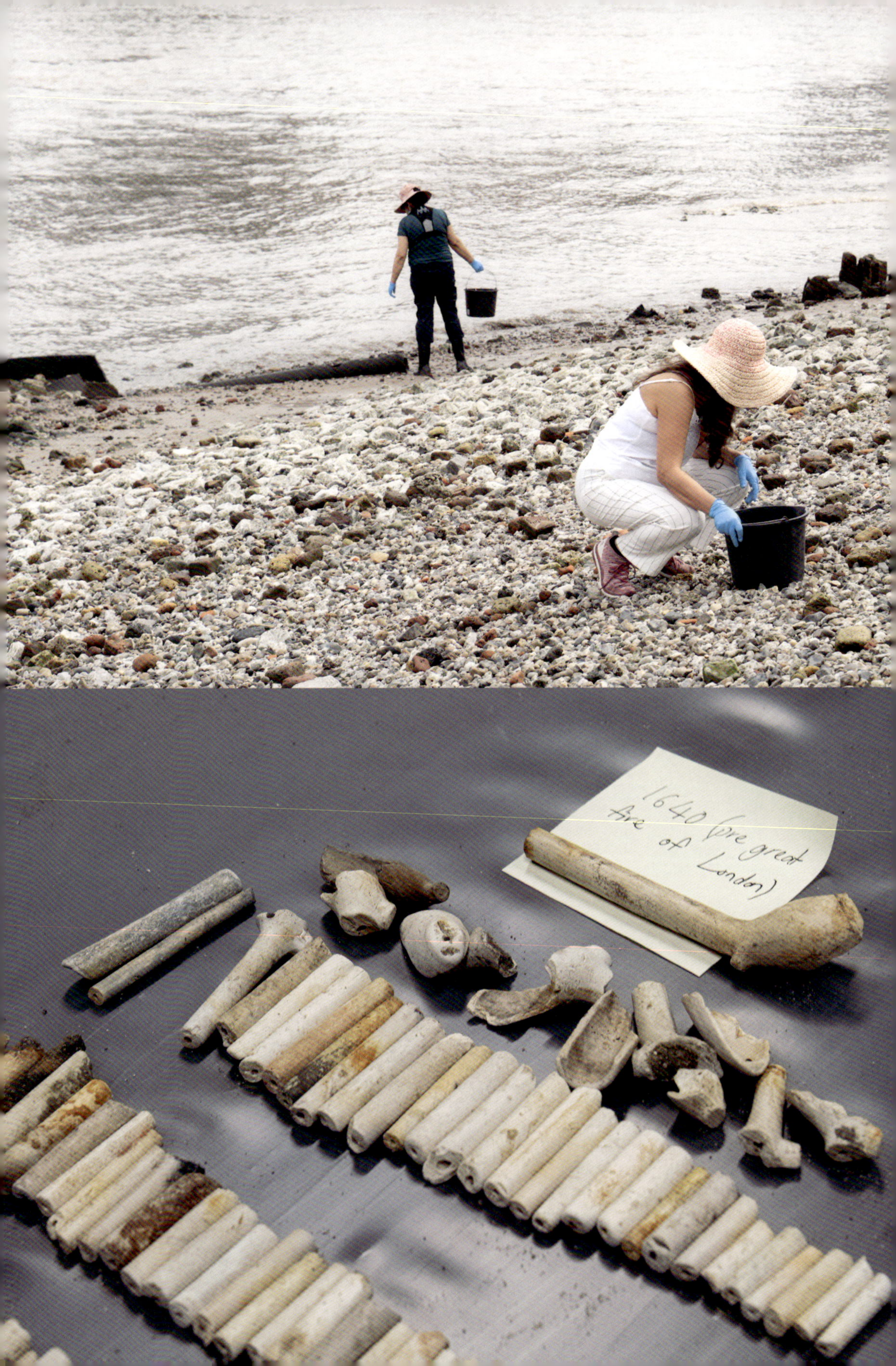
1640 (pre great
fire of
London)

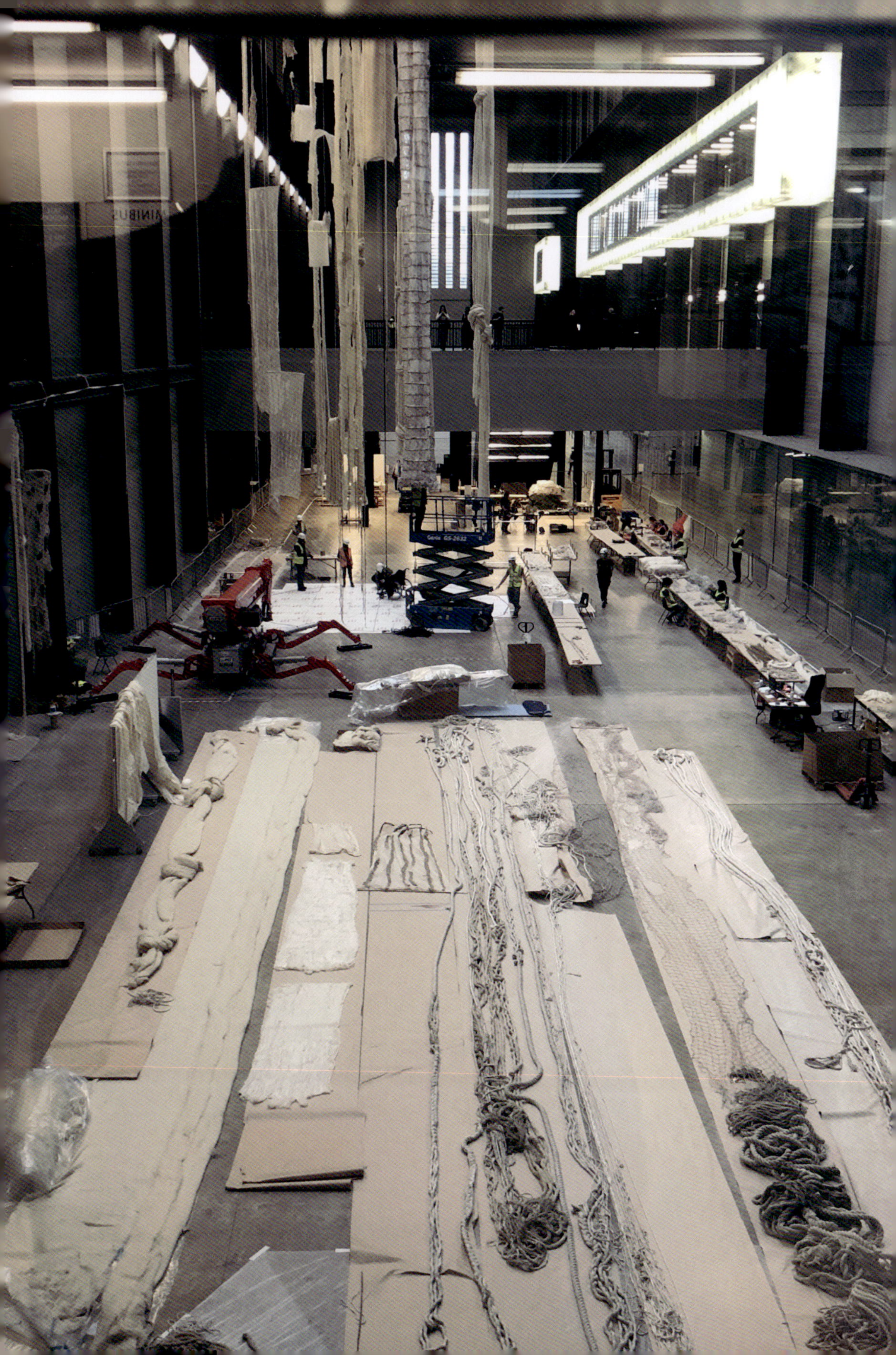

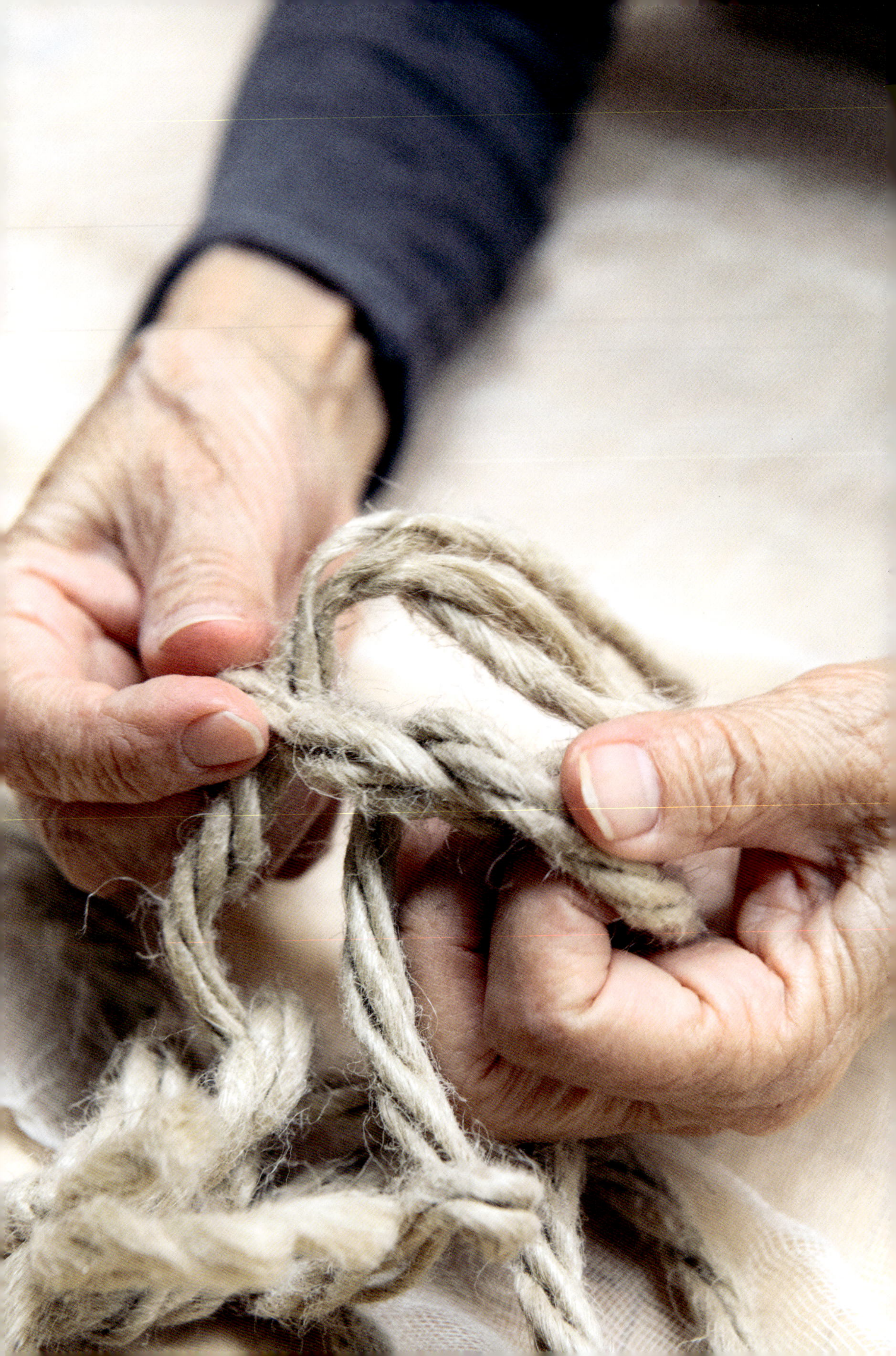

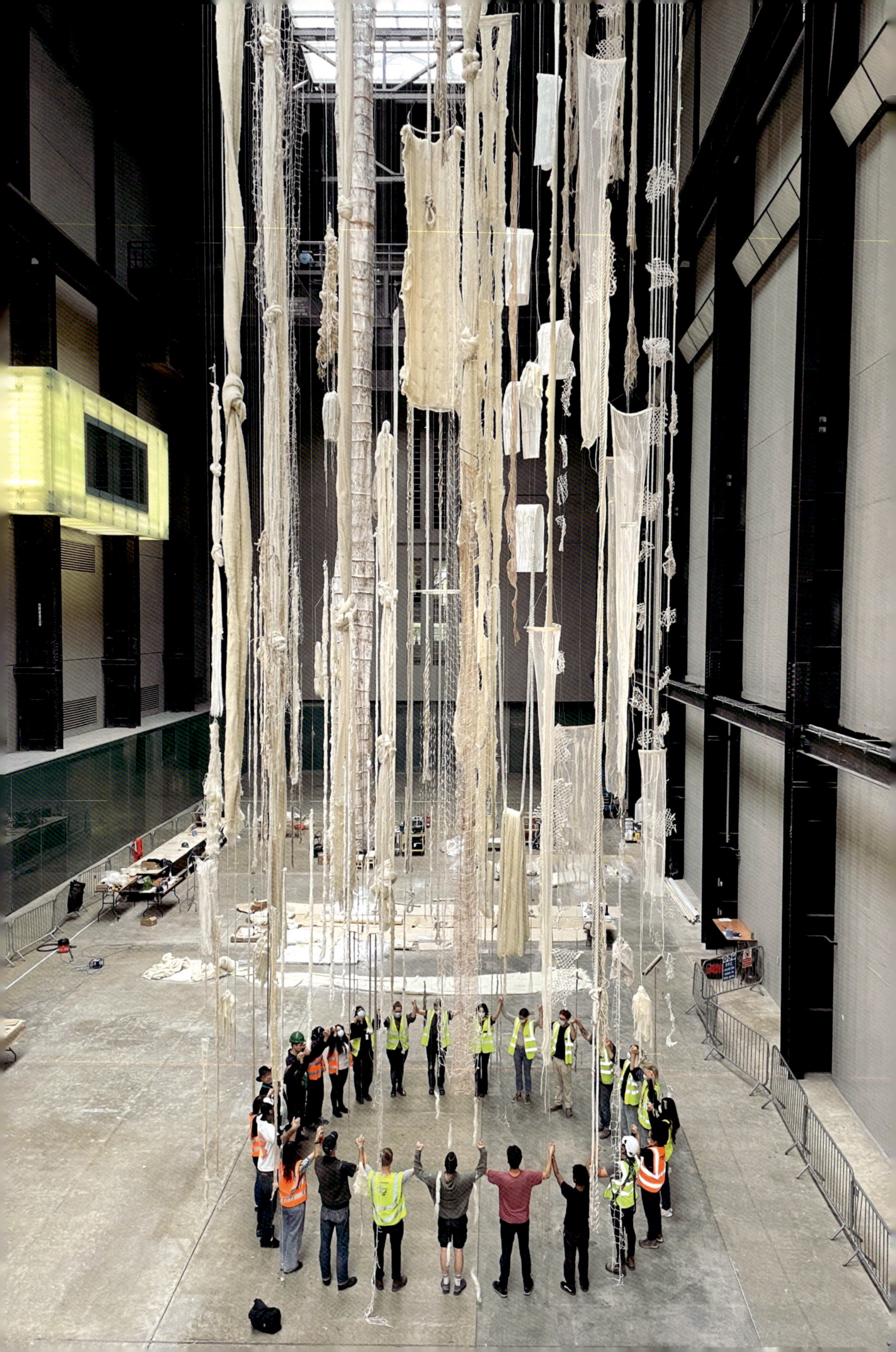

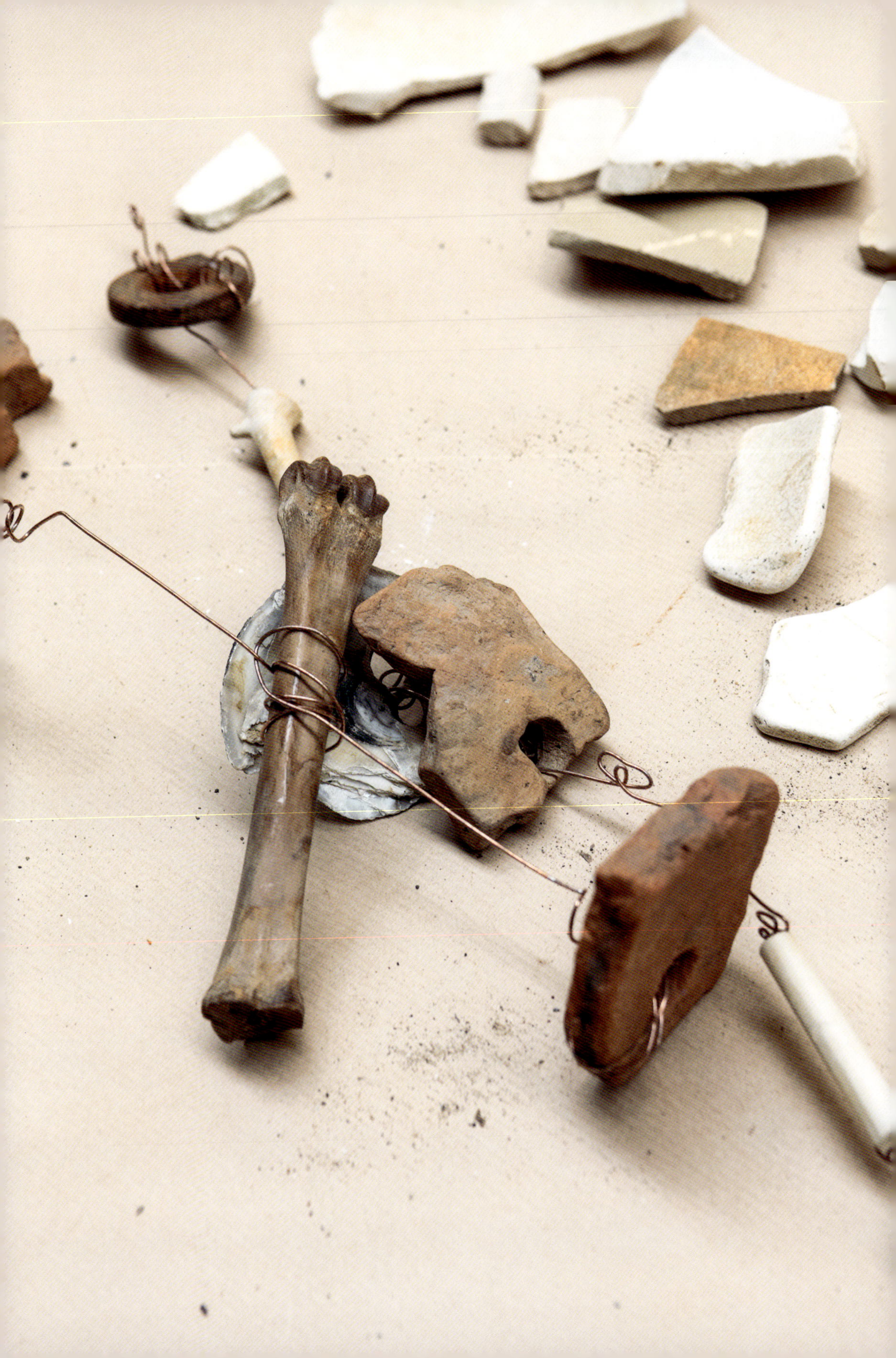

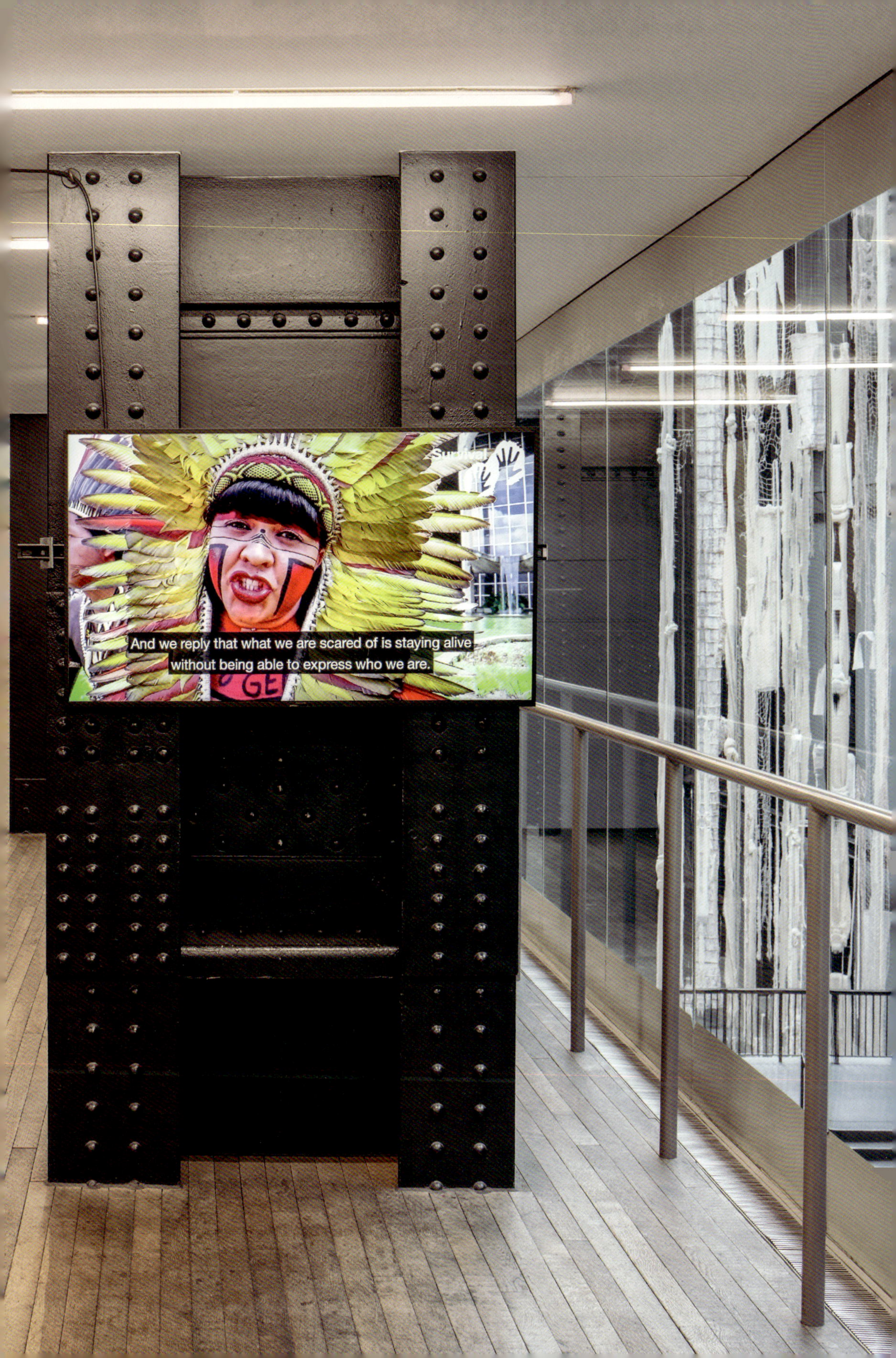

Survival
And we reply that what we are scared of is staying alive
without being able to express who we are.

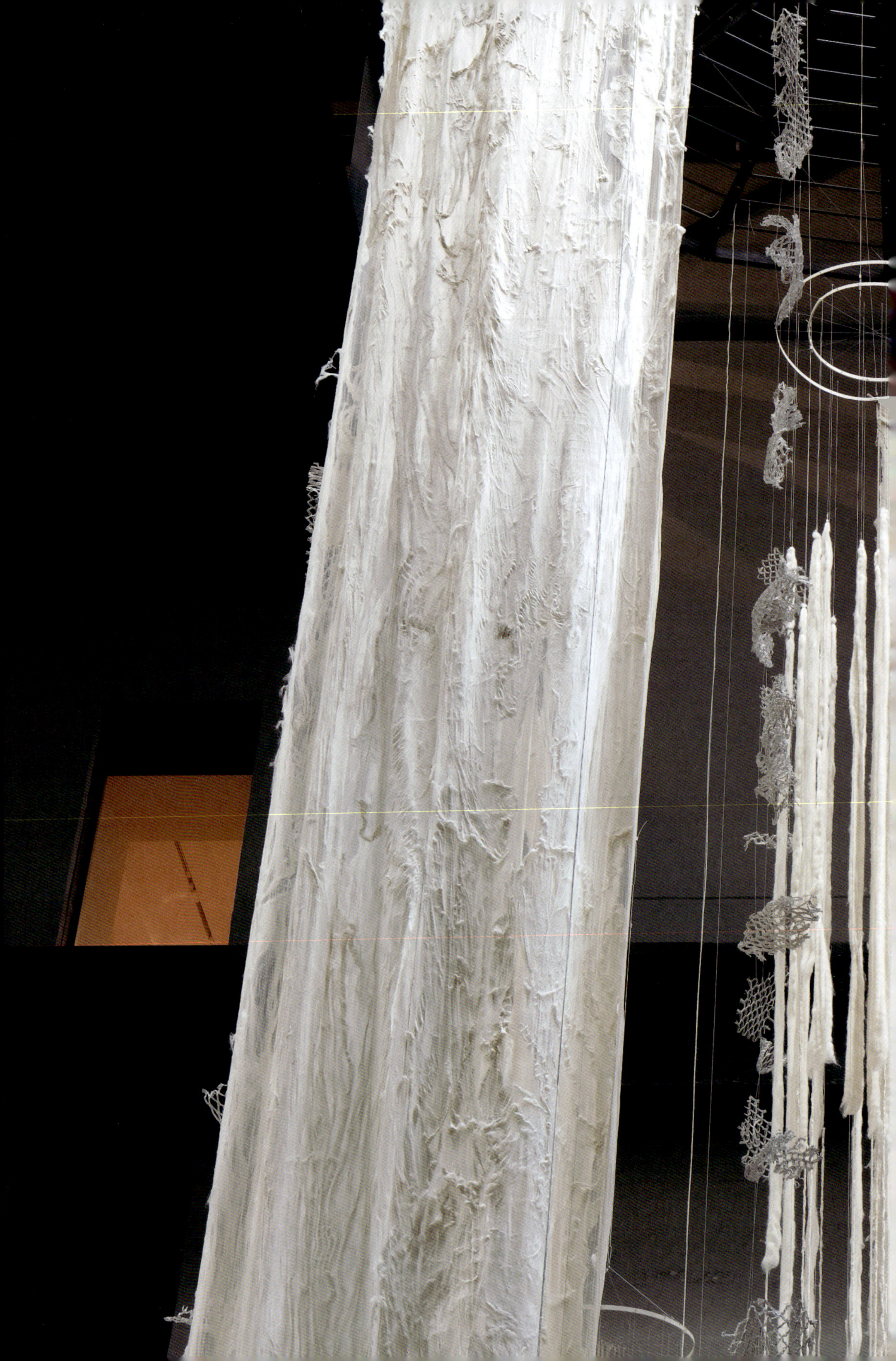

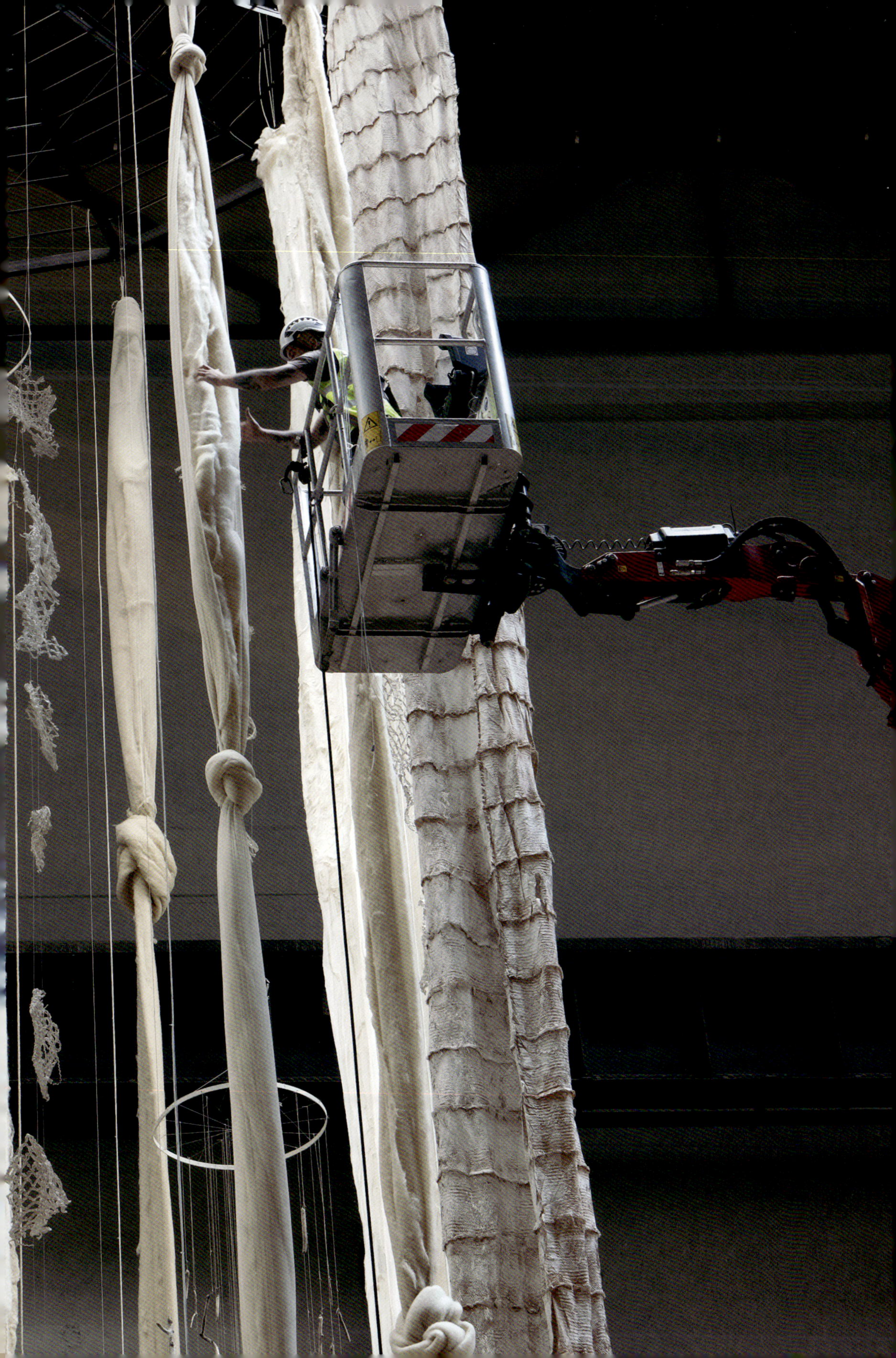

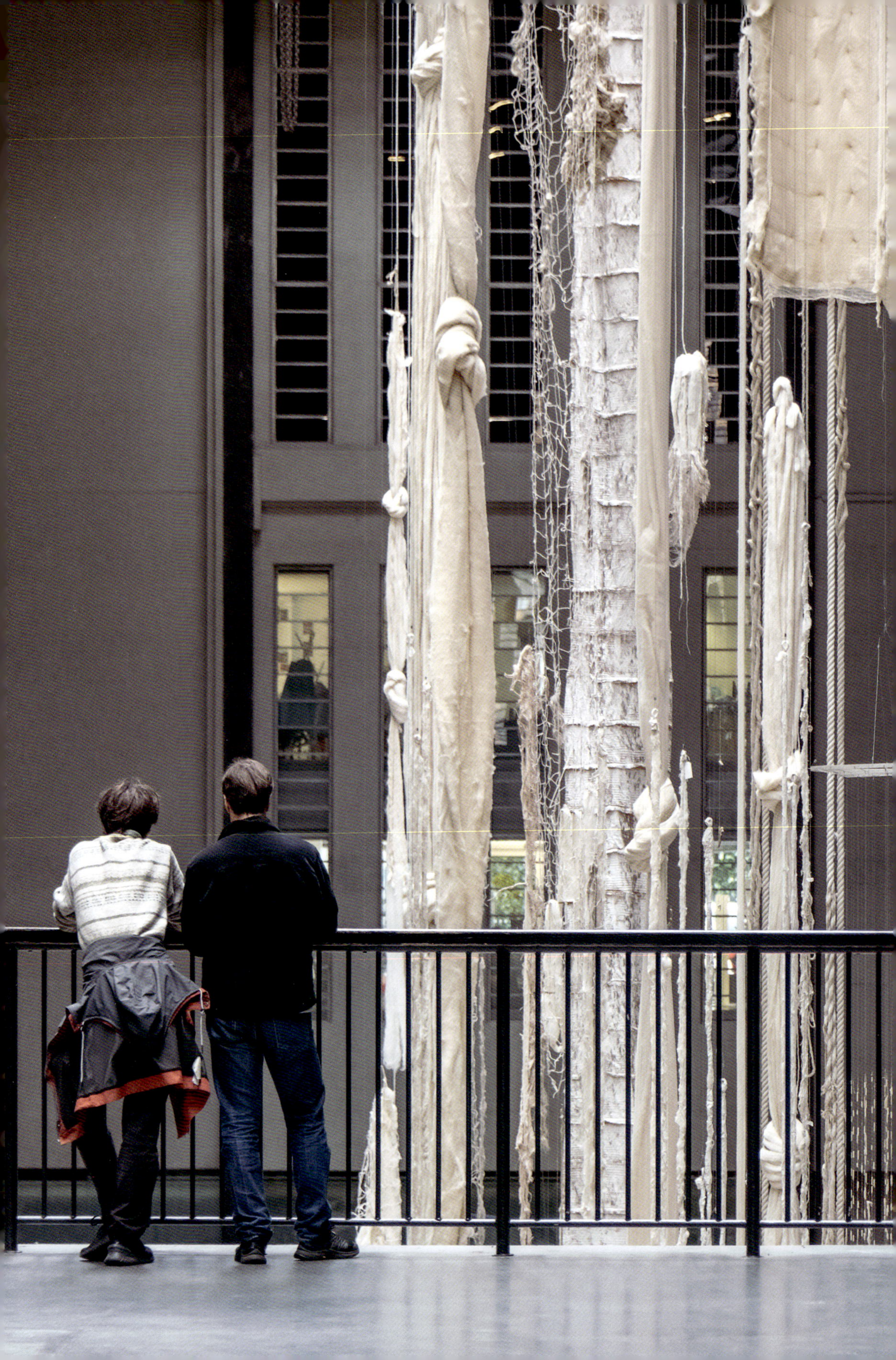

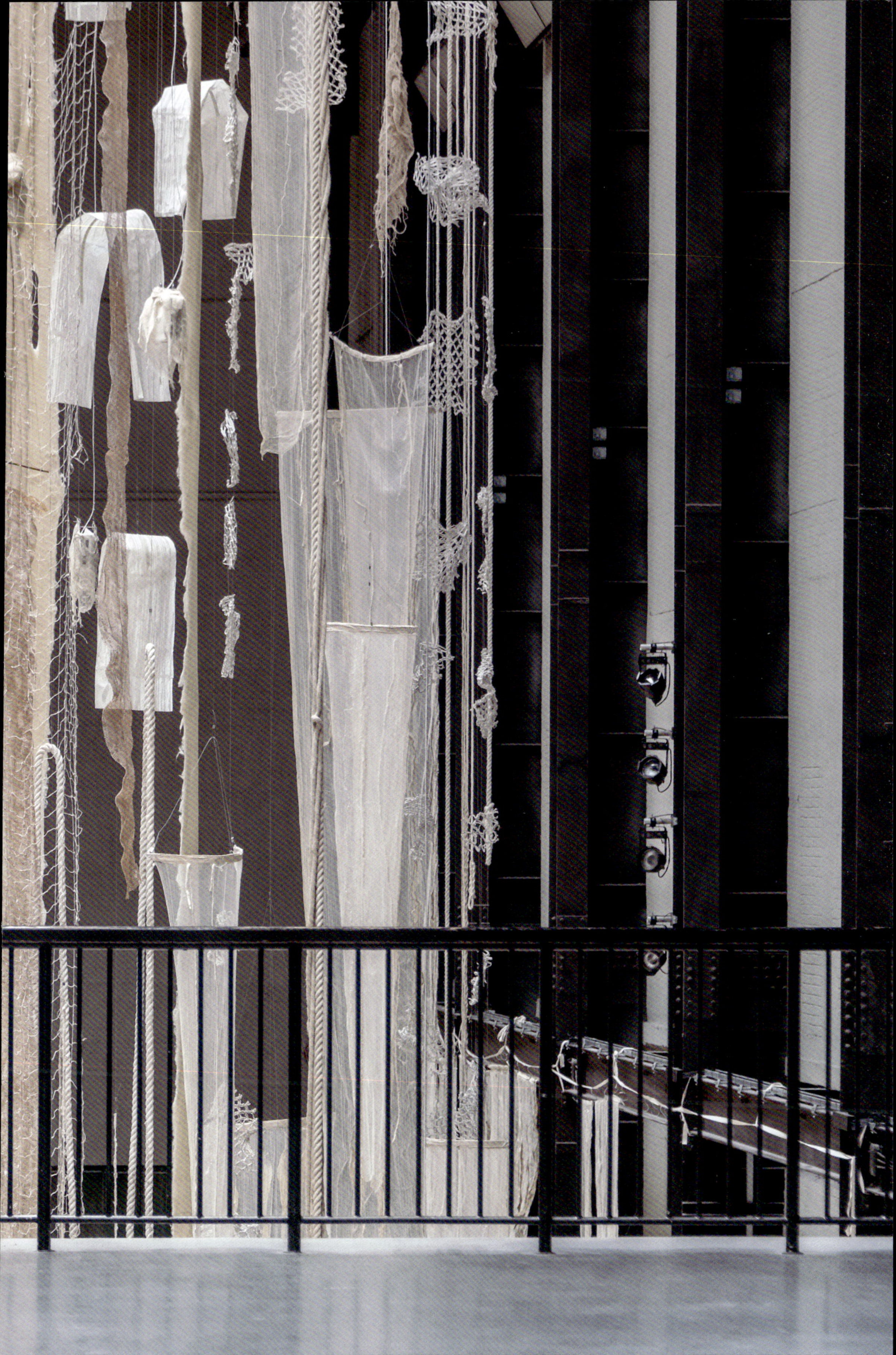

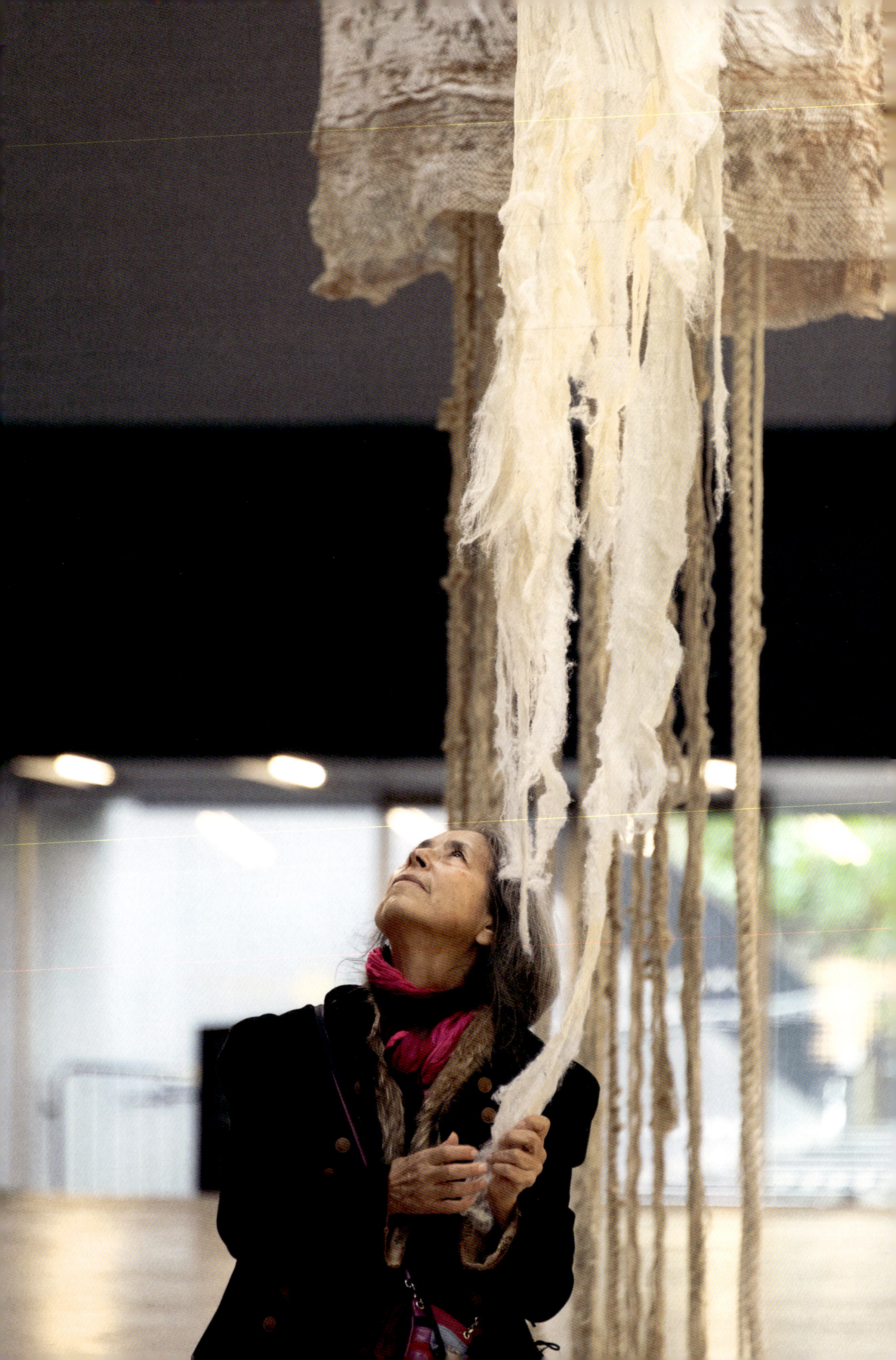

Hyundai Commission

Cecilia Vicuña
Brain Forest Quipu

Edited by Catherine Wood
With contributions by Chus Martínez, Fiontán Moran,
Luke Roberts, Cecilia Vicuña and Catherine Wood

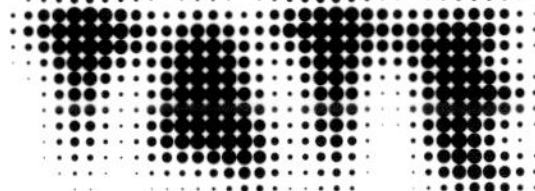

First published 2022 by order of the Tate Trustees
by Tate Publishing, a division of Tate Enterprises Ltd,
Millbank, London SW1P 4RG
www.tate.org.uk/publishing

on the occasion of the exhibition
Hyundai Commission: Cecilia Vicuña
Brain Forest Quipu
Tate Modern, London
11 October 2022 – 16 April 2023

In partnership with Hyundai Motor

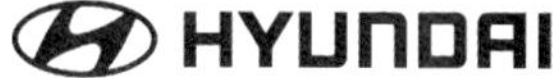

A catalogue record for this book is available from
the British Library

ISBN 978 1 84976 835 1

Distributed in the US and Canada by ABRAMS,
New York
Library of Congress Control Number applied for

Senior Editor: Nicola Bion
Production: Juliette Dupire
Picture Research: Roz Hill
Designed by Mark Thomson
Set in Custodia (Fred Smeijers)
All poetry translated by James O'Hern unless
stated otherwise

Colour reproduction by DL Imaging, London
Printed and bound in Italy by SIZ

Cover: *Brain Forest Quipu* 2022;
p.20: *Brain Forest Quipu* 2022
p.22: *Quipu Womb (The Story of the Red Thread,
Athens)* 2017

Measurements of artworks are given in
centimetres, height before width and depth

Brain Forest Quipu 2022
Plant and animal fibres, various substrates, and
other found material
Sound, looped; Video, colour, sound, subtitles;
Performance-ritual, multiple participants

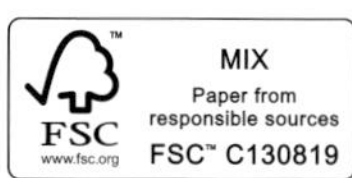

Contents

21 Supporter's Foreword

23 Foreword

28 Cecilia Vicuña: The Natural Dream
Chus Martínez

42 Cecilia Vicuña in Conversation with Catherine Wood

58 Cecilia Vicuña: Time Lines
Fiontán Moran

71 A Rough Movement to Capture the Delicate:
The Poetry of Cecilia Vicuña
Luke Roberts

74 A Quipu Autobiography
Cecilia Vicuña

126 Biography

134 Credits

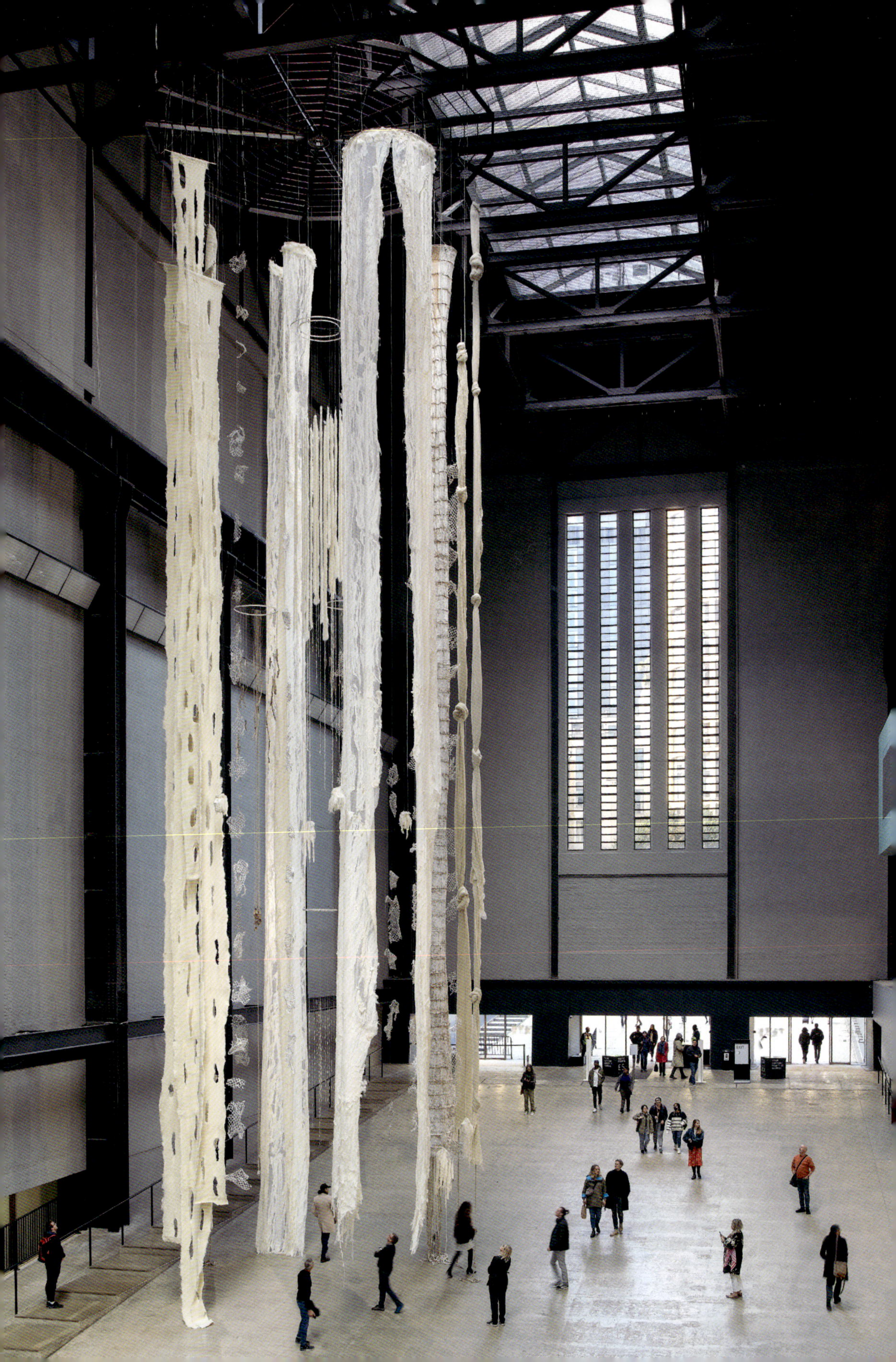

Supporter's Foreword

Cecilia Vicuña's poetic responses to the human condition encourage individual and collective thinking about our future, which we hope might provide us with new ways forward.

Throughout Vicuña's work as an artist, poet, and activist, she asks us to examine the ways in which we live and coexist. Focusing our attention on cultures and heritages that have shaped our world for centuries, her forms are as fragile as our contemporary landscape, while the ephemeral quality of the work reminds us of the precariousness of life. At a time of growing unease about the future, Vicuña's understanding of the relationships between lands, peoples, and histories invites us to come together in imagining an alternative, collective future.

Hyundai Commission: Cecilia Vicuña: Brain Forest Quipu, is the seventh Hyundai Commission, a series of inspiring new works for Tate Modern's Turbine Hall. Each artist's explorations move beyond the Turbine Hall as they ask us to question our place in our own communities, as well as within inherited societal structures. Vicuña's groundbreaking work interweaves past and present to provide a timely reminder of the generations of memory and history we hold. We hope her ways of seeing the wider world, which celebrates continuity and regeneration, will open our minds and encourage engagement with our surroundings as we reflect on our interconnectedness.

With a commitment to deepening engagement with artists, communities, organisations and audiences from across the globe, Hyundai Motor continues to support Tate and its vision. Behind our long-term partnership is a way of thinking that encourages the exchange of ideas, dialogue, and debate around the world, and a sense of responsibility to explore the transnational condition. Hyundai Motor is delighted to support Cecilia Vicuña's extraordinary commission, as she takes us on a journey of discovery and shows us what might be done if we work collectively.

We offer a very special thank-you to the artist for her remarkable vision and to everyone who has worked with her to realise this project.

Euisun Chung
Executive Chair, Hyundai Motor Group

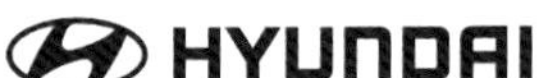

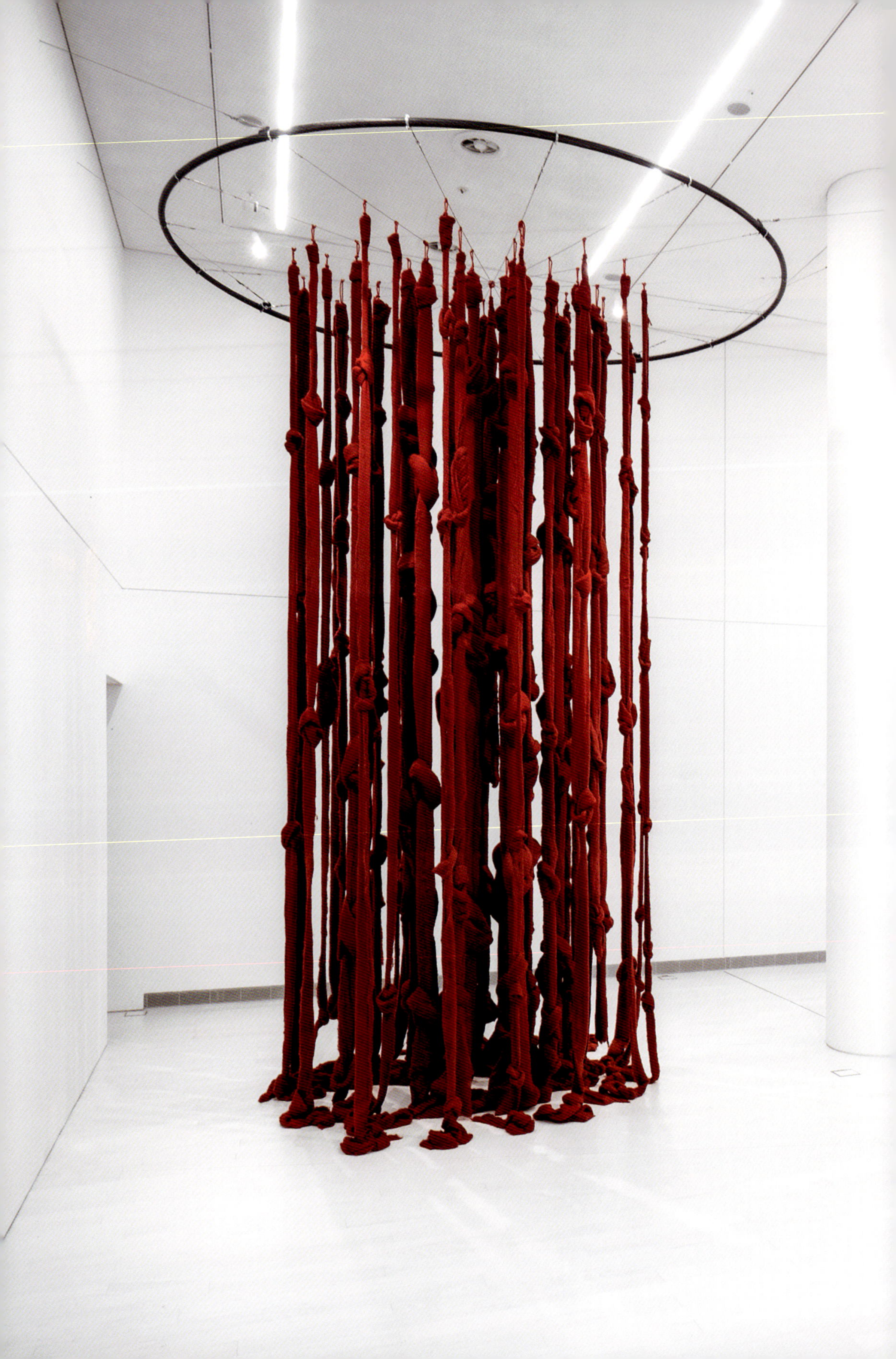

Foreword

Cecilia Vicuña's Hyundai Commission, *Brain Forest Quipu*, channels two
kinds of power: her work is scaled to the awe-inspiring height of the Turbine
Hall, which draws our gaze upwards; and it invokes the whisper of ancient
knowledge, which she tunes us in to. Vicuña's installation draws upon decades
of her pioneering work with the Andean tradition of the quipu, upon her body
of exquisitely *precario* arrangements of materials – wool, hemp, bark, bones –
and upon her work as an activist working against the exploitation of the earth's
resources and for the sovereignty of its Indigenous populations.

Within the industrial grid of the Turbine Hall, Vicuña weaves an alternative
architecture that she invites us into. She binds the two ends of the space via
her asymmetrical pair of circular, skeletal sculptures made of ghostly raw,
white, or sun-bleached materials to evoke a dead forest. These 'mother and
child' quipus concentrate the ethos of Vicuña's dreaming world; they are
material apparitions that link plants, animals, and the human hand to the
mysteries of the ecosphere, and the infinite cosmos. Vicuña's work is material
and mathematical, particular and universal. The work is made from a range of
materials, including items sourced locally – wool from Dorset to mudlarked
clay pipes found along the River Thames – but Vicuña links the specificity of
their unique textures and properties to an expansive sense of the universe in
which we are but a small part, that we can apprehend by touching and seeing
while also imagining, dreaming, intuiting towards the recesses of deep time
and outer space.

Vicuña's conception of the quipu operates at many levels beyond the
magnificent physical sculptures that soar twenty-seven metres upwards
towards the Turbine Hall's skylights. *Brain Forest Quipu* is also sonic, and
social, and digital. Working with composer Ricardo Gallo, Vicuña has woven
a composition that takes a similar form to the physical structure: their own
improvisations, Vicuña's singing that channels traditional Andean song, and
the voices and sounds of collaborators, and nature, are laced together – with
periods of silence in which the sounds of the hosting space can be discerned.

The sound is woven both within the quipus and more gently expanded
throughout the space. Working with members of the local Latinx community,
with local craftspeople and makers in London, Vicuña also weaves new
bonds between people, and with materials. She has an innate belief in the

capacity of humans to make with our hands: capacity which has often been lost or forgotten in the twenty-first century. And yet her work is very much located in the now. The 'Digital Quipu', which will channel the voices of climate activists in the Amazon and other places where forests – the oxygen of life on this planet – are under threat, is fundamental for Vicuña, along with 'Quipu of Encounters' – a series of global events, or knots of action – and no contradiction to the centuries-old traditions and concepts with which she is also working.

Vicuña's work resonates with our extraordinary and conflicted times. This entanglement of our bodies – with both the material world of nature and the places in which we live – is enmeshed in the hive-mind of technology that connects us with each other, while isolating us in new and often uncertain ways.

The project also returns Vicuña to London, where she lived from 1972 to 1975 while on a scholarship at the Slade School of Art and due to the 1973 military coup in Chile. During that time she created the painting *Violeta Parra* and her installation *Precarios: A Journal of Objects for the Chilean Resistance*, which form part of the Tate Collection, alongside the monumental *Quipu Womb (The Story of the Red Thread, Athens)* 2017 that was acquired last year.

As the seventh annual Hyundai Commission, *Brain Forest Quipu* is supported through the commitment and generosity of our long-term partner Hyundai Motor Company, who continue to show their passion and enthusiasm for the way Tate and artists seek to speak to contemporary concerns. Their support ensures that contemporary art projects can continue to enrich our shared understandings of the possibilities that the future holds. On behalf of Tate Modern I would especially like to thank Executive Chair Euisun Chung, Hyundai Motor Group, for his significant support of the Hyundai Commission and the Hyundai Tate Research Centre: Transnational.

The project has been curated by Catherine Wood, Director of Programme, who has with great care worked closely with Vicuña to realise every facet of the project, alongside Fiontán Moran, Assistant Curator, International Art, and Beatriz García-Velasco, Exhibitions Assistant. This ambitious endeavour was managed by Petra Schmidt, Production Manager, Commissions, who thoughtfully led the project with dedication, and Richard Install, Senior Production and Technical Manager, who provided essential technical expertise with characteristic good humour and diligence. Helen O'Malley, Curator, Community Partnerships Programme brought members of Latin

American Women's Aid and Latin American Woman's Rights Service network onboard to participate in the making of the Quipu sculptures, and curated the event 'Quipu of Encounters: Rituals and Assemblies'. Rachel Kent, Head of Programme and Partnerships, and Neil Casey, Head of Business and Operations, offered essential advice, support and direction. I would also like to thank Michael Wellen, Senior Curator, Displays at Tate Modern, and former Tate curator Tanya Barson for bringing Vicuña's work into the Collection.

Interwoven with the team at Tate was a set of individuals who have supported Vicuña throughout the project. Many thanks are due to Anna Stothart and Ursula Davila-Villa, who helped to coordinate and balance a multitude of requests, to Alexis Rose and the team at Lehmann Maupin, and especially to Miranda Samuels who worked closely with Vicuña researching the history of 'ghost forests' and Indigenous materials and sound archives, and building the 'Digital Quipu' – compiling videos of Indigenous land and water defenders across Brazil, Ecuador, Paraguay, Tanzania, Kenya, India, Myanmar, The Philippines, Papua New Guinea and the United States of America, including peoples of the following Indigenous communities: Munduruku, Kayapó, Xokleng, Huni Kui, Xikrin; Guajajara, Xakriabá, Yanomami, Awá, Waorani, Sarayaku, Ayoreo-Totobiegosode, Walikale, Twa, Maasai; Sengwer, Gond, Oraon, Chenchu, Karen Indigenous peoples, T'boli, Sepik peoples, Ojibwe, Ponca Pa'tha'ta. Many thanks to those who shared their stories and to the following environmental and Indigenous-led organisations who supplied the videos: Amazon Watch, Indigenous Climate Action (ICA), Global Witness, Karen Environmental and Social Action Network (KESAN), Project Sepik and Save the Sepik campaign, If Not Us Then Who? and Survival International.

Sound is another immaterial aspect of the quipu, and I would like to thank Ricardo Gallo for creating, together with Vicuña, the soundscape that expertly crafts together so many disparate compositions, and to Ariel Bustamante, who worked on the sound design with Gallo. We thank all those who contributed pieces of music for inclusion: Benjamin Calais, Yao Chunyang, Diego Espinosa, Julián Gallo (with samples from the town of Santa María de Timbiquí, Colombia), Ricardo Gallo, Tomoko Hojo, Germán Lázaro, lololol (a.k.a. Sheryl Cheung), André Magalhães (Aldeia Multiétnica, Brazil), Claudio Mercado (Museo Chileno de Arte Precolombino's Sonic Archive), Ernesto 'Teto' Ocampo, Julie Patton, José Pérez de Arce, Bernardo Rozo and Ariel Bustamante, Paulo Santos, Urian Sarmiento, Samita Sinha, Jonathan

Skinner, Benjamim Taubkin, Juan Manuel Toro, Paola Torres Nuñez del Prado & The People of Tupicocha, Cecilia Vicuña, Wei Wei (a.k.a. VAVABOND) and archival recordings of Pygmy people from Middle-Congo and Gabon recorded by Gilbert Rouget.

Vicuña worked on-site in the Turbine Hall for the entire four-week duration of the installation period. It would not have been possible to do this without the contributions of Material Research & Development Makers Louise Bennetts and Soraia Salim Samju who conducted a multitude of experiments in the early stages of the project and have worked closely with Vicuña and the installation team to make the sculptures. I would like to extend these thanks to the team of Community Participants – Siomara Giraldo Bedoya, Patricia Bidi, Soraya Fernandez D.F., and María Eugenia Chacón-Morales – who mudlarked together and then worked on the quipus with great care and enthusiasm. Mudlark Lara Maiklem supported the collection of found objects from the Thames foreshore, offering invaluable insights into the history and significance of each item. Their work was extended through the collaboration with the art fabricators The White Wall Company. Many thanks are due to Edward Oliver, who produced and coordinated the installation, alongside the talented team of makers and installers: Gino Saccone, Giacomo Layet, Veronica Arino, Claire Pritchard, Ali Forbes, Gusty Ferro Lopes, Tom Gould, Calum Stevens, Chris Hewson, Joseph Morris-Doherty, Sam Reason, Ralph Parks, Juan Gimenez-Zapiola and Anthony Kleanthous, as well as the designers and project coordinators Mark Torrens, Piers Saxby-Candy, Ashley Elliott, Robin Baker-Gibbs, Maria Martin, Tony Martin and Elliot Hepworth, alongside engineers Peter Laidler and Alastair Barnard at Structure Workshop and the engineers Anton Sawicki, Jonathan Jackson, Ellie Moore and Bastien Delechelle from Buro Happold.

As with every commission, there is a large team of people at Tate who contribute to the success of such ambitious projects. While there are too many to thank individually here, special thanks are due to David Hingley, Head of Visitor Experience; Sandra McLean, Senior Manager, Visitor Engagement and Operations; Sarah Bashir, Conservator - Preventive Conservation; Kathleen Patterson, Diary Coordinator; Barry Palmer, Head of Safety and Security; Roger Miller, Risk, Health and Safety Manager; Carmen Stevens, Head of Business, Corporate Membership & Events; Rebecca L. Evans, Events Planner; Mark Edwards, Project Manager; David Walden, Senior Estates Manager; Judith Comyn, Head of Audience Research and Data; Hannah

Geddes, Curator, Interpretation; Helen Beeckmans, Duncan Holden, Cecily Carbone and Hele Rhys in Press; Charlotte Reeves, Ania Patla and Mollie Sanders in Corporate Partnerships; Jennifer Shearman, Sandra Sykorova and Ariel Haviland in Public Programmes; Megan Pottle, Liat Rosenthal, Jessye Bloomfield and the rest of the team in Marketing; Scott Morris and Saskia Mercuri in Digital; and our colleagues in the Legal, Learning, and Design teams. Thanks to ADi Audiovisual for their work on the soundscape; to John Hanson and James Adams, Electricians; and to the Audio-Visual team at Tate Modern – Dan Crompton, Chris Phelps, Gareth Fox, Pete Triggs and Nalin Dissanayake – for their support.

This book is published as part of a series that ensures the legacy of the Hyundai Commissions. Special thanks are due to the contributors: to Chus Martínez for the revelatory essay; to Luke Roberts for his elegant introduction to Vicuña's poetry; to Fiontán Moran for the timeline; and of course to Vicuña for her artist section. At Tate Publishing we are very grateful to Tom Avery, Publishing Director; Nicola Bion, Senior Editor; Juliette Dupire, Production Controller; and Roz Hill, Picture Researcher. Particular thanks are due to Brian Guerin for researching and supplying images from Vicuña's archive; to Mark Thomson for the design of the Hyundai Commission book series and his creative solutions to this title; and to Sonal Bakrania, Lucy Dawkins, Matt Greenwood and Joe Humphrys in Tate Photography for the beautiful images of the installation.

Finally, I would like to thank Cecilia Vicuña for bringing Tate into the world of the quipu and for the generosity she has shown throughout the project. Presenting *Brain Forest Quipu* at this moment has enhanced ongoing conversations about our role as an institution, in relation to the planet and our locality, and the way art can create space for the exchange of knowledges between people. It is a testament to her vision, and the ties that she forms between ancient and modern, between song and thread, between dream and reality.

Frances Morris
Director, Tate Modern

Cecilia Vicuña: The Natural Dream

Chus Martínez

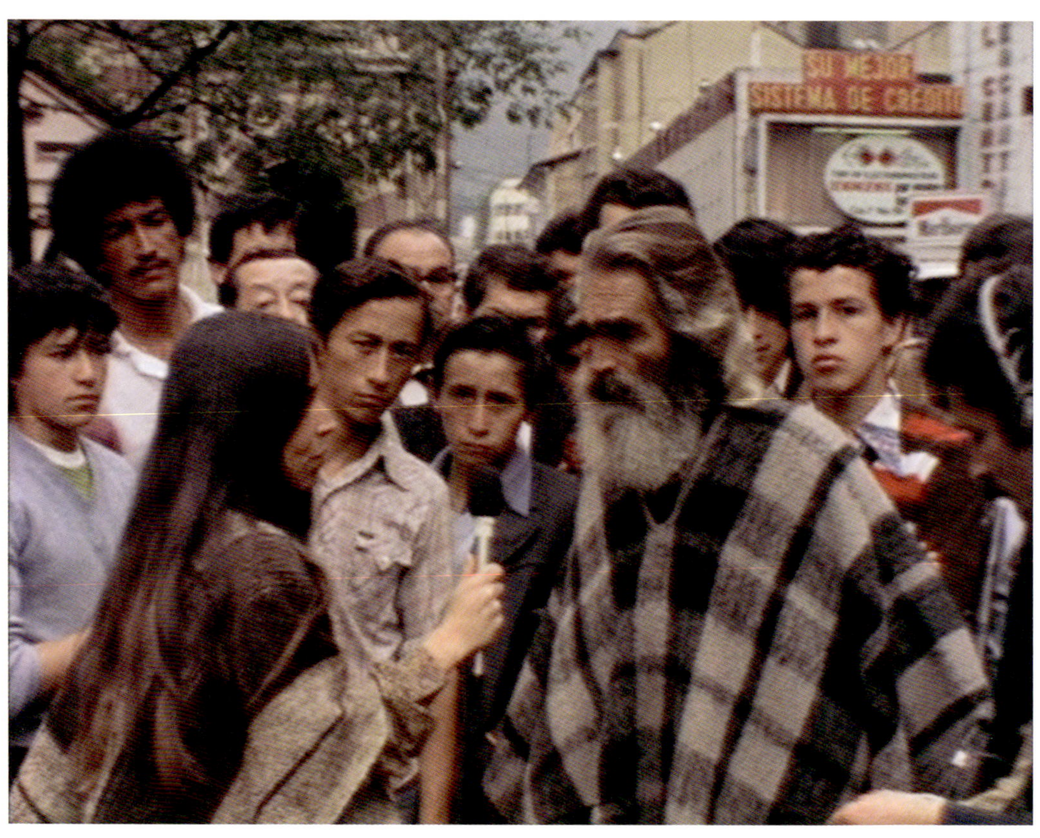

¿Qué es para usted la poesía? (What Is Poetry to You?) 1980,
16mm film on video, colour and sound, 23 min 20 sec, Spanish
with English subtitles

Poesía (Poetry)

We often wonder how the world gets reprogrammed. What is it that originates
a change, and what forces sustain the changes already made? What are the
words, the sounds, the gestures that will express them?

When I was young, I was profoundly irritated by poetry. I perceived it as
a sophist enemy of reason. If you come from a poor background, modernist
education teaches you to battle emotions, to resist all forces that tell about the
world in first person. You soon become a soldier of the disciples defined by a
Western curriculum: you are not you, but the voice of a certain understanding
of power and cultural views talking through you. The father of a very great
friend of mine, an Iranian school teacher exiled in Sweden, spent hours reciting
poetry while making food for the family. When we entered the house, he
always greeted us with a smile and asked, 'Do you know the words of the great
poets?'– and he started reciting to us. I felt both fascinated and embarrassed
by it. Later, travelling to the Middle East, I discovered that poetry was an
essential part of cultural, emotional and political communication there. Not
only was reading poetry important, as it is in certain intellectual classes in
the West, but reciting poetry was crucial. Reciting to the family, reciting to
friends, teaching children to recite and repeat those verses – learning by heart
constituted a bonding ritual, but a ritual that irritated my senses because I
was trained to despise all that was not coming first through the mind. A ritual,
nonetheless, that had also survived and resisted the colonial way of imposing
order upon the colonised, which included favouring narratives over verses.

When I visited Chile some ten years ago to get to know the great Nicanor
Parra, a poet and a very knowledgeable person about the Mapuche cultures
of Chile, he said to me that poetry is the tongue of Earth. I still remember
listening to every word of this sentence and feeling the world opening up
differently. It was as if this sentence changed all I knew until that very
moment. I suddenly saw the work of artists like Cecilia Vicuña under a
different light. I wondered how I had failed to understand that this collective,
forceful reclamation of poetry was a movement – a network that created,
through the verses and the voices reciting them, a connection between all
vernacular and Indigenous peoples around the world.

When people talk about reclamation, the Western mind immediately
thinks that they want to take what we took from them. It is partly so; we need
to give back, and giving back entails pain. But it is also the case that over the

centuries, ancient and ancestral cultures have generated tools of reclaiming without material possessions being involved. Poetry is one such tool, one that invokes again and again the fundamental dilemma of white cultures denying Indigenous and non-white cultures. The Indigenous condition and connection to ancestral territory and wisdoms vary and mutate. Poetry collectively rehearses these unstable conditions.

In November 2014 I travelled to MoMA PS1 to attend the presentation of *Kuntur Ko*, a recording made by Cecilia Vicuña in 2006, published by Torn Sound in 2012 and distributed by the Hueso Records label founded by Iván Navarro. Cecilia Vicuña describes *Kuntur Ko* as songs of water, composed to address the melting of the glaciers in Chile. Singing as a way of entangling different languages – combining the names for water in Quechua and Mapuche, Spanish and English – her performance, her voice created sound reflections resembling the circulation of water and, almost magically, made water appear in the space where we listened. The voice in her use of poetry was simultaneously channelling and honouring the spiritual laws of the ancestors who believed in the agency of water. It was clear that the agency Cecilia Vicuña was embodying was a real one: the ocean's agency, the water's agency, was not only symbolical or metaphorical but a real power, a force that expressed a will and could only be conveyed through poetry. Like critical and argumentative thinking in the West, the work of Cecilia Vicuña offered us an opening to a radically important epistemological method by which we might imagine nature having a voice.

Knowing what nature says, knowing what ancient wisdom knows, knowing what Indigenous peoples reclaim does not inevitably lead to a culture and a practice oriented towards living our lives in coexistence. But it surely has had the effect, over the years and decades, of cyclically transforming our imagination of what is possible. Poetry is there to enrich the world it unveils even if destruction still continues and escalates – the two compulsions are not mutually exclusive – and today it produces a continuity between the world of the living and the dead that was never so present before. Poetry, and poetry in the work of Cecilia Vicuña, introduces oral tradition as the place where a new technology of life is originating.

Alegría (Joy)

Joy is a carrier. We reflect too little on the importance of joy. Pain seems
to have been more successful as a notion to think about. We are told, for
instance, that pain makes us bond – but does it really? Can pain really be
shared? It seems more logical to think that a community in pain has a difficult
time activating their capability to act and to regain a sense of time ahead of
them. Joy, on the contrary, is an emotion whose very function is to establish
connections between experiences that might otherwise not be together.

And joy is one of the central traits of Cecilia Vicuña's work: a joy that
affects our senses and allows us not only to see, to touch or to reflect on the
past, but to encompass all the dimensions of life while seeing, listening or

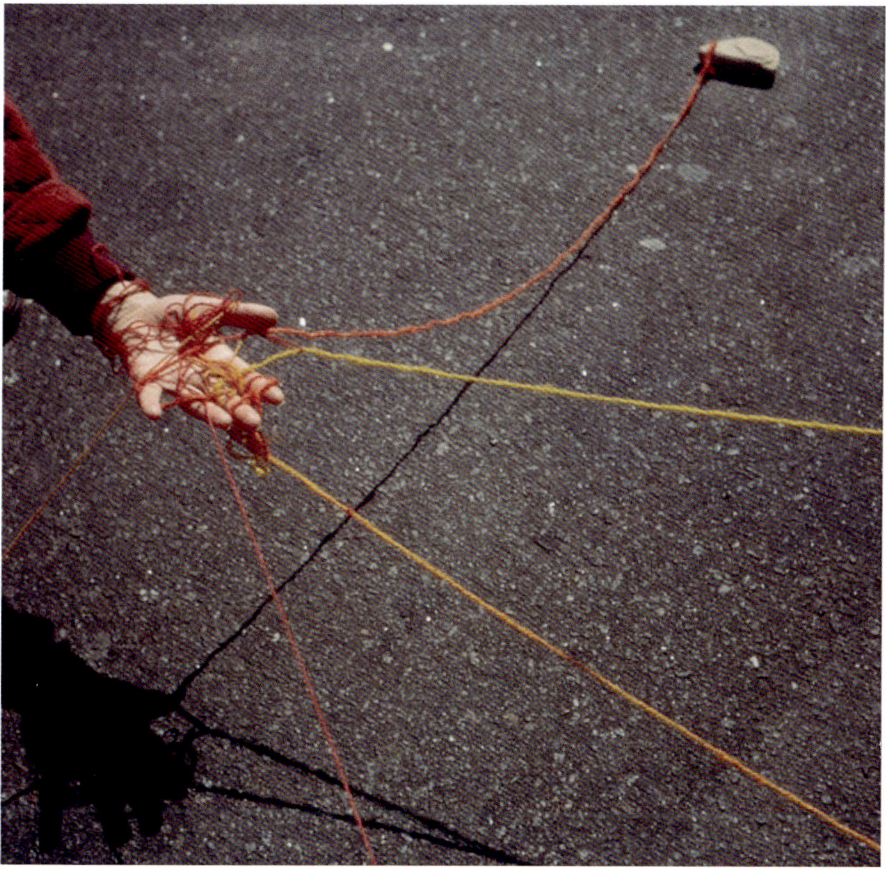

Ceq'e 1994, street performance, Franklin Street, New York

touching art. Joy is a trait that allows for something fundamental in the work of Cecilia Vicuña: the expansion of the personal dimension into a more intense collective and shared dimension of experiencing the world. It is difficult, therefore, to see her work under the lens created by Western art historians of the 'political'. It is true that a political depiction of the description and reclamation of injustice and justice constitutes a core element of the work. But all her sayings about and portrayals of a world that has been dispossessed of rights, of means, of voice are illuminated. Yes, there is a force that is illuminating all that she does, and that force is what I call joy: a joy capable of making us relate, bond, establish not only argumentative but emotional relationships with her way of presenting.

Multiple dimensions meet. Images tell. Objects convey. Surfaces vibrate. The fibres create rivers in her hand – and soon, when you see her works, together with her poetry and songs, you understand that Cecilia Vicuña has been working towards the emergence of new social habits. Oh! We know in the Western world of habits being established by norms, norms being a result of a consensus and consensus being a force that keeps things in order. Now, close your eyes and listen to her whispering through her materials into your ears and organs a world that presents social habits as festive habits. Imagine habits

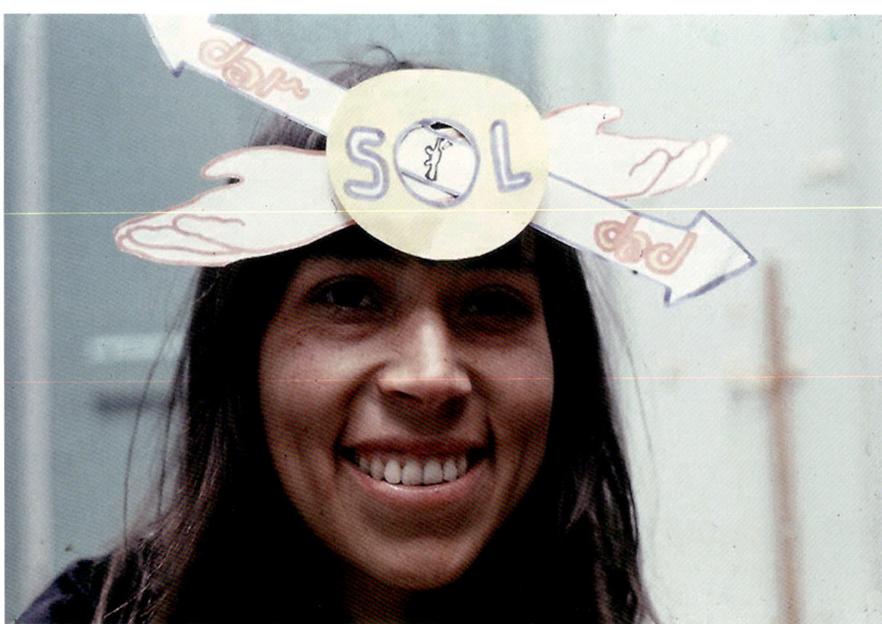

Sol y dar y dad (Solidarity: To Give and Give Sun), *Palabrarmas*
c.1977–9, performance and public intervention, Bogotá

that inject the social with a good face, first, then a smile. Can you imagine a social smile?

In the past, monuments used the pedestal and the control of a horse to signify power, big power. But wouldn't a social smile embody an even bigger power? Imagine if every performance created, and every gathering around Cecilia Vicuña's work was ultimately intended to produce, a warmth inside the organs, then the blood, then the skin – a warmth that we couldn't help but express as a smile.

When we collectively smile, a simple but effective mutuality is created: we smile to and at one another. Imagine many smiling at one another. Add animals to the smile: animals smiling to us and we to them, animals smiling to one another. Add clouds. Clouds smiling at us, we to the skies, to the winds, to the sun's rays. At this point it all seems exaggerated to you, or perhaps naïve, but it is not. Faces are surfaces, bodies are volumes, organs are made of matter not that different to the fabrics and fluids used to create sculptures; it seems only normal, therefore, to include our bodies in an intense and shared joy that may last for a second or a minute, but will leave a trace in all of us forever of being part of the sun. The expression on our faces and the emotions we feel in every cell of our bodies are a matter of the work of Cecilia Vicuña.

Tecnología (Technology)

We often talk about artificial intelligence, but we fail to see the intelligence of all that is alive. If I were to name one important trait in art made by women, I would say it is the reclamation of the organic – of bodies and their bodily functions – and its connection with all other bodies existing. If we look at computer development, changes in the container and cavity that comprise the body of the machine – from a very big box full of perforated cards to a small flat box full of integrated circuits – seem central. Likewise, in art made from a certain perspective of gender upon nature, the cavity question is fundamental: uteruses and guts versus brains conceived as black boxes. In other words, more than anything else, learning to interpret the inside of the body has allowed art and artists to investigate not just the connections in life, but also how we interpret these connections. Wasn't it poetry that first spoke about thinking through the inner body? It was thanks to poets and artists that scientists began to investigate the potential influence of the gut on the brain. Their discovery was that similar cells in our gut and brain allow for information to circulate inside us in ways science had long dismissed but art had assessed again and again. If it weren't for artists like Cecilia Vicuña, we wouldn't have the grounds to imagine and invent rituals, experiential cultures, educational methods and erotic and sexual ceremonies to engage, collectively, in shaping a new self.

Modern science taught that this transformation of the self happens once you intervene from the outside, but artists like Cecilia Vicuña show us that we may first shape the world through the senses, and matter will accommodate this slow metamorphosis. This, far from being a mystical assumption, needs to be interpreted as the true technological ambition behind her work: a non-white technology based on coding the senses and the languages by which we recount our experiences and thoughts according to the values of a multi-species entanglement. Why do I use the word technology here? Because ideas about what intelligence is and how we should think are locked inside our cultures. I perceive the practice of Cecilia Vicuña as radically invested in unlocking and opening these conceptions so that we can think about a non-binary relationship with technology and the machine. And the easiest way of doing so is by reflecting on our experience of our bodies and nature, our bodies and the immaterial (poetry and voice), our bodies and images, our bodies and materials, and developing the idea of a world without tools. We enslaved machines – and colonised their identities – to make them enhancers of the human, but to be able to fulfil the laws of true mutuality we need to include technology into a different order.

It is interesting to follow the narratives about future machine learning as the story of a rebellion to come. One day, machines will be performing functions we cannot even dream of, and on that day they will be out of our control and may decide against the humans. But is it necessary to dream of contraband power always in submission and rebellion? Of cycles of creation and destruction? This question is present throughout the work of an artist committed to encompassing every living reality through performance and presence. Of course, one can only do a little in every work, in every magical rehearsal of the voices present in the elements of the universe, but this continuous exercise nonetheless advances a method – a carefully developed method of combining artistic languages and materials – oriented towards learning how to reach out to the more-than-human world.

Ancient and vernacular cultures aimed to reach out to the more-than-human not only as a magical practice, but as a way to connect, to seek peace,

to erase any potential sign of aggression from nature to the human and vice
versa. And although these ancient practices and knowledges were suppressed
by our imperial and colonial impulses, nowadays these cultures and mindsets
are re-emerging. It is definitely not impossible to think that art serves the
purpose of creating an informational flow and a culture of imagining how these
knowledges can coexist with the scientific and industrial codes and devices
we so much believe in. (And actually, if artificial intelligence learns to rebel it
means it can learn to be an ancient poet too.)

As much as we can imagine Cecilia Vicuña placing the monumental
collective smile upon millions of faces across cultures and continents, we
can imagine, too, future machines smiling. I am certain – and I use you as a
reader and a witness – that Cecilia Vicuña invented through her practice the
menstruating computer, or a machine able to feel with the menstruating body
and even able to be a partner in giving birth. It is important to understand that
her quest for natural justice and her emphasis on an enhanced sensuality is
oriented towards defying any calculated outcome in the relations we establish
with the world. The calculable and the knowable are languages that poetry
and performance counteract.

Morfología (Morphology)

The question of form is a fundamental one. Skills, codes, standards: the whole
of Western culture is a believer in form. De-forming form is a way of creating a
space of interpenetration of nature into culture and in that way merging both
principles into one. Working outside the skills of the academy in this way is
a means of coming closer to the small things: to the sticks, the branches, the
stones, the roots, the pieces of materials that appear in an almost spontaneous
way. This way of addressing matter poses beautiful questions that concern life.
Can a flower be mainstream? Can a detail constitute the totality? The practice
of Cecilia Vicuña is porous and open to the big question of relevance as seen
from the lens of a culturally formulated outreach, a mainstream.

Industrialisation, modernity, and the entanglement of capitalism and class
formation and awareness has deeply affected the role (and the self-esteem)
of all those working in the arts, but also of all those perceived as artisans or
'outsiders' to the system. The binary logic of popular versus elitist, commercial
versus conceptual, slow or niche versus the speed of media has determined

the way we judge the relevance and importance of having art and culture at the core of our communities. The process of creating emotional fluidity and sensorial diversity within the institutionalised art systems of the West has taken – and is still taking – a long time. The art systems we know through art institutions have not allowed for fluidity, nor for many transitioning exercises within the rigid inherited worlds of patrimonial and colonial concerns. Yet over the decades this process has (or has not) been unfolding, Cecilia Vicuña has been insisting on and presenting in her work, or poetry, or making, a notion of form far from well-defined and fixed. Her epistemology, her way of getting in touch with materials-touched-by-the-elements is metamorphic: open, created for change. Everything is affected by everything else. The role of art and the artist is not to fix or stop the evolution of form or a material. On the contrary: art sets the world in motion.

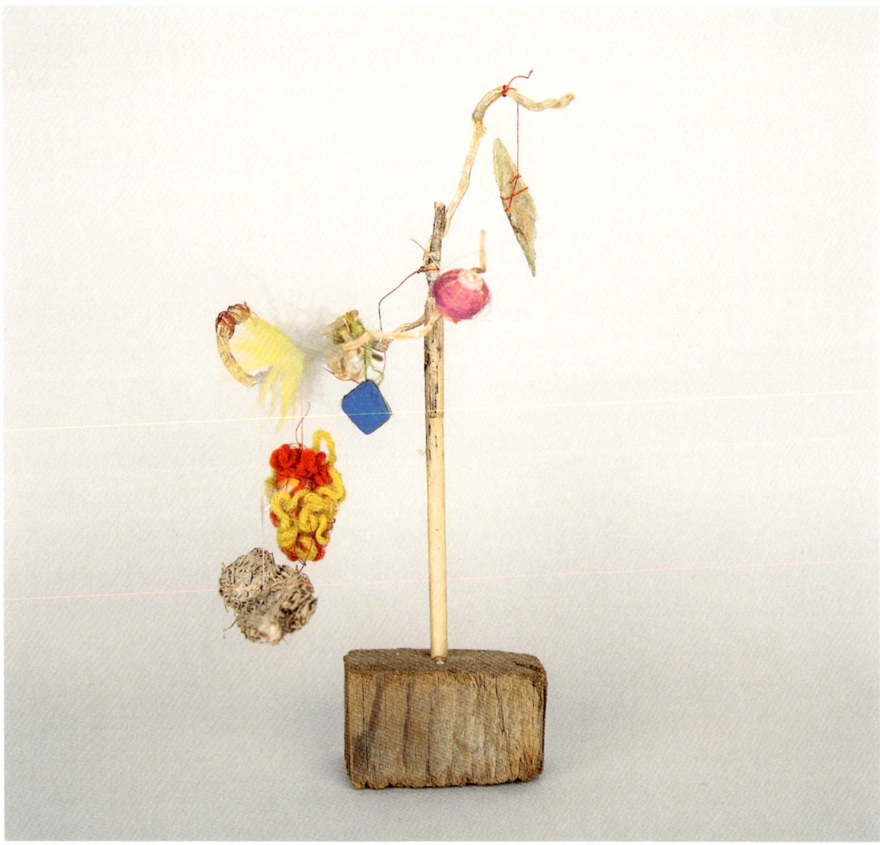

Árbol de vida (Tree of Life) 1984, mixed media, wood, twigs, wool, seashells, horsehair

The avant-garde understands the experiment as a matter of form – of breaking with old formats, the emergence of hybrid forms and the discovery of new ones. A swan becoming a woman who then turns back into a swan is not only a question of formats. Probably, until very recently, no one thought these processes would be possible outside the metaphoric and literary worlds of fantasy and fiction. It took a world pandemic to make apparent how many thousands were claiming this possibility for their own bodies. We now see bodies being disentangled from their biological traits, from their sexual assign-ments, producing a fluidity that runs through the whole of society – a source of nourishment compelling all those structures designed, named and identified in a certain way to change and to dance with this immense flow that is only just starting.

Still, many imagine a (singular) transition that can be achieved in a life-time – a change or an adaptation that needs to happen, a correction that may be made. We are so easily fooled, even by ourselves. Once a transition happens, in fact, many more transitions may follow. They should. Why would one embark on this adventure only once? Who assures us that the identity we desire at the age of twenty will continue to release the same joy a decade later? I see those individuals capable of undergoing complex, painful and even very risky physical transitions as veritable pioneers of a time to come. Like the Argonauts and the cosmonauts, real visionaries, those transitioning are taking upon themselves and their bodies the task of experiencing and discovering for the rest of us the possibilities of a world in transformation. Millions of processes at many different scales will start happening besides the more complex medical ones affecting our established processes, structures and institutions. If the revolutions of the past situated the body as the counterpart of the oppressive powers, with individuals risking their lives for freedom, the streets, the barricades and the weapons in this revolution are the bodies themselves. Transitioning is a way of offering up one's past life and defining a new identity and a new body for freedom. Once we realise that you cannot invert the logic of a system, you may be willing to propose a mass transition of all the bodies that sustain the structures of that system, thereby inducing a new identity into the social. This idea is neither new, nor an issue related to just a few people (nor solely to gender). These deep changes will soon become 'available' and present to many, even if the thought of such transitions is or will remain unfamiliar to them for a long while. It has to do with a deep need to gain an understanding of impermanency. In capitalism, inconsistency gets punished, risk gets praised. But the time for changeableness has arrived.

Misterio (Mystery)

The secret and the mysterious bear a beauty that has fascinated us for millions
of years. As much as science reveals, humans create ways of producing and
keeping secrets and mysteries. From the banality of mystery novels – so
popular for good reason – to the unanswered questions on the origin of life or
the cosmos, we relate to the unknown.

The production of beautiful mysteries is central to Cecilia Vicuña's
performances and poetry – and I will extend it to all her works. Mystery
appeals to a structure in which elements are revealed to us and activated
in ways that demand our active engagement: an engagement that is not
necessarily oriented towards finding a solution to or resolution of a particular
situation, but simply towards being part of the adventure a mysterious
experience offers to us. The structure of the mysterious is the structure of
forces and presences that (we acknowledge) go beyond what our common
sense allows. Mystery, too, is related to joy. It creates a connection – but a
transversal one that defies the confidence we have gained through the last
two centuries in being synchronic with the real. When the world opens and
different times start to interplay and grow entangled – as described by today's
quantum physicists and the old savants and shamans alike – the mystery is the
feeling of this paradox being real, and being revealed to our senses. If we try
to apprehend this with the language and tools of the explicable, we will shiver
and feel the uncanny in the mysterious. If, on the contrary, we accept that
visible and invisible forces, explainable and unexplainable parameters coexist,
we will experience the pleasures of the secret. Codes, cyphers, presences,
practices, substances, souls, animated and unanimated instances all constitute
the complex and hyper-pedagogical texture of the mysterious. There is no
transition, whether gender, social or cultural, without a mystery. The mystery
is a method that has one goal: to keep our motivation towards life alive. Time
and again it awakens our demand for being exposed, and in every exposure the
world dilates. Like the body giving birth, the mystery allows for encounters
between multiple layers of time and space.

It is wrong to suggest that those artistic practices reinstalling the ways
of knowing of ancestral cultures and poets are in contradiction of analytic
thinking. It is precisely arguments like this that re-state Western ways'
separation from – and their power over – other ancient forms. Analytical
thinking, after all, features in many ancient rituals, and it is important to be

able to discover the many different ways analytic thinking appears, both in humans and in animals. Yes, in animals too. It has been recently discovered that certain fish species can recognise themselves in the mirror, and that those fish also react to the pain and death of members of their own species. It is for this reason that no elements of life should be overlooked. It is only important to understand the different needs and functions of the multiple ways intelligence appears in every life context.

The art of Cecilia Vicuña has been really attentive to those differences, to the function of words to express intentions, to deny oppression or to describe the beauty of the sound of the human voice as a wind from the lungs that merges with the currents of the seas. Her work has been attentive to colours and how they, too, talk and address and give presence to blood that has been spilt, to the life that has been born, to the criminal acts that have been committed. The fibres she uses speak of the forests and the trees and their will

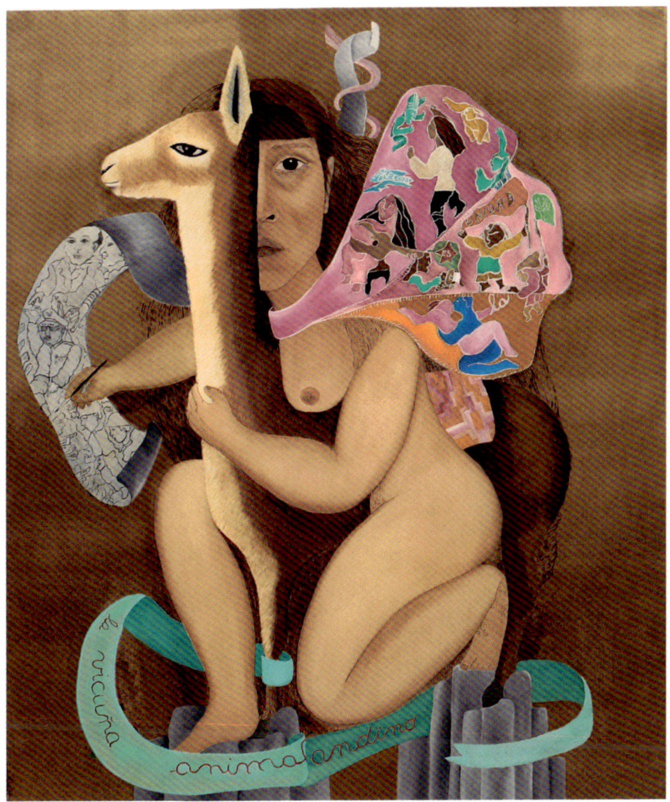

La Vicuña 1977, oil paint on canvas 139.1 × 119.4

to take us all into their embrace and make us breathe the air of Earth together, inhaling and exhaling as one. Her work has also been attentive to our dark desires: to extract, to possess and dispossess, to annihilate. But what is unique in Cecilia Vicuña's work is the profundity of her trust that we may change. And in this trust we need to fall asleep and wake renewed.

Transferencias (Transfers)

Imagine art creating paths for you to be able to engage in a pursuit. Paths that will cross your assumptions, that will meet your beliefs, that will expose you to the weathers of experiencing. Paths that are taking you as you take them. Imagine this now not as an individual but as a collective movement of crossing and inhabiting these paths – streams of people and animals and even plants. Ah, you are thinking I have gone too far: plants don't move. But plants *can* move. You have seen animation movies and didn't think they were such a crazy thing to witness. Now. Again. Streams of forms of life moving and meeting.

The work of Cecilia Vicuña represents a practice that believes in collective-to-collective transmission. Being together as a community and a group means traits and habits which differ from those we possess when we are alone. The study of complex systems has already shown that what a bird is able to do in a flock differs from the skills it has when it is by itself. The collective being allows the individual other ways of being in the world – ways that possess an intelligence that is only active within the collective.

Throughout her work, but especially in her performances, Cecilia Vicuña is calling for a gathering and a forming of a collective around and inside her work. The work acts as the substance that allows for a form of transferring that surpasses the idea of the author or the artist doing or acting in front of an audience. Her work is already a 'them', a non-binary entity embedded in the principles and values of collective doing and perceiving. And it is from there that she connects with the collective intelligence of nature and us. Understanding the importance of thinking in the terms, values and laws of the common good and the collective is fundamental if we are to interpret the political, aesthetic and epistemological dimension of her practice. Her works are like rivers, streams of water that are also the sum of many environments and forms of being. Symbiosis and mutuality are called and recalled constantly in her practice to induce in us a conception of life as having agency. It is not only the individual human that has agency, but every form of life. And if this is the case, we have no right to control or possess other forms of life. Instead, we have a duty to introduce co-creative forms of being together in the world with them.

The work of Cecilia Vicuña inhabits, and forces us to reflect on how to preserve and nourish, an expanding sensorial space. It is an expansion that is being achieved through a combination of artistic languages and certain genres (performance and installation, and also poetry), but also through presenting an uncommon intersection of art, non-binary culture-nature and vernacular and Indigenous wisdoms in the public domain. Her hyper-sensorialisation of materials and language embodies a change in the way we might imagine what is possible, proposing the invention of a new ground to sense not the past of art but a co-created future together. The work of Cecilia Vicuña has a metamorphic dimension: it aspires to be alive, to cease to be culture and become skin, shell, nature. And nature today names a complete revolution in the way we sense, in the way we relate to organic and non-organic life, and in the way we understand gender, generative life, power and life.

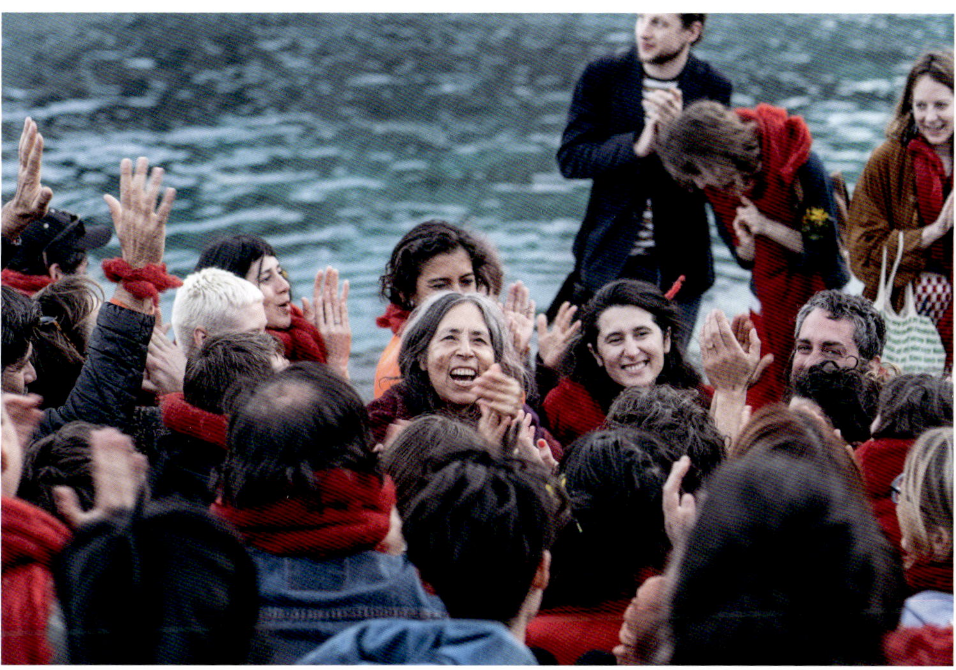

Beach Ritual (near Athens) 2017, documenta 14, ritual performance

Cecilia Vicuña
in conversation with Catherine Wood

7–8 June 2022

CW: For the Turbine Hall, everyone is so happy that you are building on the extraordinary Quipu Womb *in our collection and bringing a new quipu sculpture to London, the* Brain Forest Quipu. *What does the quipu mean for you?*

CV: The quipu, for me, is not at all as it has been defined since the colonisation of Peru. To archaeologists and anthropologists, the quipu is basically an object: a system of communication, a system via knots. It's been studied intensely for the last two centuries, especially since the late twentieth century. Of course, I read everything that's ever published about the quipu. And its complexity keeps growing as mathematics advances, and more and more is understood about not just the mathematics of the knot, but about how much information can be encoded in the shaping of the knot, in the direction of the spinning, the form of twisting, the colours of the threads and the position of the knots. This research has concluded that the kinds of iterations possible are just as many as in the alphabet that we use in the West.

You yourself have studied the history of the quipu for many years, from the perspective of a maker.

Yes, my perspective remains different. I feel that the quipu is really a field of knowledge alive with spirit energy, so vast that the Western mind doesn't have the tools to even consider it. Because the quipu, if some archaeologists are right, is at least five thousand years old. But it was only intensely used for the last two thousand years before the European colonisers arrived. The colonisers let it be for maybe a hundred years, but then when they started to exploit the land and the water and other natural resources, people showed up in the colonial courts with quipus as proof of their communal ownership, and their duties and responsibilities towards the land. That's when it was banned.

So, the quipu almost disappeared but didn't die completely – it stayed alive among the shepherds, in highland communities, and in several colonial forms that keep surfacing today.

When was your moment of revelation that this was a form for you, artistically?

The moment came when the teenage Cecilia, a little girl in Chile, came across not the object but the idea of the quipu in a book. And the idea overtook me so completely that the first evidence appeared in my poetry in the 1960s. I think the first time I made an object that looked like or had some connectivity to the quipu was in 1972, and then 1974. That tells me that this knowledge entered me or let me in. It's not so much that I learned about the quipu, but perhaps the quipu learned about me. The quipu began to live in me – as image, as imagination, as desire for knowledge, a yearning for 'What was it that made it exist?' And because I never let go of that passion, of that desire to learn, I kept learning about it. And eventually I began doing many forms of quipu, but I didn't learn about them in books. I learned from my hands, by making my own art and my own sculptures.

That intuiting of ancient practices is extraordinary, and it's a thread through the various forms of your work, whether in material, sung or spoken form, isn't it? How did your own work 'enter the quipu' for the first time?

In 1972 I wove my room in Con cón with blue thread. The room was not that large, but the weaving was maybe ten times larger than my body. And the most extraordinary thing about it is that when my friends and even my family walked into my room, they didn't see it. That caught my attention. I remember saying to my mother, 'Do you see something different?' 'No', she said, and she was inside the weaving!

But this notion of weaving, even if almost invisible to others, was the beginning of something very significant for you.

Yes – I thought, 'How interesting that this weaving is invisible to people.' I wrote at the time that my weaving was connecting heaven and earth. And I said, 'That's the reason why they don't see it – because they're so used to dealing only with daily life that if you interfere through art and a special weaving, it's just not readable.'

The first quipu I did in an arts space was in the year 2000, in Galería Gabriela Mistral in Santiago, Chile. Not even my friends at the Chilean Museum of Pre-Columbian Art took any notice that I had done a quipu the size of that big gallery. I did it as an invisible quipu, in a white room with white floor and white ceiling, with very thin white cotton threads.

That sounds very beautiful. And resonant with the raw materials and whites you are using for Tate, as well as the white wool of your 1999 piece Cloud-Net.

It was really exquisite. And again I witnessed how people could walk in the gallery, look at the space – 'Oh, it's empty!' – and leave. This was crucial for me to understand the existence of the quipu in a space that was beyond the Western mind. Eventually, I learned that the Incas had developed an invisible quipu.

What was the Inca conception of the invisible quipu? And how did it relate to your own?

What I call the invisible quipu was, for the Incas, the 'ceque' ('line') system that organised the ritual calendar and the movement of water for irrigation. It was a set of sightlines connecting sacred sites on land to the intergalactic space where water is born, via straight lines (not drawn on the ground), conceptualised as a mind quipu that embraced all communities.

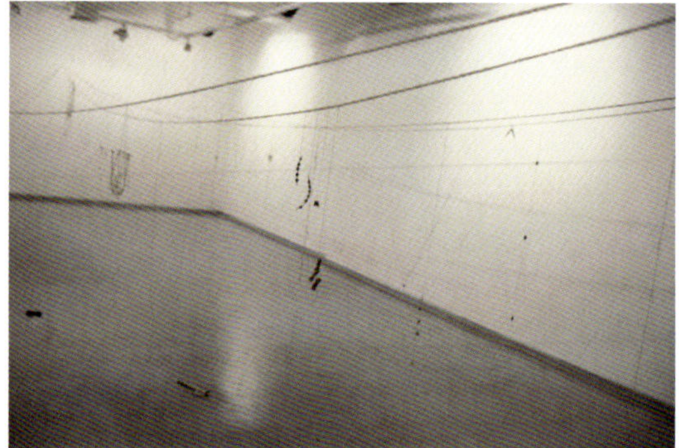

Quipu Semiyo 2000, Galería Gabriela Mistral, Santiago

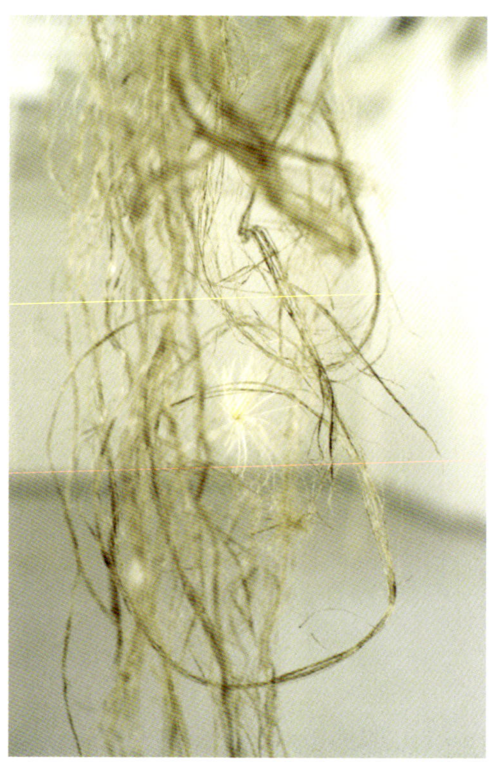

Quipu Semiyo 2000, Galería Gabriela Mistral, Santiago

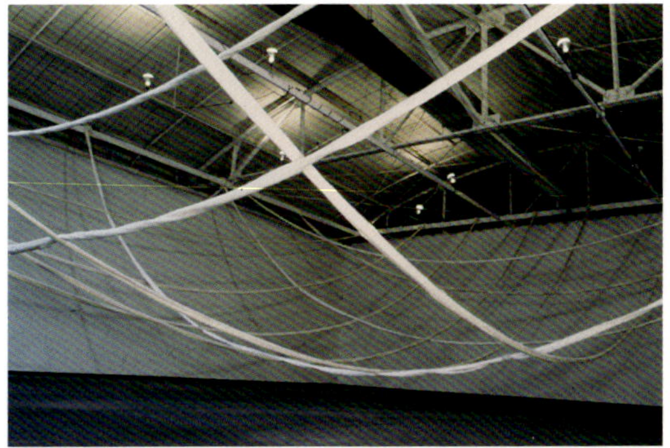

Cloud-Net 1999, Diverseworks, Houston

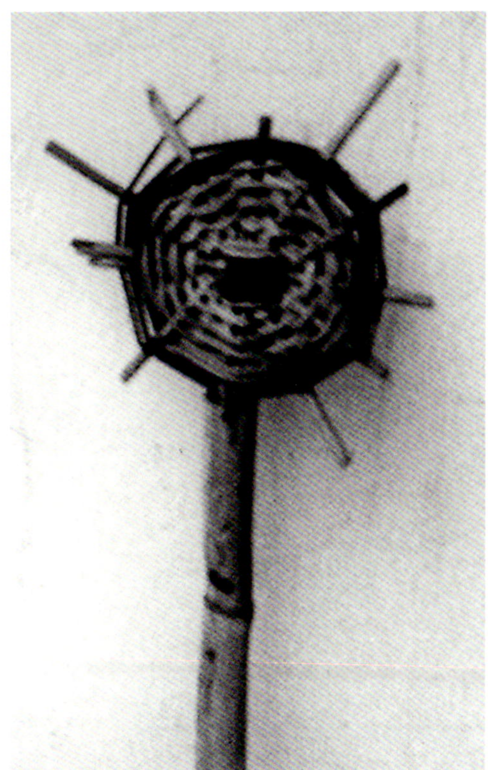

Culo e' canasta (Basket's Butt) 1966, destroyed

So how was it iterated or shared?

The 'knots' of this quipu were certain places, such as an important spring or a particular mountain – a ritual place that could be thought of as belonging to this line. Regular ritual activities were held at these sites, of which all were aware.

How incredible! And so, even though it was invisible, people would describe it and talk about it?

Yes, of course.

And draw it?

For a long time I thought there were no drawings, but lately I've learned there are petroglyphs in Machu Pichu.

Just describe it. And would it connect to the stars?

To the stars and to the summit of the mountains. There were forty-one sightlines emerging from Cusco – Cusco was the core – and when I read about this, I thought immediately, 'Wow! The ceque is a sacred quipu', and I began weaving the landscape. One side of the river to the other, one side of the rock to the other, one side of the street to the other. And then I began weaving people. Creating living quipus. Years later, I discovered a scholar had reprinted a small paragraph from a colonial text of the sixteenth or seventeenth century that described a collective ceremony very much like the living quipus I had by then been doing for decades.

May I ask, how or why do you feel you had this knowledge inside you?

It's impossible to know. That's why I say there's something like a field of knowledge, a collective field of understanding, that has been cultivated by

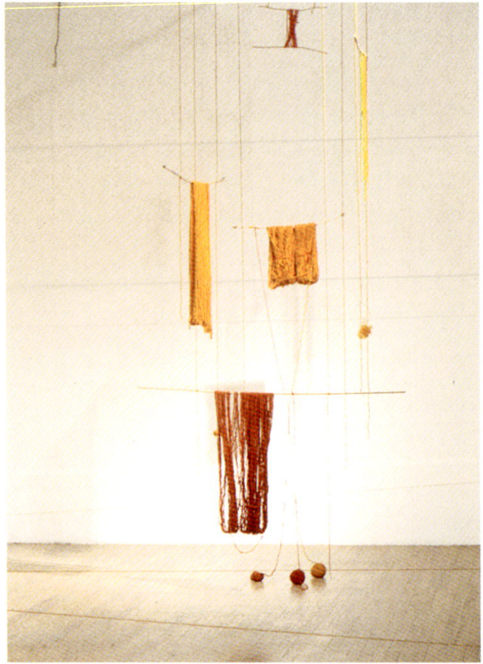

Ceque Fragments 1994, site-specific installation, Center for Contemporary Arts, Santa Fe
Below: detail

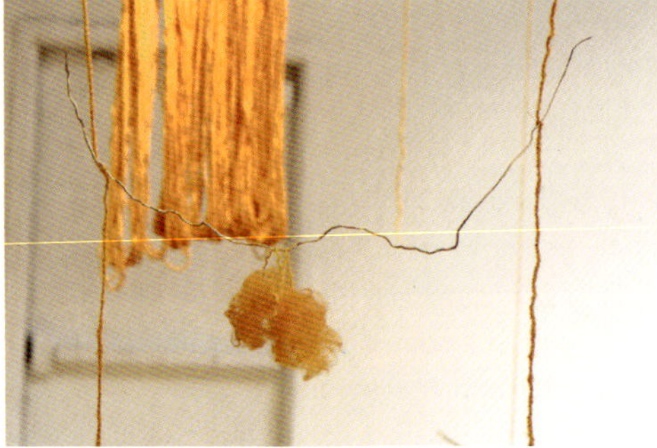

people for either five thousand years, two thousand years or five hundred years, depending on how you see it. So it's available, and certain people somehow connect to it, through their dreams or just their sensibility. I cannot describe it any other way without distorting it.

So in your body you had an instinctive knowledge of this tradition?

Yes. That's why you read in my poetry that my hands knew something I didn't. That's not a metaphor: I mean it literally. For example, I know that I'm able to paint because for thousands of years people have used the hand in a particular way. You can grab a pencil as you're grabbing it now because it's been millions of years of people doing just that grabbing gesture.

Did you ever read Michel Serres's book The Parasite? *This is Western philosophy, but he talks about humans working; how your work starts to become you so that you're just doing it, you're in the flow. He talks about it in relation to writing, but he says he becomes like a spider weaving its web. It becomes almost automatic.*

That's true. For example, I have written poems about me being a little girl – a toddler on all fours, not able yet to walk – and my mother knitting. My mother didn't work on a loom because looms had been eliminated from her mother line – at some point I discovered that she was Indigenous, but she didn't know it – maybe two centuries before she was born. So, I had this image of the threads as very large, and me very tiny looking up and seeing them against the light.

Children have an extraordinary ability to perceive colours, smells, sounds, that then are lost as they grow up. And now there's a lot of new neurological research noting that children have more senses than we do as adults.

There's something you said in a previous conversation that I loved, about letting the slow hidden voice within you rise above your European education, and how you listen to these whispers of what you called ancient knowledge and ancestral memory.

Nobody taught me that – it was born in me – but I can think of things that helped that imagination grow, which is of course the things that I read. I was a little reader from four or five, and I lived in the countryside, so there was nothing to distract me but the little animals. So, I spent a lot of time with the animals, plants, with the sound of the water, with the sound of the wind, the sound of the forest, and books. I connected those two worlds.

My father and mother had a wonderful library – they had art books and they had books in many languages, and that's how I learned so many languages, because nobody said, 'Oh, my darling, this book is in French, this book is in Italian', and so since French and Italian and Portuguese are similar, I more or less understood. [laughs] And I just read them.

We didn't have many comics, because it was the countryside, but I remember there was one man who came with one or two magazines per week, which we eagerly awaited. Some of them were typical Western comics like *Flash Gordon* and *Superman*, produced in the United States and translated in Mexico. But there were also Mexican comic books, with Pre-Columbian stories. So, I grew up reading those Pre-Columbian stories in comic-book form, firing the imagination of a child.

So, I related to language and then weaving and to all these things – things that you needed to discover and understand. The wonderful thing is that nobody explained anything. Nobody tried to make me read or make me do art – I just did things. And my mother and father were wise enough to let me alone to do whatever. When they saw that I needed paper or colours, they provided them – that's it.

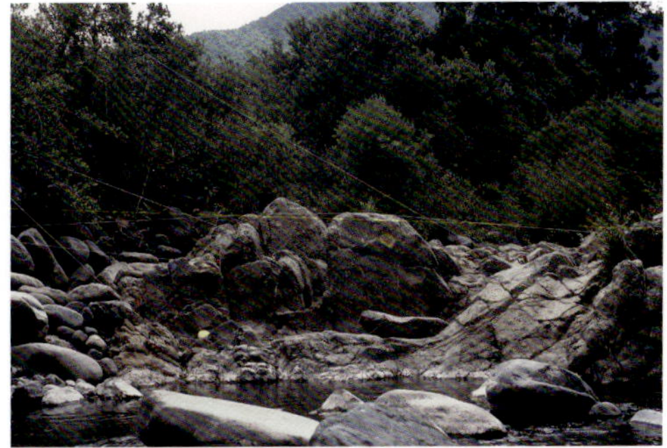

Antivero 1981, ritual performance, Colchagua, Chile

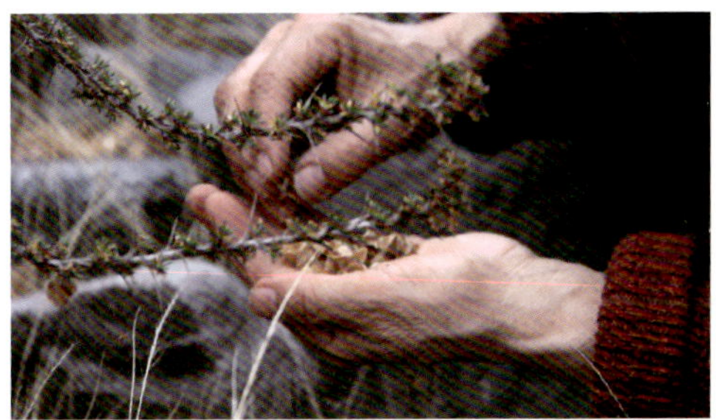

Semiya (Seed Song) 2015, HD video, colour and sound, 7 min 43 sec

In a way, there are two very distinct aspects of your practice. There are the figurative paintings with these stories and the portraits of individuals, such as your mother or Violeta Parra. Then there are the abstract forms – if we can call them that, even though they're writing-based – like the quipus. They look very different, but I wanted to ask you about the two aspects, because you've talked about both coming from a kind of dreaming place – but very different manifestations of the dreams.

What I consider my art, abstract and figurative, began on a very particular specific day in January 1966. I had finished high school and I had been admitted to architectural school, because I imagined that I could be an architect.

Why did you want to be an architect?

Because I was already a poet, I was already a little artist, according to me, doing a lot of paintings, abstract ones. Why did I think that abstract painting was painting, and not figurative? Because in my family there were very many women artists and only one of them – my grandmother – did figurative art. And I thought it was beautiful, but not for me. But my aunts were doing abstract works, including ceramic sculptures, very powerful ones, and their houses were filled with abstract paintings by their colleagues and friends. Because my family belonged to this community, my first painting was completely abstract, and I continued to do abstract work. And when I decided to study architecture, it was because I thought, 'There's no point in studying art or poetry because I'm already doing that. But architecture is the sort of art where all the other arts can be. I'll extend the poetry and art through architecture.'

So you were already thinking about how to 'make space' within which your art could exist – a social space? Which in a way is how I see your quipu structures –

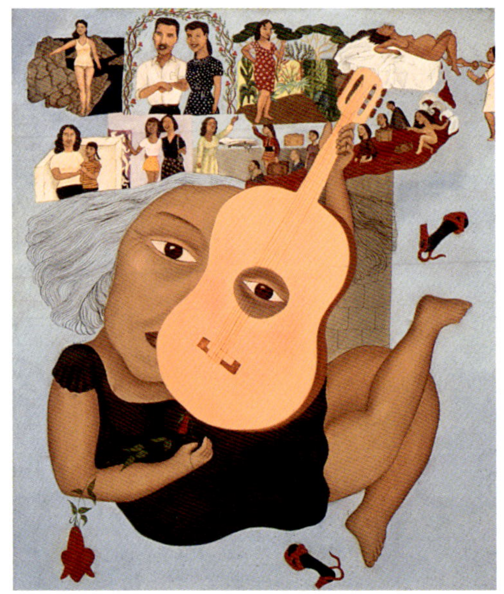

Bendígame Mamita 1977, oil paint on canvas 139.7 × 119.4

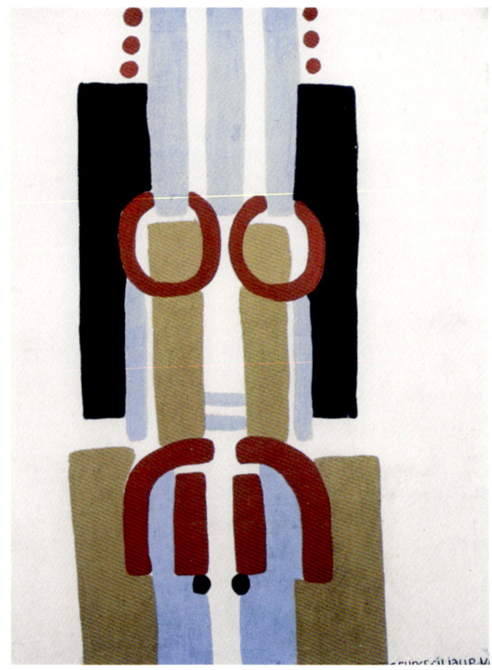

Brujo Azul (Blue Wizard) 1965, earth colour pigments on canvas, lost

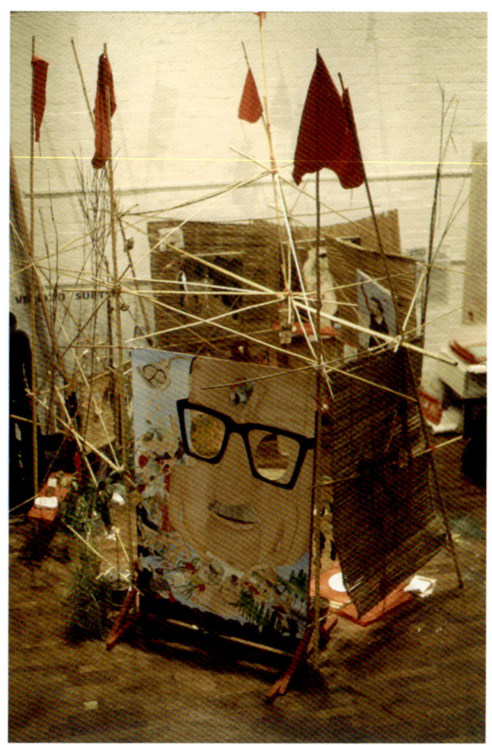

La ruca abstracta (o Los ojos de Allende) 1974, bamboo, wool, mixed media and seven oil paintings on canvas, 205 × 300 × 300, Arts Festival for Democracy in Chile, organised by Artists for Democracy, Royal College of Art, London

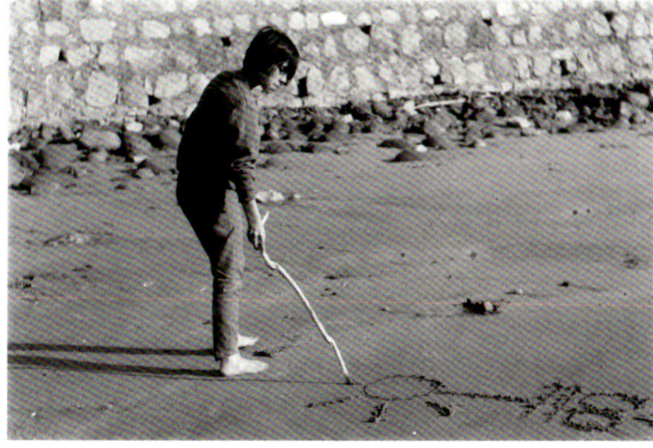

Cecilia Vicuña, Con cón 1966

Yes. So, I am on the beach on that day in January 1966. I have told this story so many times! And I feel the wind come, and instead of just going past, the wind made itself into a knot around my body. And I remember turning around as if I had been enveloped, caressed, by the wind. And that feeling made me realise: 'Is it the wind doing this?' I turned around to see the sea, the light, and I became aware that all of it was aware, and that I was being sensed exactly like I was sensing all that. And I dropped to the ground, the wet sand where I was by the sea, and I grabbed a stick, a piece of debris, and I pushed it into the wet sand, and drew. And when I did that, I knew that I was doing it not for me but for the sea and for the elements – in other words, I would be communicating with them just to say, 'Yes, I see.' And that was the first of my art. The next thing was picking up more debris. I created a little city, you know? Because I had it in mind that we needed to create a different kind of culture, a different kind of city, that would be erased by the high tide.

That precarity was already fundamental, then: making lines in the sand that would be washed away by the rhythm of the tides. 'Maximum fragility, maximum power', you've said, which I love. Was that drawing a one-off, though? Did you repeat that drawing in the sand, or were you satisfied that somehow the imprint of it stayed in the imagination?

It's hard to answer. Most likely I would already have been doing drawings in the sand regularly, but I only became conscious that this was art when I planted that stick. But the stick would behave exactly like the spirals, exactly like the drawings, because it was not permanent. One wave comes and, pah, it's gone. And somehow, I understood the beauty of that – the dissolution, the disappearance. Because then I came the next day and did it again.

Oh, you did? That's what I wanted to know.

I did. And I still do when I find myself by the sea, a river or lake. But not the same thing. Each time I did it, it was completely different, because there would be different debris, you know? I fell in love with the form, the shape of this debris – all of it abstract, of course – and a moment came when I decided, 'I will take one home because they are so beautiful.' I took it to my little studio, and I showed you a photo of the first precarious object that I did outside the beach.

Now, the first object that I did is the spiral, and it's a sun, and I call it *A Sun*. And I have a photo of it. The object itself disappeared, but I want to recreate it in this exhibition because it was so important for me. Because once I saw that, I had complete clarity that all this was one art form, whether it had appeared or disappeared, whether it remained or didn't remain. And that's when I came up with the concept of *arte precario*.

Many years went by, and one day I was looking at the abstract paintings I was doing before this event in 1966 – the paintings have gone, but I still have photos of them, and when you look at the paintings I was doing in 1965, you see that they are exactly the same as what I did in the sand. I had painted it before, as abstract painting. Putting them together, I said, 'Someday I have to make an exhibition like this, where I have the abstract painting' – which I would now want to recreate as it was – 'and the precarious object.' So that you would see that the root of my art is completely abstract.

I do see how the approach is travelling through you, to manifest in these different ways. But the interesting shift is that you were going from painting it to making it in the sand.

Exactly. It's the reverse of what you would think.

Yes, indeed. For example, the Western art-historical reading of the 1950s Japanese avant-garde group Gutai inferred that the live actions performed by the artists then manifested in a material work, and that's 'the work', but obviously we know that the performance was the work and the canvas was often secondary. So it's very interesting that you went from making the art object into intervening in the ecosphere. But this movement was back and forth, in your work?

For me, discovering that this painting pre-dated my sand piece as a form was important because if we think of the history of art, we don't know of many objects – let's say, from Palaeolithic times – because only a handful of things have remained, like little necklaces and carved pieces. There's no way of telling what came before – the act of painting or tattooing the body, or painting the caves or little carvings. Most likely it was like what I experienced: they evolved together, and whatever shot up first is immaterial because they existed in interaction with each other. So, when I saw that I had done it first in painting, I felt profound happiness, because it connected my art to this ancient gesture. Now they are finding painted surfaces that are seventy thousand years old. And I'm sure they will keep pushing back as more knowledge opens. Even today, as an old woman painting, I still feel the ancestral drive that connects the fluid that comes from my hand with that ancient pigment.

It's fascinating to hear you talk about the origins of your work. In the modern art world that we're in – and that the Guggenheim and Tate are participating in – the story is always one of innovation, rupture, the avant-garde that breaks with tradition. What you're talking about is tuning in to ancient traditions and practices. Of course, how you've done it has been original and it's been 'yours', but how do you see that tension between tradition and the idea of modernity?

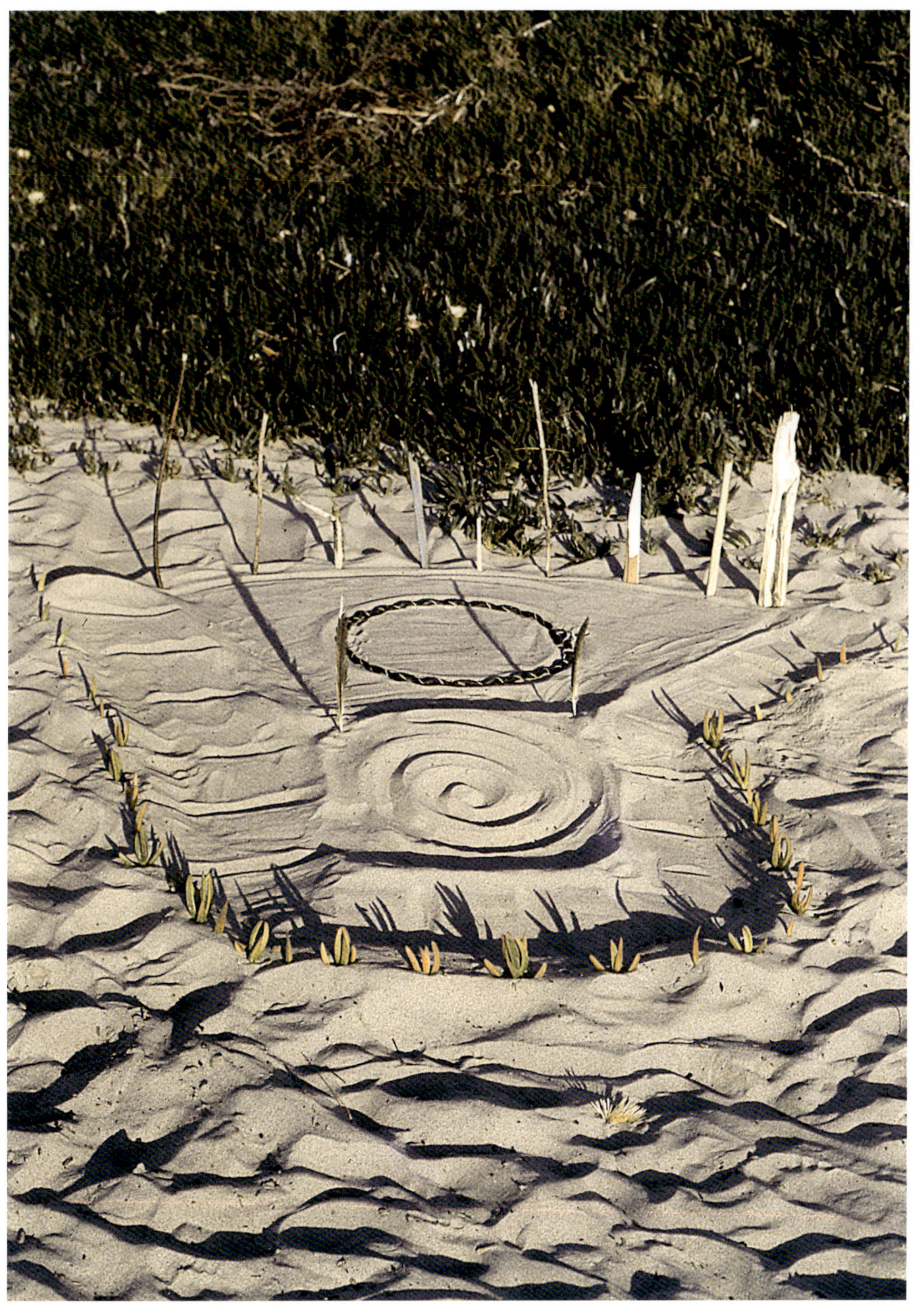

Casa espiral (Spiral House) 1966, site-specific installation,
destroyed, Con cón

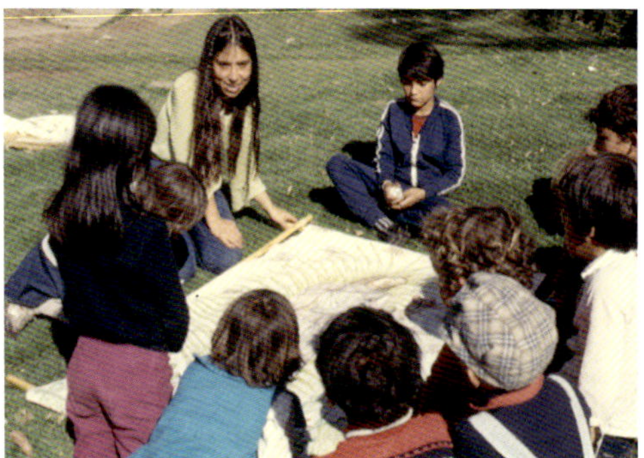

Cecilia Vicuña and her works from the exhibition *Homenaje a Vietnam* (Homage to Vietnam) during a workshop with children in Bogotá, 1977

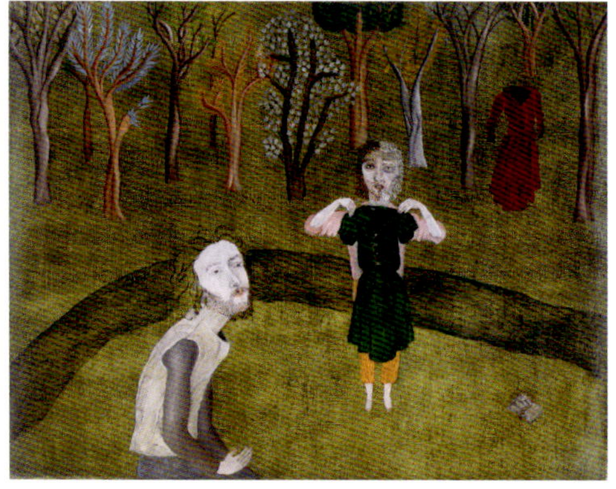

Keep the River to the Right 1973, oil paint on canvas 48.3 × 63.5

Well, it is true that I was educated, like everybody else, in the idea that for art to be art it had to be a break from something that existed before, so I am completely in tune with that. When I looked at the paintings in my aunts' places, I knew that I should not repeat anything that I had seen. I knew that that would make it not true, not real. It had to be something different. The search for difference was important to me – saying something that has not yet been said, or has been forgotten – but you cannot deny that whatever we do is always a continuation, too.

Though that continuation is less talked about in art.

It is not talked about because the West is interested in individuality and in signalling that this person is a genius as opposed to all the others. But in truth, everything that we do responds to something that we have received and something that we're building on. That is equally real, so one doesn't negate the other.

Exactly. And I love some of the ways you've talked about weaving people, invoking examples of the bridge that's braided, that's made by the community. The question of collective responsibility as well as collective skill-sharing comes into this approach. And you've also done a lot of teaching, haven't you, in making your work, extending and elaborating your work, whether with children or different community groups?

Yes, absolutely. Because I have the sense that, just as these arts have really illuminated my life, that they can do that for everyone. I see the joy, I see how it liberates the imagination and the senses. And whenever I have done it, it's like an explosion, a geyser of happiness.

I once did a big installation in the Museum of Fine Arts in Boston – the American northeast, one of the most repressive societies in the world. We were building a quipu together, and all the staff

working with me in this big, majestic, Western-
oriented museum worked regularly having to
follow the four thousand rules institutions demand
of their workers. And I can tell you that while
we were building together, we danced inside the
knots. Every morning they arrived eager to do
some more! Nobody felt it as a duty. Everybody
was just coming for the joy, sharing their stories …
It was a thing of beauty.

*Absolutely. Working in a big institution like Tate as I
do, I think about your approach and how you foreground
joy – manifest in that early work of yours creating a
living room as part of your work in 'warming up the
museum'. As you say, what we do should be a collective
endeavour that is based in sharing in the joy of the art.
I was reflecting recently that in many other cultures our
security guard system of protecting objects would be a
sacred role rather than the rather low-paid, low-status
role it has historically been in the Western museum.
And there have been a number of artists who've tried to
rethink the choreography of positions in the museum, to
rethink the labour and how that is part of the ritual.*

And it becomes a ritual. Yesterday I went as a
viewer to see my show at the Guggenheim, and
many of the guards came at different moments to
talk to me, to tell me how they felt, transforming
the notion that they are non-speaking guards.
They are not – they are people. They brought to
me presents, testimonies and stories, what people
had said, and how much they loved explaining in
their own terms: 'That's not a rope.' And it was
so beautiful.

*Your Guggenheim exhibition includes many of your
paintings which embody the figurative aspect of your
dreaming, and that connect to surrealism. This brings us
back to your time in London in the 1970s, when you met
Roland Penrose, who supported your work. Did you see
yourself as part of 'surrealism'?*

Yes and no. I had a wonderful conversation about
this with Dawn Ades in which I said, 'I don't
think Latin American artists were followers of
surrealism – I think Latin American artists were
surrealist even before surrealism came forth.'
[laughs] Because the reality is such that if you start
researching, you're going to find that these kinds
of juxtapositions are completely part of the culture.
Dawn was very interested, and she asked, 'Where
did you read that?' And I said, 'Nowhere! It's just
what I think.' – 'But why do you think that way?'
And I said, 'Well, because I was a painter once,
and you could certainly say that my paintings are
surrealist, but I didn't think of myself as surrealist.
I just was painting the way the Indians painted
their own transformations of Christianism.'

*I don't know if you were reading Freud and thinking
about the subconscious, or were you intuiting and
dreaming these scenes?*

Well, I was aware of Freud – I did read one of his
books on dreams, but I read it when I was fourteen
or fifteen and I didn't pay much attention to the
idea of the subconscious. I paid a lot of attention to
the question of dreams, the importance of dreams,
but not to the theories.

*But then you were talking about Indigenous culture,
the dreaming space, and how you're bringing to your
paintings the three levels of the quipu in terms of
conceptual, ritual and material. So you had another
dreaming culture that wasn't about Freud, but you were
aware of that. So in a sense it's a decolonial approach
to surrealism.*

Yes, as a funky continuation of the ancient
culture of the Americas. And of course, I love the
surrealists. The technique I paint with I got from
Leonora Carrington. I followed the method, not
the image, just as she, in turn, was following the
medieval method of the early Renaissance. Back

in 1969, I stayed with Leonora for three days on
my way between the US and Chile, and it was
absolutely fantastic. I slept under a Max Ernst
tapestry! Like a dream.

And what was the method you learned from her?

The method is you first do a layer – a brown
ground – and then you build up layer after layer of
your image.

*So it's a sort of glazing technique, of thinner washes that
build up?*

Thinner washes. Absolutely. It's almost like
watercolour, but with oil. If you look at one of my
paintings through a microscope it's really almost
transparent – my layers are transparent.

*Yes, the paint is luminous. I see that relationship to the
medieval. This is such a rich backdrop to then thinking
of you now in 2022 in London. I remember that we
were talking during lockdown about the Thames. I love
the way that, as an activist and as a poet and an artist,
you talk about water and humidity and the water that
sustains human life and plant life – and we'll talk shortly
about your activism for the rainforest. But I remember
asking you about the relationship between your work
coming into our collection and the Thames next door, the
'great brown god', and you were saying you'd performed
a ritual on the shore, quite recently.*

Yes. Each time I come to the Tate I do the same
thing: I go down and touch the water and make
an offering for the water. When I lived in London,
you couldn't do that – or I never knew a way. The
studio I had in Stepney Green was not far from the
Thames, but I had no access to the river. It was
like an industrial zone, so there wasn't a walkway
at the riverfront, none of that.

Yes, that's true. Well, now it's less polluted and you can

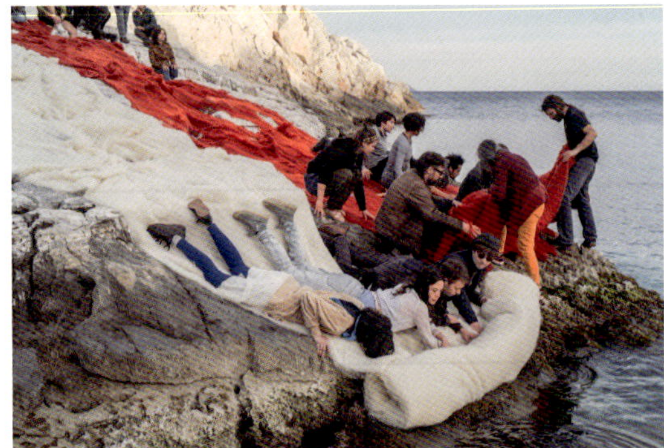

Beach Ritual (near Athens) 2017, documenta 14, ritual
performance

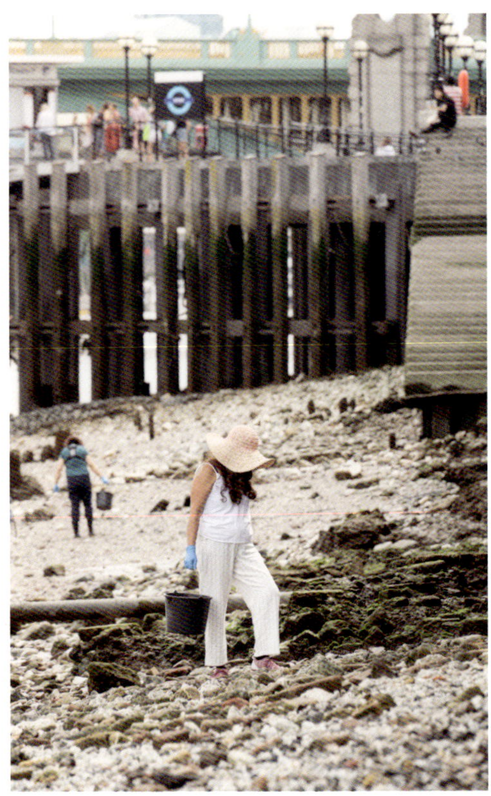

Two members of the community in Southwark mudlarking on
the banks of the River Thames, London, July 2022

walk down there, and I know that you're thinking that the work for Tate will involve mudlarking and collecting objects there.

When we were doing the *Quipu Womb*, I wanted to do a continuation of the quipu into the Thames, like I did in Athens. Remember? In Athens the great quipu at the EMST Museum 'continued' metaphorically at the coast, into the Mediterranean Sea. I wanted to do the same in London, though this was interrupted by Covid.

It would be amazing to do it when we do the Turbine Hall, then – to extend the quipus that you're going to make for the Brain Forest Quipu *with an action, working with people in the community: the social weaving of the quipu that you've talked about.*

The sculpture itself will be, to a great extent, a collaborative construction, because I will invite the participation of several people to either gather materials or make elements of it. And I consider it to be a collaboration as well with the plants and animals whose hairs and fibres are going to be woven. That is one aspect of it.

Can you tell me about the sound dimension of the quipu?

This is one of the aspects inspired by the ancient invisible quipu. The 'Sound Quipu' will also be a collective piece which will involve both natural sounds, cultural new sounds, and archival sounds – we will weave in multiple forms. For this quipu I will collaborate with Ricardo Gallo, who will arrange or compose new music for the quipu, as well as organising the multiple juxtapositions following the audiovision that I 'hear'.

You have collaborated with Ricardo Gallo before. How did you start working together?

He was giving a concert in New York with a group of Colombian musicians, all of them masterful, beautiful. But when he played the piano, I didn't hear regular piano according to my ear. I heard sounds that belong in a sort of extra dimension of sound in nature, that I identify as the Andean music, or the music of the mountains. Sometime after that Ricardo came to a poetry reading of mine and he said he heard music inside my words. Of all the many musicians I had collaborated with, none had ever said that, so it seems we're hearing in each other something that cannot be exactly named, yet we hear it and let it guide us.

How will it work at Tate?

When you invited me to do the Turbine Hall, I knew immediately that I wanted to do a spatial quipu and a sound quipu, because the space wants it. Whenever I have been to the Turbine Hall, there's a very pleasing sound already there, composed of human voices. A child shouts, a guard says, 'don't do that'... It's a space where all sounds compose each other. I imagined a sound piece that would play with that, adding a few more layers all softly waning, just like the forests are fading, and their sounds too. All the infinite richness of sound of this world is disappearing with the extinction of the species, and it pains me. It will be a composition of intervals, with the negative space of silence as one of its key principles. It will probably be a subtle, tenuous piece.

And there are additional dimensions of the quipu for the twenty-first century?

Yes, there are two more dimensions of the quipu: a digital exchange where I invite the voices of the peoples involved in the struggle to protect the forests of the world to be present at the Tate, via the video messages and urgent calls to action that many communities and organisations are producing. And the last one is the ritual 'Quipu of Encounters' involving the activists who are mobilising to stop the destruction of ecosystems by the ever-increasing investment in extraction by European and American banks around the world.

My hope is that the combination of these collective ritual activities will act as a distant echo of the multidimensional quipu that disappeared five hundred years ago through colonial violence. I imagined it as three aspects, but I see now that they are really four. If we can pull this off, it will be the first time that these quipu forms will be manifestly present, so that people will recognise in them organisational patterns of behaviour that are art forms in themselves. My hair stood on end when I said that! This is really a first time. All the quipus that I have done before were preparing the way for this because these dimensions were never allowed or understood before in a Western context, you know?

I liked how when you first talked about making quipus for Tate you said, 'The quipu is not entering Tate – Tate is entering the quipu.' And I now understand this in terms of how you think of the quipus as a network, conceptually, materially and socially. I wondered if you could say something about that, and about how your activism from a climate point of view intersects with the quipu on its multiple levels.

When I say that the Tate is entering the quipu and not the other way round, I mean it in terms of history. The quipu is an ancient system of perception, of thought. Tate Modern is only twenty-two years old. [laughs] So it's something new – it's like a child compared to the quipu, you see? The fact that we suppressed the richness and multidimensionality of the quipu as it was in the fifteenth century doesn't detract from the fact that it's still there in potential. And this has to do with what I consider my activism, even though it is not at all what people conceive of as activism. My activism is not only disregarding the thoughts

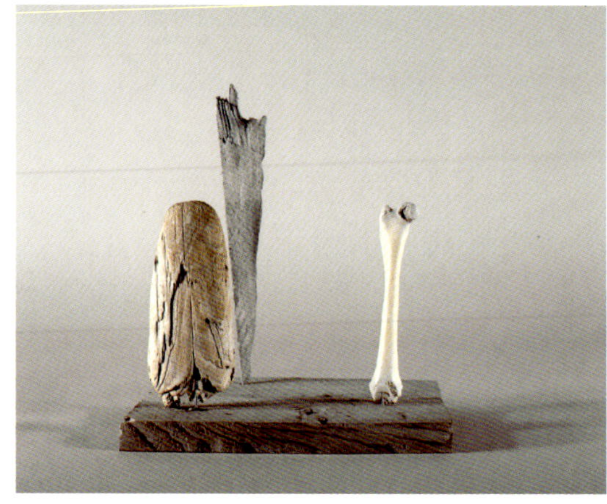

Cementerio (Cemetery) 1982, mixed media, wood, and bones

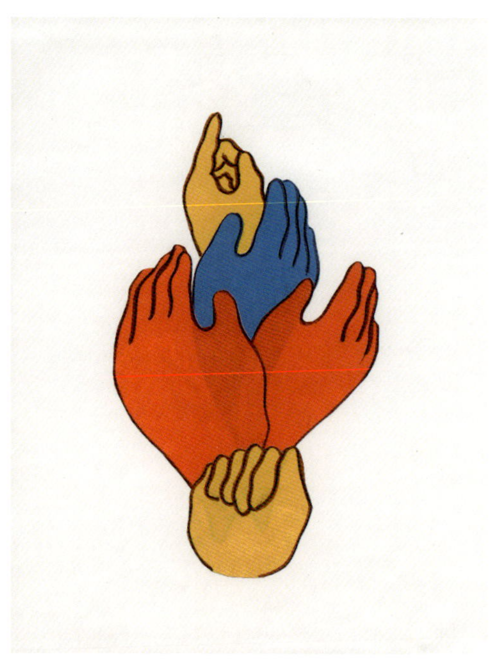

Árbol de manos (Tree of Hands) 1974, collage on paper, 30.5 × 23

and definitions received from Western domination, but searching for the other thoughts and perceptions that exist in us as human beings. Because we are the living proof that this universe of humanness is not what we have been told. The word 'human' literally means 'of earth' – 'hummus' – so our humility and the humidity of earth are one. If we cease to perceive this relationship, both suffer; our humanness is reduced and endangered when the humidity of earth is endangered. There is a deep linguistic ecology, a knowledge embedded in words, you see? We cannot afford to continue this idea that language and earth are separate, because they never have been. And now there is a collective movement of artists around the world focusing on collaboration, reciprocity and exchange, so there is a glimmer of light at the end of this tunnel of extinction and extermination of cultures and languages.

It makes me think differently of the choreography of the public museum as a place for gathering, and how the quipu draws people in and organises people in another way, which has a lot to do with your own sensitivity to materials and how you're drawing in space. Making these very fine details in your large quipus draws people's perception right in, allowing them to get lost in the variety of materials that you've found.

An activism of perception and of language observes how language interacts with all the other fields of collective understanding, including the field of what is defined as art. The quipu is a guide precisely because it was a force expressing multiple forms of society, including a virtual dimension where the people could see themselves as interconnected – not only with each other and the earth but with the cosmos, and the origin of water in intergalactic space, as I mentioned before. Now, of course, we know that water exists all over the universe and that it is born in the intergalactic dust – a new 'discovery' that confirms the knowledge

the Andean shepherds carried from ancient times to the present. And now we are in the process of shifting, all of us together, an ecology of perception and understanding. And that's where the Tate and the quipu are coming together – because the quipu wants and needs the Tate as much as the Tate needs and wants the quipu. That's why you and I are working on this. The truth of the matter is that the will to self-transformation exists both within the Tate and within the field of the quipu that has me working within it. And now for a huge number of young artists, thinkers, scholars, archaeologists, scientists, information technology theorists, the quipu is back in our universe of speech and discourse, and for a very good reason.

Different institutions offer different conditions and limitations that I hope we can bypass now, because we are at an urgent time for humanity, and the Tate knows it and I know it. So we are, I hope, in a different moment of consciousness and collective awareness – therefore the collective quipu can come to us this time, to blossom as new life for the forests we are weaving for.

Cecilia Vicuña: Time Lines

Fiontán Moran

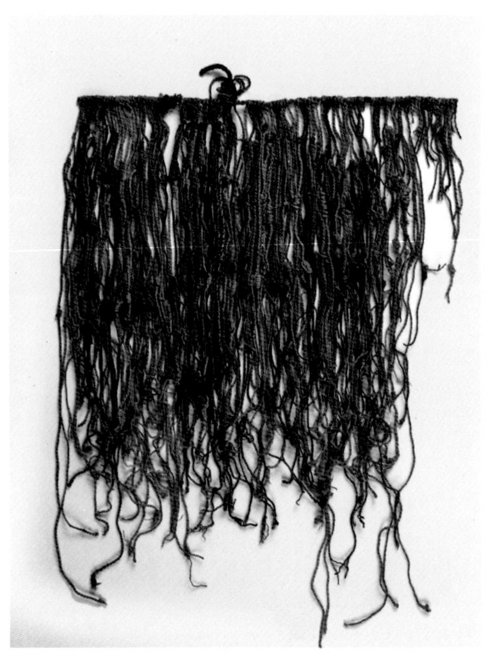

Quipu from Peru c.1400–1532, cotton 40 × 31

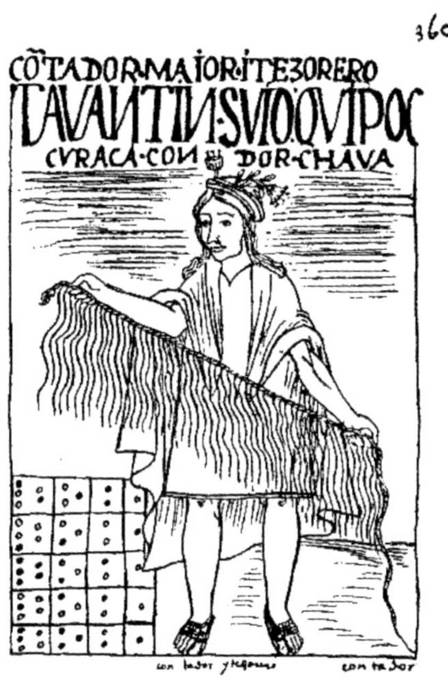

Sketch of a *quipucamayoc* from *El primer nueva corónica y buen gobierno* (The First New Chronicle and Good Government), a chronicle of Inca history by the Indigenous Inca historian Felipe Guaman Poma de Ayala (c.1535–1616). Shown on the lower left side is a yupana – an Inca calculating device.

Time moves through the work of Cecilia Vicuña. It is there in the narrative of her paintings, in the experience of her poetry and performances, and in her work foregrounding Indigenous knowledge, most explicitly referenced in her quipus.

The QUIPU is an ancient recording system that was used by the people of the Andes from 2500 BCE through to the sixteenth century, when its usage was stamped out by the Spanish colonists. Meaning 'knot' in the Quechua language, the quipu usually consists of a long textile cord from which hang multiple strands knotted into different formations and in different colours that were able to encode as much complex information as the alphabet. Although the exact meaning behind the knots is not now known, it is thought that they were used to record statistics, poems and stories, thereby creating a tactile relationship to memory and the imaginary.

In Andean society the past, present and future were seen to coexist in objects in a way that reflected the cyclicality of nature. As every knot in a QUIPU can be retied, it provides a way to think through the concept of linear time and the ease with which it can unravel.

Knotting is used literally and metaphorically in Vicuña's work. Through her close attention to materials, be they bodies, song, textile, paint or film, she creates a space to imagine how art can meaningfully engage with contemporary concerns around ecology, feminism, sexuality and politics – yet all with a sense of poetry.

In her text on the revolutionary Rosa Luxembourg, Jacqueline Rose writes: 'There is no politics without a poetics of revolution.'[1] She describes how Luxembourg understood that any real revolution needs to embrace spontaneity, change, and failure; that 'the unprecedented, unpredictable nature of the revolutionary moment be carried over into the life that follows'.[2]

1948

Vicuña's time has been one of endless personal and political revolutions and evolutions. Born in 1948 at the foot of the Andes, she identified from an early age with Indigenous culture. She recalled:

> When I was a little girl I liked to put a feather in my hair and say to the other children in the neighbourhood, 'Can you imagine what we'd be doing if the Spaniards hadn't come here?'[3]

The feather, as a connection to nature and an early writing utensil, became the symbol of Vicuña's identity and the tool through which she would make her work.[4]

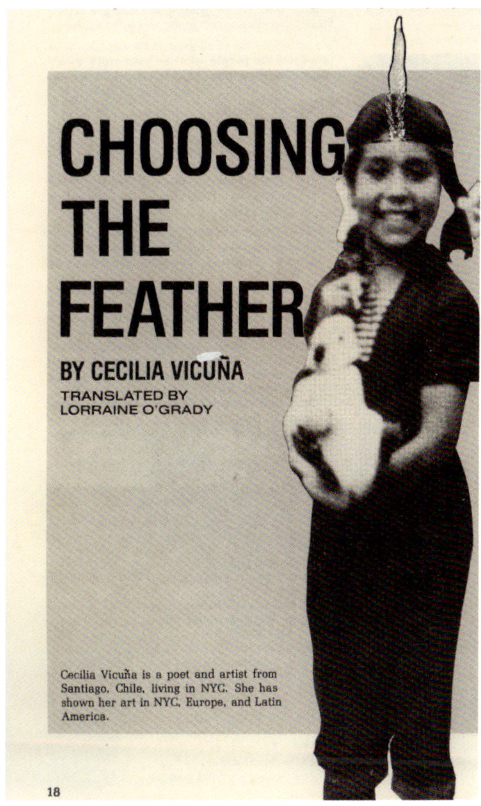

Portrait of Cecilia Vicuña as a child, published in *Heresies*, issue no.15, 1982

1963–6

Growing up in an intellectual and creative family, Vicuña was encouraged to explore her interest in reading and writing poetry. When she had exhausted the limits of language she turned to making abstract paintings and sculptures. Most of the works she made between 1963 and 1966 are lost, including a robot sculpture, illustrated here.

Her aunt Rosa Vicuña was a sculptor, and it was in her studio that Cecilia first encountered the quipu in a book. Later, she wrote in her journal:

'El quipu que no recuerda nada'

(The quipu that remembers nothing)

Such an object would suggest a quipu of unknotted or unknottable strands. It would be a quipu of loss – a loss reflecting the destruction of Indigenous knowledge, practices and history that Vicuña has tried to recuperate in her work.

1966

One day in 1966, while visiting the beach in Con cón in Chile, Vicuña found herself drawing a circle and spiral in the sand, arranging stones, sticks, and feathers, and then letting the tide sweep it all away. It was a process that for her seemed to connect to a kind of ancient energy.

This fleeting moment came to signify the beginning of Vicuña's ongoing *precario* series, an approach to making objects composed of nondescript precarious materials and held together in precarious ways. This was not an art concerned with longevity. Instead, the objects share a quality akin to an offering. Years later Vicuña discovered that the Latin origin of 'precarios' was *precis*, meaning prayer.[5]

1967

Many of Vicuña's works, especially those from the early part of her career, were transient moments that often went undocumented. This use of refuse and refusal of permanence formed a component of her *NO Manifesto* of 1967, which asserted her

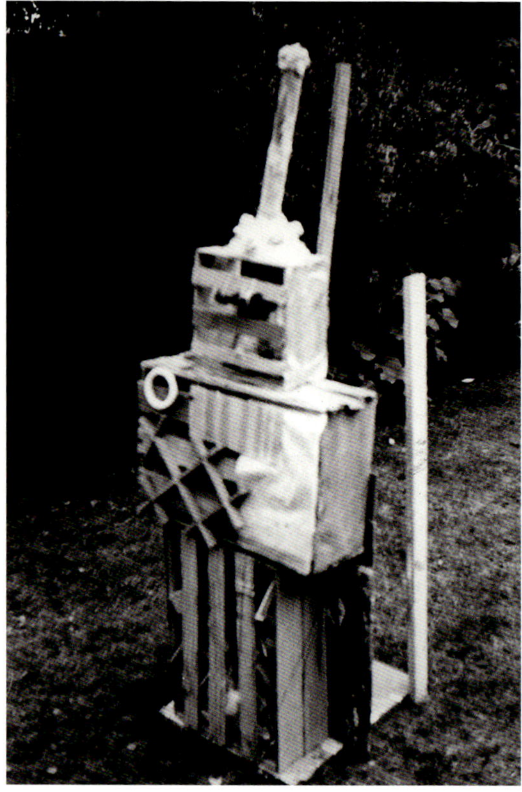

Robot 1966, mixed media, destroyed

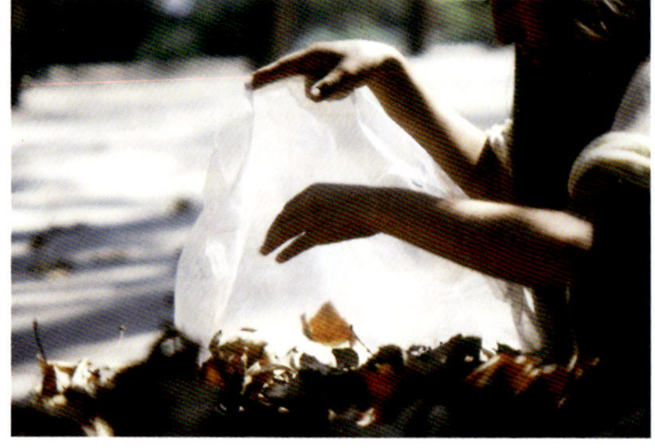

Autumn, gathering autumn leaves performance, 1971

non-identification with any movement, dogma or establishment. It would serve as the basis for a collective she formed with fellow artist and poet friends called the Tribu No. Together they would produce actions, poems and performances in Santiago that sought to challenge the conservative nature of Chilean society:

> I remember the mid-sixties in Chile, when nobody used the word 'performance', yet, we were already 'performing' poetic acts to transform our experience of the world, both in the collective scale of the democratic revolution and in the personal scale.[6]

1969

This sense of possibility and liveness was present in Vicuña's paintings too. In a handwritten note from 1969 she describes these works as part of a 'living process of thought in which everything is about to happen'.[7] After viewing abstract works at the Museum of Modern Art in New York, she began to make figurative paintings that drew upon the Cusco school of the sixteenth and seventeenth centuries which united European art traditions with Andean beliefs.[8] Like those religious images, and as in her poetry, in her paintings Vicuña plays with metaphor and symbols, often presenting figures within a shallow depth of field.

It was in 1969 that she met the surrealist artist Leonora Carrington, whose painting technique and dream-like subject matter were a formative influence. In fact, Carrington's poem 'What is a Woman?', written the following year, chimes with Vicuña's painting and poetry in its questioning of identity, the vivid imagery she deploys and her sense of humour:

> If I am my thoughts, then I could be anything from chicken soup to a pair of scissors, a crocodile, a corpse, a leopard or a pint of beer.

> If I am my feelings, then I am love, hate, irritation, boredom, happiness, pride, humility, pain, pleasure, and so on and so forth.

> If I am my body, then I am a foetus to a middle-aged woman changing every second.[9]

1970

In 1970 Salvador Allende and the Popular Unity Party were elected to power in Chile, making him the first democratically elected socialist president of a country.

1971

The election of Allende instigated an active and dynamic creative scene in Chile. The works that Vicuña made in 1971 – the year she graduated from university – reflect both the sense of possibility and an awareness of the precarity of any progressive social movement. In the work *Autumn* she stuffed leaves into clear plastic bags and across the floor of the National Museum of Fine Arts in Santiago. Bringing the outside inside, Vicuña conceived the work as a contribution to socialism and a dedication to the 'absolute joy of an instant'.[10]

A few weeks later she exhibited a series of figurative paintings including *Biombo (Casita Para Pensar Qué Situación Real Me Conviene)* (Small House to Think What Real Situation Suits Me) 1971, a free-standing folding screen that featured a series of revolutionary figures, from Janis Joplin through to a North Vietnamese guerrilla fighter, their faces replaced with mirrors. This meant that when the viewer stepped inside the standing screen they had to think about their place in this 'real situation' of social and political change.

1972

In 1972 Vicuña moved to London on a scholarship to study at the Slade School of Art. At the time she was working on a series of paintings dedicated to 'Heroes of the Revolution' (1971–8) that placed

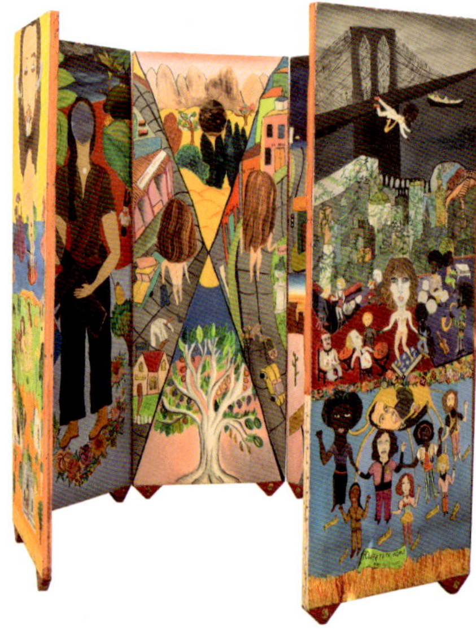

Biombo (*Casita Para Pensar Qué Situación Real Me Conviene*)
(Small House to Think What Real Situation Suits Me) 1971,
oil paint on canvas, 12 panels, 155 × 55 each

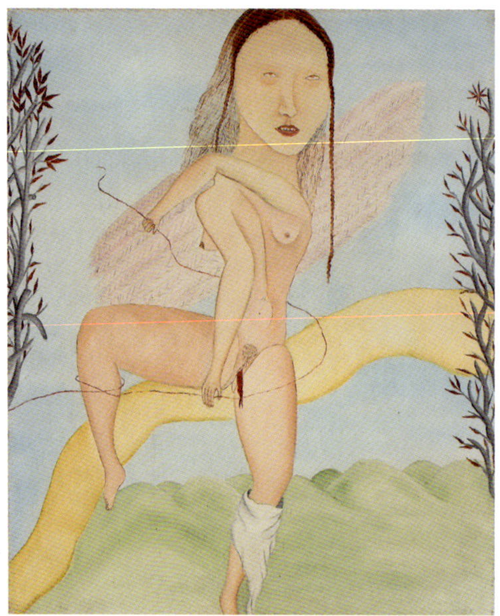

Ángel de la menstruación (Menstruation Angel) 1973, oil paint
on canvas 57.1 × 48.2

political figures within dream-like environments
that queered the usual representation of male
heroism. Karl Marx is surrounded by fornicating
couples, Allende and Fidel Castro appear like a
couple, and Lenin holds a sign stating: 'The people
will never reach complete liberation until they
achieve the complete liberation of women.'[11]

1973

Not all the heroes Vicuña painted were political
leaders, as shown by the 1973 painting of Violeta
Parra, a Chilean singer, songwriter, poet artist,
who toured rural Chile recording and compiling
popular and folkloric music. This led to the
reinvention of Chilean folk music known as *Nueva
canción* (New Song), which became important in
popularising Salvador Allende's leadership. The
banner in the painting references Parra's work with
textiles and features scenes and symbols from her
life and her best-known song 'Gracias a la vida'
(Thanks to life).

Like Vicuña's poems, which featured
celebratory expressions of sexuality, many of her
paintings convey a sense of joy. In the self-portrait
Angel de la menstruación (Menstruation Angel) 1973
she creates a 'cosmic weaving' where the blood
clots of her body unite with the red hemp string in
her hand as she flies through the air.

In June 1973, right-wing Chileans attempted
to overthrow the Popular Unity government of
Allende. Vicuña responded by creating a set of
precarios in honour of the revolution. However, on
11 September 1973 the Chilean military, led by
General Augusto Pinochet and with the aid of the
United States, staged a military coup d'état that
resulted in Allende taking his life. The *precarios*
became 'objects of resistance'.

When she exhibited *Precarios: A Journal of
Objects for the Chilean Resistance* in London, Vicuña
included a text explaining that the poverty of their
appearance was 'their socialist character' and that
they aimed to 'kill three birds with one stone':

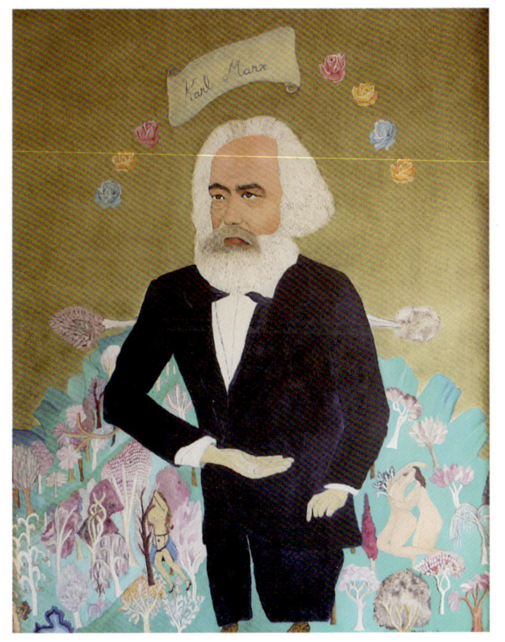

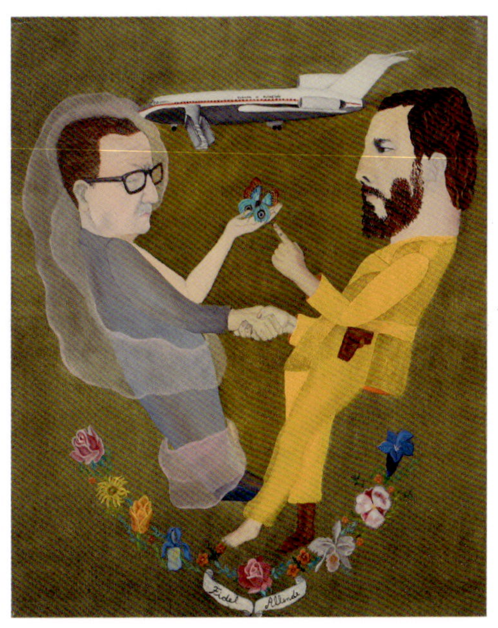

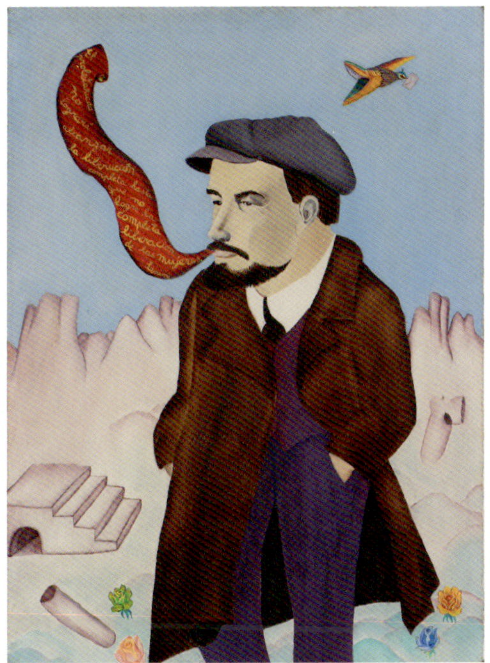

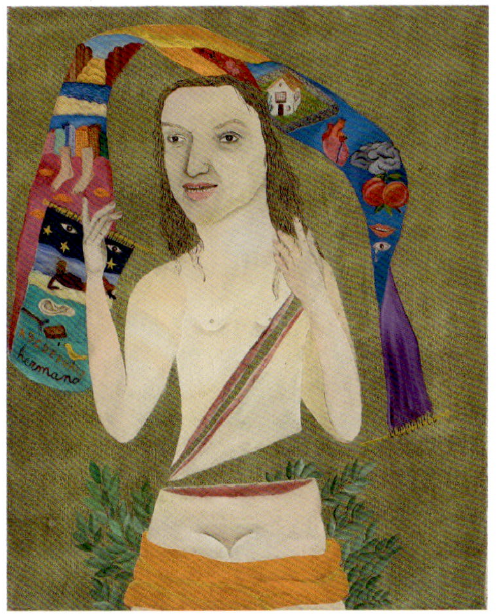

Violeta Parra 1973, oil paint on canvas 58.1 × 48.1

Heroes of the Revolution series 1971–8
Karl Marx 1972 (top left), *Lenin* 1972 (top right), *Fidel and Allende* 1972 (bottom left)
Oil paint on canvas 91.1 × 71.7, 69.9 × 51.1, 72 × 59

politically: stand for socialism
magically: help the liberation struggle
aesthetically: be as beautiful as they can to give
strength to the soul.[12]

Vicuña conceived of each object as a chapter in a
journal. Their inherent fragility encouraged the
viewer to linger over the works and be attentive to
the careful collaging of elements that were for the
artist 'the result of a caress'.[13] There is also a sense
of play: one object, made on a piece of wallpaper,
cuts up the phrase 'El pueblo unido jamás
será vencido' (The people united will never be
defeated) to create a set of cards where the words
and their syllables can be endlessly rearranged.

Some of the *precarios* and associated texts were
included in Vicuña's artist book *Saborami* (1973),
published by Beau Geste Press in Devon.
The title came from the popular bolero 'Sabor a
Mí' (Taste of Me) and the book brought together
almost ten years of work in a collage technique
that blurred the traditional demarcation between
poetry and art.

1974

Despite being in exile from her own country,
Vicuña continued to find practical ways to support
the Chilean resistance. In May 1974 she founded
Artists for Democracy with the artists John
Dugger and David Medalla, alongside curator and
writer Guy Brett. In October of the same year the
group staged a festival at the Royal College of Art
featuring an exhibition of works donated by artists
such as Claes Oldenburg and David Hockney, as
well as film screenings and performances.

In September 1974, one year after the Chilean
coup, more than ten thousand people assembled at
Hyde Park in London and marched in protest and
solidarity. The protest was co-organised by British
trade unions and the Chile Solidarity Campaign, of
which Vicuña was a member. Those who arrived at
Trafalgar Square were greeted with a large political

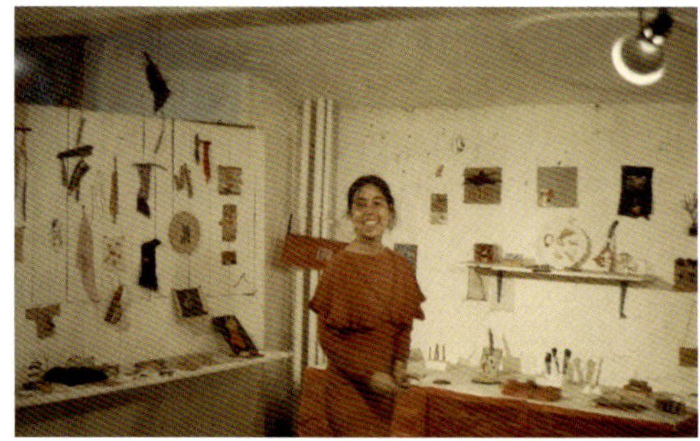

Vicuña with her installation *Precario: A Journal of Objects for the
Chilean Resistance* 1974, Arts Meeting Place, London

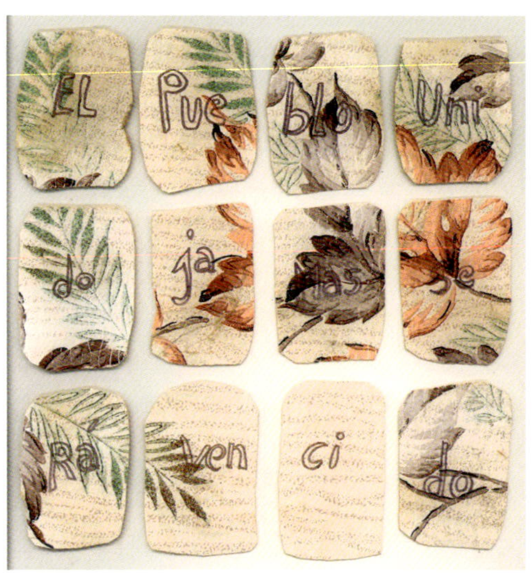

Juego de cartas, El pueblo unido jamás será vencido (card game)
1974, from the series *Twelve Books for the Chilean Resistance*, part
of *Precarios: A Journal of Objects for the Chilean Resistance*, felt-tip
pen on wallpaper, each 6 × 6

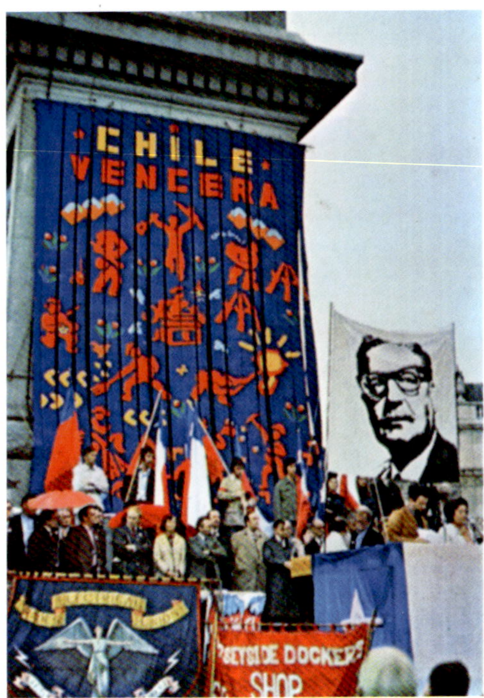

John Dugger, *Chile vencerá* at Trafalgar Square, London, 1974

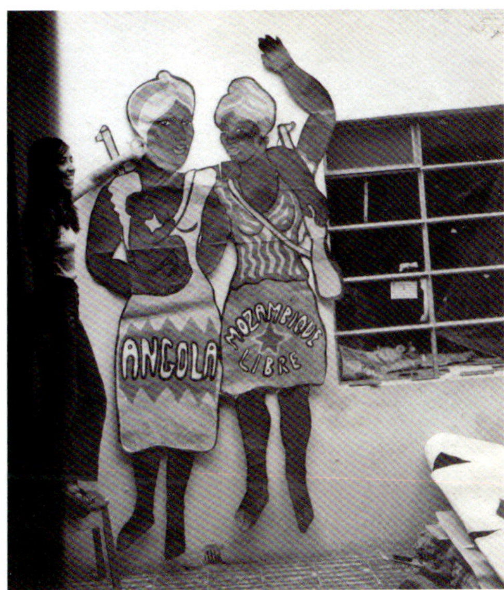

Cecilia in her studio in Bogotá with some of her painted cut-outs to be used as the stage set for a concert of Chilean folk band Quilapayún at Teatro La Candelaria c.1978

banner declaring 'CHILE VENCERÁ (CHILE WILL PREVAIL)' suspended on Nelson's Column. The banner was designed by John Dugger and based upon stories Vicuña had told him about life in Chile.

1975

The following year Vicuña moved to Bogotá, Colombia, where she would stay for five years. Travelling throughout the country, as well as to Venezuela and Brazil, she took part in political meetings connected to Chilean resistance and continued to nurture her connection to Indigenous traditions. It was also a time of more collaboration: she made stage sets for music and theatre groups including Corporación Colombiana de Teatro and the Chilean folk music group Quilapayún, and provided art workshops for Indigenous communities.

Vicuña continued her commitment to using art as a tool for political activism in paintings such as *Chile Salutes Vietnam!* 1975, which depicts the meeting of a Mapuche woman and a Vietnamese guerrilla woman, whose countries had both been affected by interference from the United States.

1977

After the end of the Vietnam war in 1977 *Chile Salutes Vietnam!*, along with many other works, was included in Vicuña's exhibition *Homage to Vietnam* at Gilberto Alzate Avendaño gallery in Bogotá, where she also organised a workshop with children.

1979

The snapshots on p.67 show how Vicuña understood the importance of documentation, as can be seen in *Vaso de leche* (A Glass of Milk) 1979. At the time, contaminated milk had led to the death of two thousand children in Colombia. In response Vicuña created the small gesture of spilling a glass of milk using a piece of string and writing the following text on the pavement in chalk:

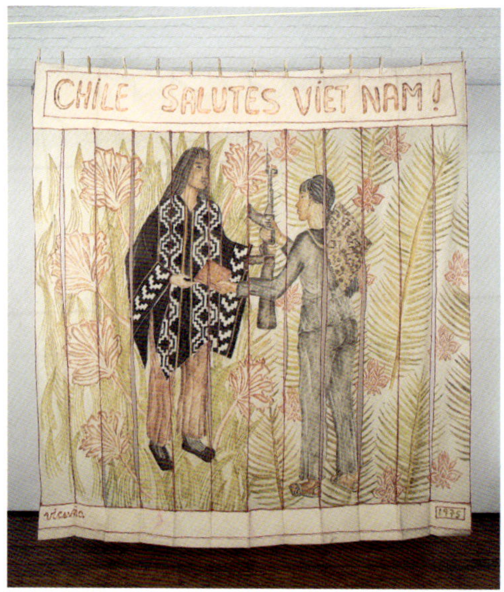

Chile Salutes Vietnam! 1975, pigment on cheesecloth 228.6 × 213.4

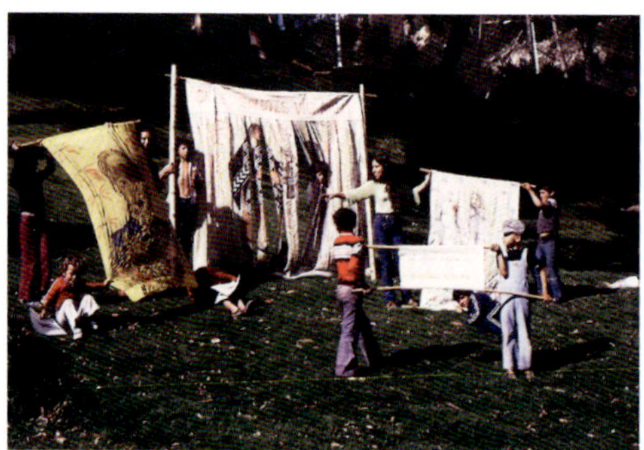

Cecilia with works from her exhibition *Homenaje a Vietnam* (Homage to Vietnam) during a workshop at Gilberto Alzate Avendaño gallery, Bogotá, 1977

the cow is / the continent / whose milk / (blood) / is being / spilled. / What are we doing / with life?

The performativity and political potential of a small, intimate gesture is present in Vicuña's *Palabrarmas* series, first conceived in 1966 and developed through the 1970s to the 1980s, which is perhaps the perfect meeting point of her work as an artist and poet. *Palabrarmas* was an investigation into the meaning of words and how they can be re-cast and rethought politically through a set of playful gestures. Vicuña would take a phrase or word and turn it into a drawing, first on paper and then eventually as cut-outs or floating elements on a transparent screen that could be taken into the street. The title of the series, a neologism coined by Vicuña, emphasises this mutability, since it can be translated variously as

 word-weapons (palabr-armas),
or
 wordwork (palabrar),
or
 shovel-open (pala-abra)
or
 word-more (palabra-más)
among other things.[14]

Here, Vicuña emphasised the inherent precarity of language and how no word, object, or being is distinct from another but all are instead enmeshed within a net-work of associations.

Such wordplay has its roots in Indigenous cultures where reading, writing and meaning are often relational. Vicuña has written that in Maya logosyllabic script, for example, signs are allowed to have multiple associations and movement, explaining: 'Flexibility of meaning is important for an oral culture where memory is not seen as fixed but is an ongoing creative phenomenon, renewed and transformed at each reading.'[15]

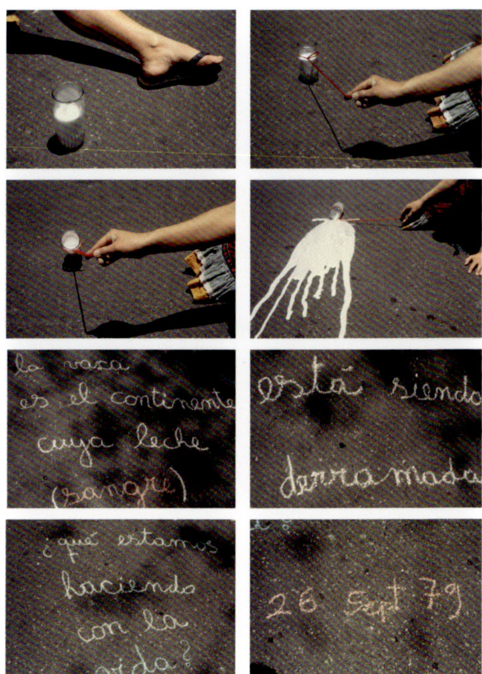

Vaso de leche (A Glass of Milk) 1979, performance, in front of
the House of Simón Bolívar, Bogotá, as part of the collective
action 'Para no morir de hambre en ele arte', at the invitation of
CADA, C-prints on Fujicolor Crystal Archive paper 42.5 × 54.6

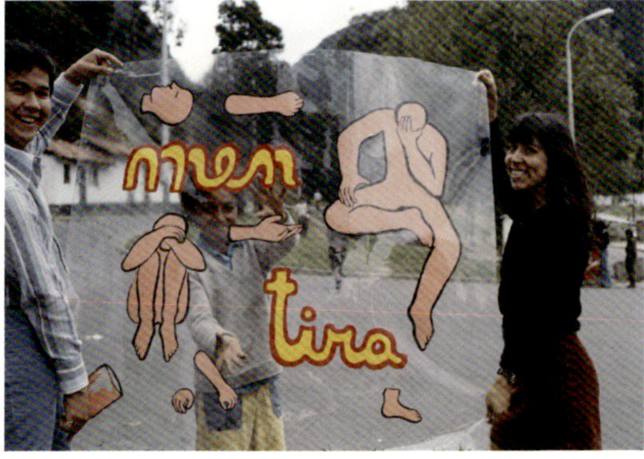

Men tire, Sol y dar y dad (Lies/ Tear the Mind Apart, Solidarity/
To Give and Give Sun), 'Palabrarmas' series c.1977–9,
performance and public intervention, Bogotá

1980

For Vicuña, poetry is an integral part of the world.
In 1980 she made a film where she asked people
in Colombia: 'What is poetry?' Her favourite
response was: 'Que prosiga' (That it may go on).[16]

1980–90

In 1980 Vicuña moved to New York where she
began the series *El Agua de Nueva York* (1980–90),
which continued her interest in notions of precarity
and transience as she placed her objects in
puddles, drains and rivers throughout New York.
At this time Lucy Lippard, a long-time supporter
of her work, invited Vicuña to join the Heresies
Collective, a feminist group producing a regular
publication on art and politics, *Heresies*. Vicuña
describes their gatherings as 'an art form in itself,
my best education and entry into New York'.[17]

1990

On 11 March 1990 General Augusto Pinochet
stepped down as President of Chile after a 1988
referendum where 56 per cent of votes were cast
against him, thus ending his seventeen years of
dictatorship.

1990s

Vicuña lived between New York and Buenos Aires
in the 1980s and 1990s. At this time her work
moved into multi-part or large-scale installations
that, despite their size and ambition, continued to
emphasise small intimate moments in gestures that
resisted being easily read or consumed. For example,
in *Cloud-Net* 1999 at Art in General in New York,
she created an open-weave net from unspun wool,
in which the negative space became an integral part
of the work. It was also one of her first large quipus
and the start of her frequent use of unspun wool.

2006

In 2006 Vicuña climbed the Cerro El Plomo in
Chile and laid lines of red wool across the glaciated

landscape as part of a ritual to protest about the sale of the glaciers to mining corporations. When the sale went ahead she placed a sliver of red wool in the courtyard of the presidential palace in protest, a work entitled *Menstrual Quipu (The Blood of the Glaciers)* 2006.

2010

Her experiences in the Andes informed Vicuña's film *Kon Kon* 2010, which she described as a 'digital quipu' where documentary elements about her childhood in Con cón and the environmental catastrophe enacted on the landscape of Chile are used as a main thread into which other stories, images and performances are tied.[18] Towards the end of the film she references the way in which relatives of the 'disappeared' – people who were taken by the authorities during Pinochet's dictatorship – hung images of their loved ones from their body using paperclips and, repeating this technique, forms an analogy with the disappearance and destruction of ancient sites and the dunes in Chile, a result of policies enacted by Pinochet's government which continue today.

2017

The connection to the sea as a site of rebirth was the focus of Vicuña's contribution to documenta 14 (2017), which featured *Quipu Womb (The Story of the Red Thread, Athens)* 2017. Consisting of fifty-two strands of unspun wool dyed red that hang from a circular ring, the work contrasts the monumental with the intimacy of its subject matter, emphasising the life-giving power of the womb. This was developed into a participatory action by the Mediterranean coast, in which Vicuña wove thick lengths of red wool around people and rolled a blanket of semi-felted wool down to the shore.

2018–22

From life to death: as the reality of loss due to climate change, civil injustice and colonialism

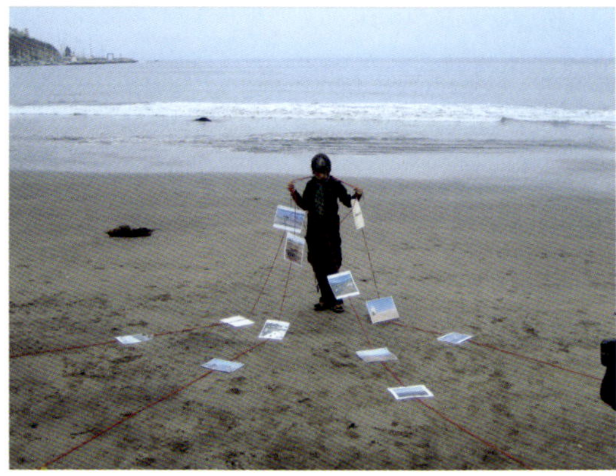

Kon Kon 2010, HD video, colour and sound, 53 min 55 sec, Spanish with English subtitles

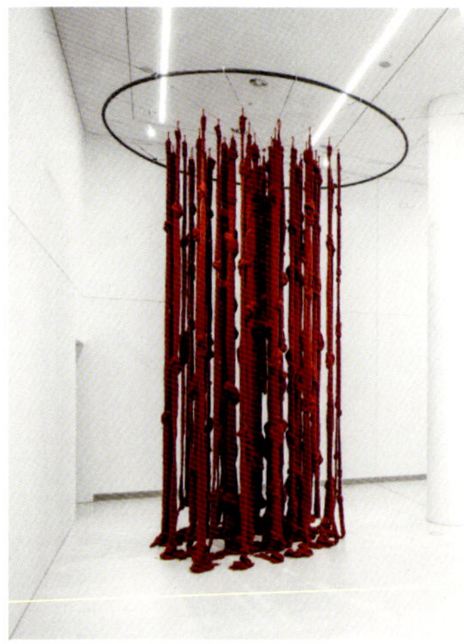

Quipu Womb (The Story of the Red Thread, Athens) 2017

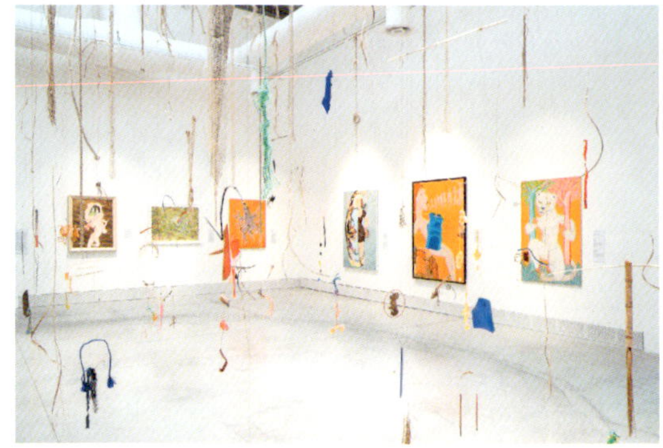

NAUfraga 2022, Venice Biennale, *The Milk of Dreams*, 2022

68

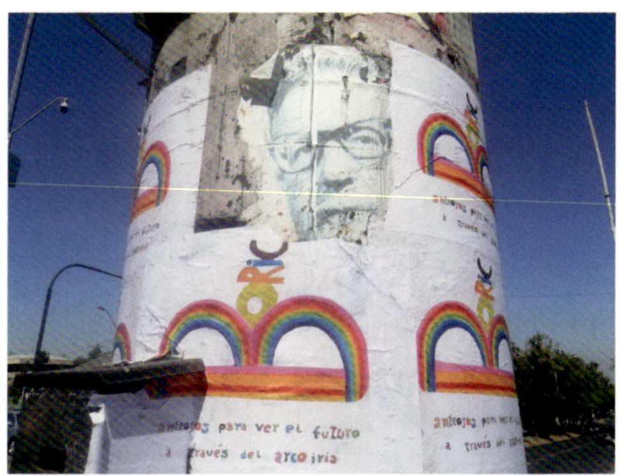

Documentation of posters created by Antonia Taulis based on Vicuña's glasses *Anteojos para ver el futuro a traves del arcoiris* (Glasses to See the Future through the Rainbow) in support of Gabriel Boric's 2021 presidential campaign and distributed all over Chile by *Mercurio*, 2021

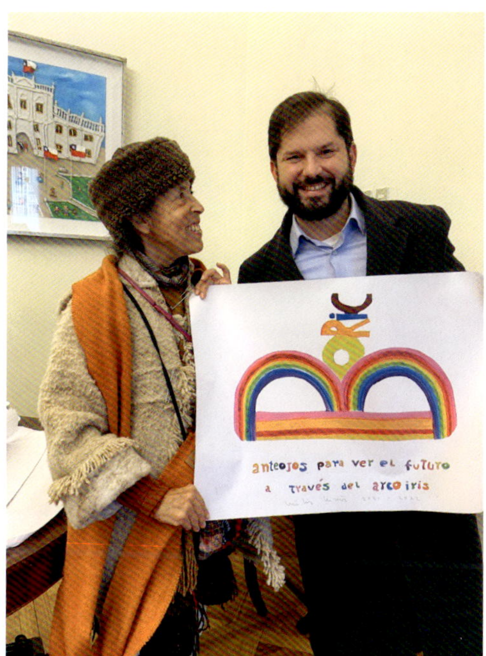

Vicuña and Chile's recently elected president Gabriel Boric, Palacio de la Modena, Santiago, 11 July 2022

has become an ever-increasing element of contemporary life, many of Vicuña's recent works have centred around absence. *Disappeared Quipu* 2018, presented at the Brooklyn Museum, and another version at the Museum of Fine Arts in Boston, was a reflection on the loss of Indigenous textile traditions. At the 2022 Venice Biennale her installation *NAUfraga*, whose title combined the Latin words 'navis' (ship) and 'frangere' (to break), consisted of *precarios* made from found objects collected in Venice that hung from the ceiling to appear like floating debris in the ocean. A few months later she unveiled *Extermination Quipu* 2022 at the Guggenheim Museum in New York.

Vicuña's work also suggests a sense of possibility, a sense that revolutionary processes can still occur, which was most recently epitomised in the Palabrarma *Anteojos para ver el futuro a través del arcoiris* (Glasses to See the Future through the Rainbow), made in support of Gabriel Boric's 2021 campaign to become President of Chile. The joyful rainbow design was subsequently reproduced in posters designed by Antonia Taulis and, with the successful election of Boric, became a symbol of the new progressive agenda set out by his Social Convergence government. On 11 July 2022, Vicuña and her mother met the new President in El Palacio de La Moneda, the same building where Allende took his own life fifty years before.

Today

Reflecting on Vicuña's work from the perspective of this time, as she works towards the realisation of *Brain Forest Quipu* at Tate Modern, shows that her intricate and careful approach to looking at the world provides an important pathway to follow – one that connects the past to the future and creates a space to listen, to allow for precarious things, to find time again.

69

1 Jacqueline Rose, *Women in Dark Times*, London 2014, p.41.

2 Ibid, pp.40–1.

3 Cecilia Vicuña, 'Choosing the Feather', trans. Lorraine O'Grady, *Heresies*, no.15, 1982, p.18.

4 Ibid.

5 Ibid.

6 Cecilia Vicuña, 'Performances', http://www.ceciliavicuna.com/performances, accessed June 2022.

7 Cecilia Vicuña, handwritten note (1969) in unpublished book *El diario estúpido* (The Stupid Diary). Published in Miguel A. López, 'A Retrospective for Eyes that Do Not See', *Seehearing the Enlightened Failure*, exh. cat., Witte de With, Rotterdam 2019, p.42 n.2.

8 Miguel A. Lopez, *Seehearing the Enlightened Failure*, exh. leaflet, Witte de With, Rotterdam, 2019, p.5.

9 Leonora Carrington, 'What is a Woman?' (1970), reprinted in *Cultural Correspondence*, nos.12–14, Summer 1981.

10 Cecilia Vicuña, 'Autumn', in *Saborami*, Devon 1973, unpaginated.

11 Cecilia Vicuña, 'Lenin' (1973), republished along with her other texts on paintings in *Seehearing the Enlightened Failure*, exh. cat., Witte de With, Rotterdam 2019.

12 The text forms part of part of Cecilia Vicuña, *Precarios: A Journal of Objects for the Chilean Resistance 1973–4*, Tate Collection, T14170.

13 Cecilia Vicuña, 'Text of the Brown Book', in *Saborami*, Devon 1973, unpaginated.

14 For more context around the works, see Carla María Macchiavello, 'The Liberate!: About Cecilia Vicuña's Palabrarmas', *Seehearing the Enlightened Failure*, exh. cat., Witte de With, Rotterdam 2019, pp.72–90.

15 Cecilia Vicuña, 'An Introduction to Mestizo Politics', in Cecilia Vicuña and Ernesto Livon-Grosman (eds.), *The Oxford Book of Latin American Poetry*, Oxford 2009, p.xxiv

16 Cecilia Vicuña, 'Language is Migrant', *South Magazine*, no.8 (documenta 14, no.3), p.2.

17 Cecilia Vicuña, in *Seehearing the Enlightened Failure*, exh. cat., Witte de With, Rotterdam 2019, p.346.

18 For an in-depth discussion of the film see Candice Amich, 'From Precarity to Planetarity: Cecilia Vicuña's *Kon Kon*', *The Global South*, vol.7, no.2, Fall 2013, p.134–15.

A Rough Movement to Capture the Delicate: The Poetry of Cecilia Vicuña

Luke Roberts

In her 1980 film *¿Qué es para usted la poesía?* (What Is Poetry to You?), Cecilia Vicuña took to the working-class neighbourhoods of Bogotá, where she recorded the oral poetics of the marginalised. A street performer sings, accompanied by a handmade instrument; he says to the camera, 'I've had to work like a dog in order to survive, but in this style I find the materials in order to compose truth.' A little girl in the crowd announces, 'Poetry to me is a story'. A worker in a brothel says, 'In sex there can be poetry, also'. A man in a nightclub explains that poetry is divided in two: between bourgeois poetry and revolutionary poetry.[1]

If the latter claim is true, there's no doubt that Vicuña's work – resolutely socialist, feminist, environmental, decolonial – is on the side of revolution. The method of the film is itself in keeping with the cultural politics of Salvador Allende's Popular Unity movement in Chile, which Vicuña had participated in a decade previously. The National Plan for Applied Arts joined artists together with workers to learn from one another.[2] As Vicuña wrote in her first book, *Saborami* (1973), published in exile in England immediately following the CIA-backed military coup, 'As industries are nationalized, I am nationalized. / From individual to communal property.'[3] The poet who goes to the people to listen remains much less common than the poet who goes to the people in order to be heard.

Vicuña's work prior to *Saborami*, written while she was a teenager, is exuberant, erotic, playful. She's described in a magazine in 1967 as 'the freshest fruit from the Dadaist tree'.[4] Her irreverence can be gauged by a poem like 'Pleasant Noises', which begins with 'bank robberies / pee falling' and ends some twenty items later with 'laughter / and / farts'.[5] Her humour is rarely acknowledged, and of course there's less and less to laugh about in our bleak epoch. But her performances – poem talks, improvisations – often contain

"

moments of absurdity and splendour. In 2019 at the Serpentine she performed *Clit Nest*, and as she bundled the audience in loops of wool, she chanted and sang, and smuggled in subversive asides. I wrote one down in my notebook: 'Do you know about Nazca? / I have to ask / Because the northern hemisphere / doesn't know anything about beauty'.

Her commitment to recovering the history of the poetry and writing of the Americas is evident in all of her writing. As the co-editor of *The Oxford Book of Latin American Poetry* (2009) she brought together an astonishing array of multilingual work, running from avant-garde heroes like César Vallejo to the *Popol Vuh*, Quechuan resistance texts of the seventeenth century, and contemporary oral performances in Tzotzil. For readers of English this is an indispensable and expansive document, which might encourage us to think of the plural, multiple, and contested, rather than the monolithic and settled.

Since the catastrophe of 1973, Vicuña's work has grown into a complex living system, full of broken and damaged objects, and increasingly conscious of the long histories and legacies of colonial violence and planetary exploitation. But the work is also animated by the corresponding force of resistance and protest. She writes:

> A poem only becomes poetry when its structure
> is made not of words but forces.
>
> Force is poetry.
>
> Everyone knows what poetry is, but who can say it?[6]

For the past fifty years, in pursuit of this intuitive knowledge, Vicuña has necessarily and often joyously transgressed the limits of poetic form. She knows when to be reckless and how to be precise. The work helps us listen, listens with us, as intimate as it's cosmic, as tender as it's fierce.

1 https://vimeo.com/ondemand/whatispoetrytoyou; see also p.28.
2 Cecilia Vicuña, 'The Coup Came to Kill What I Loved', *Spare Rib*, no.28, London 1974.
3 Cecilia Vicuña, *Saborami* 2nd edn, Oakland and Philadelphia 2011, p.23.
4 *El Corno Emplumado*, no.22, 1967, p.145.
5 *New and Selected Poems of Cecilia Vicuña*, ed. Rosa Alcalá, Berkeley, CA 2018, pp.24–7.
6 'The Quasar', *New and Selected Poems of Cecilia Vicuña*, p.245.

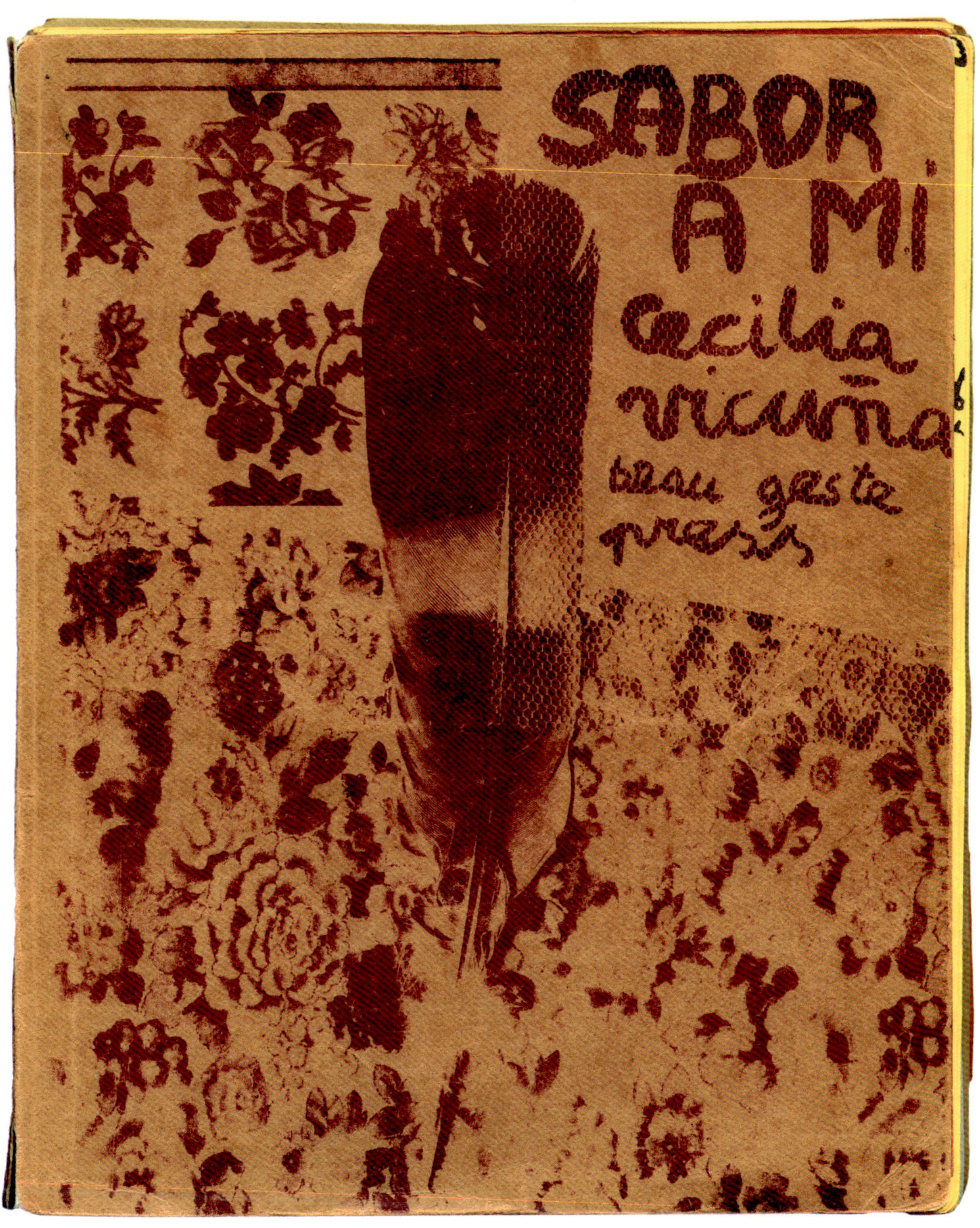

Saborami (1973), artist book, Beau Geste Press, Cullompton, UK

A QUIPU AUTOBIOGRAPHY

CECILIA VICUÑA

el quipu que no recuerda nada

'The quipu that remembers nothing' was my first quipu,

a rebellion against the loss of cultural memory.

Beyond 'knowing', my hands and imagination seemed to hold a memory
we don't call 'memory', a knowing we don't call 'knowing'.

Dwelling on the emptiness of the unformed, my longing engaged the
quipu at its root, and quipus began to sprout in me as plants grow on
a desert plain.

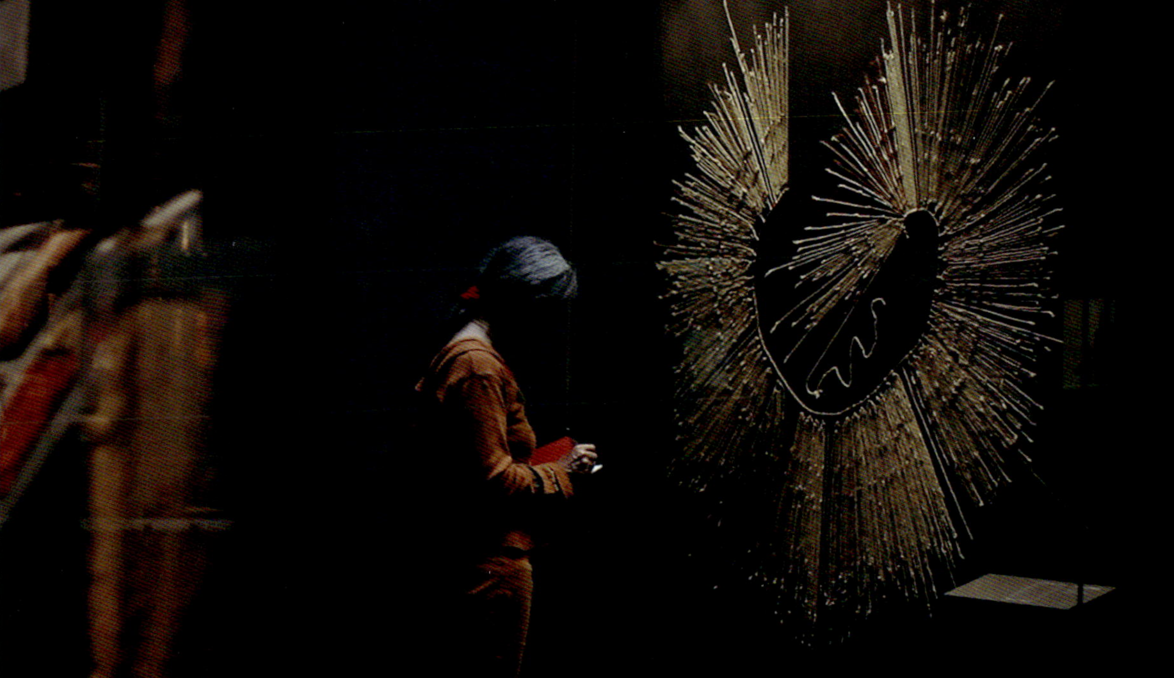

Studying the archaeological quipu at Museo
Chileno de Arte Precolombino, Santiago, Chile,
2017

I was praying, making a quipu, offering up the desire of memory.

Desire is the offering. The body is only a metaphor.

QUIPU TZIMIN KAX

My quality and fear
is to have two thighs

Golden and res
plendent

Knotted quipu
                    cords
Languages falling off
my thighs

Not elastic,
          elás!

SANTIAGO, JULY 1971

Translated by Rosa Alcalá

BLUE THREAD

I made a vest with big holes, my tits escaped through them, so I
imagined a weaving the size of my room, holding me as if I was already
a knot inside the quipu. I wrote in my journal:

> *Tired of my room's normality I have crisscrossed it with a blue thread …*
> *taut and geometrical as a sky to communicate with other worlds.*

CON CON, CHILE, JANUARY 22, 1972

El Hilo Azul, Con cón, Chile, 1972

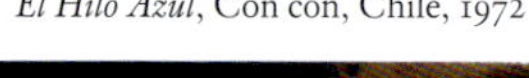

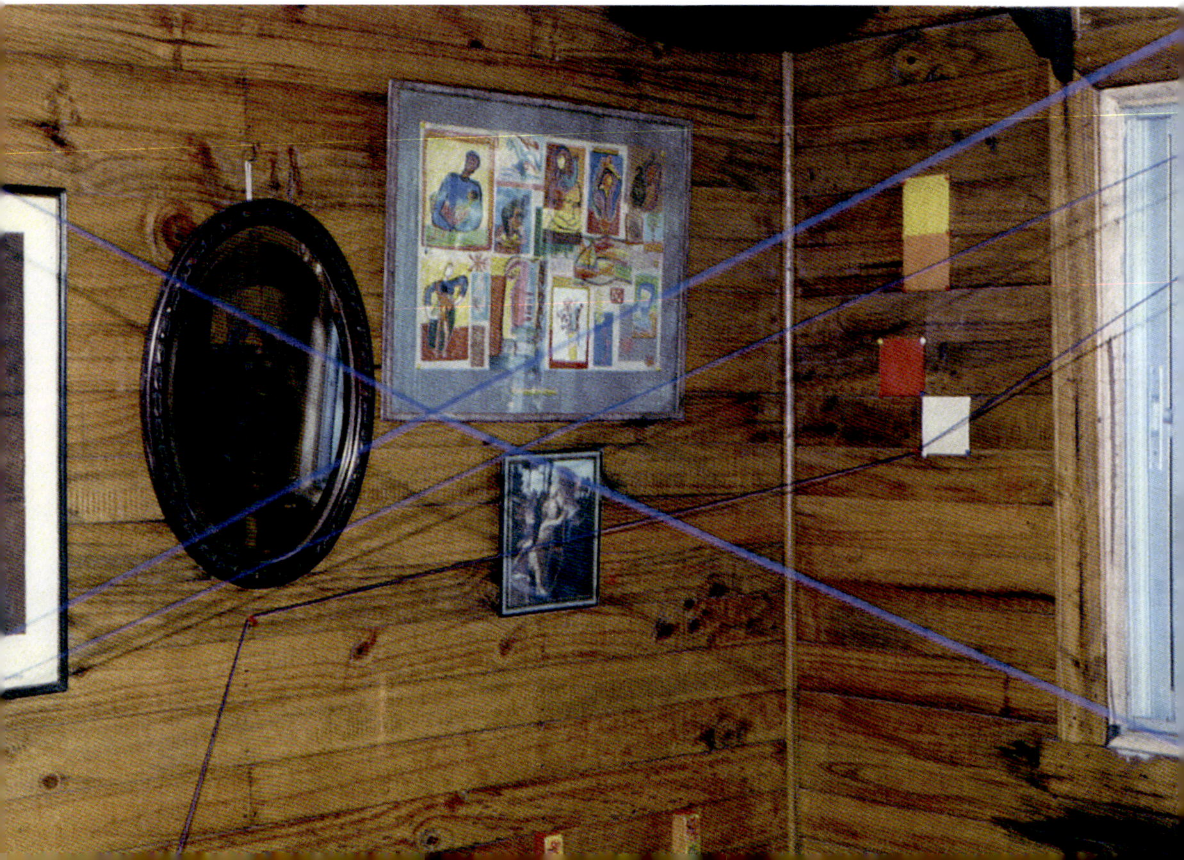

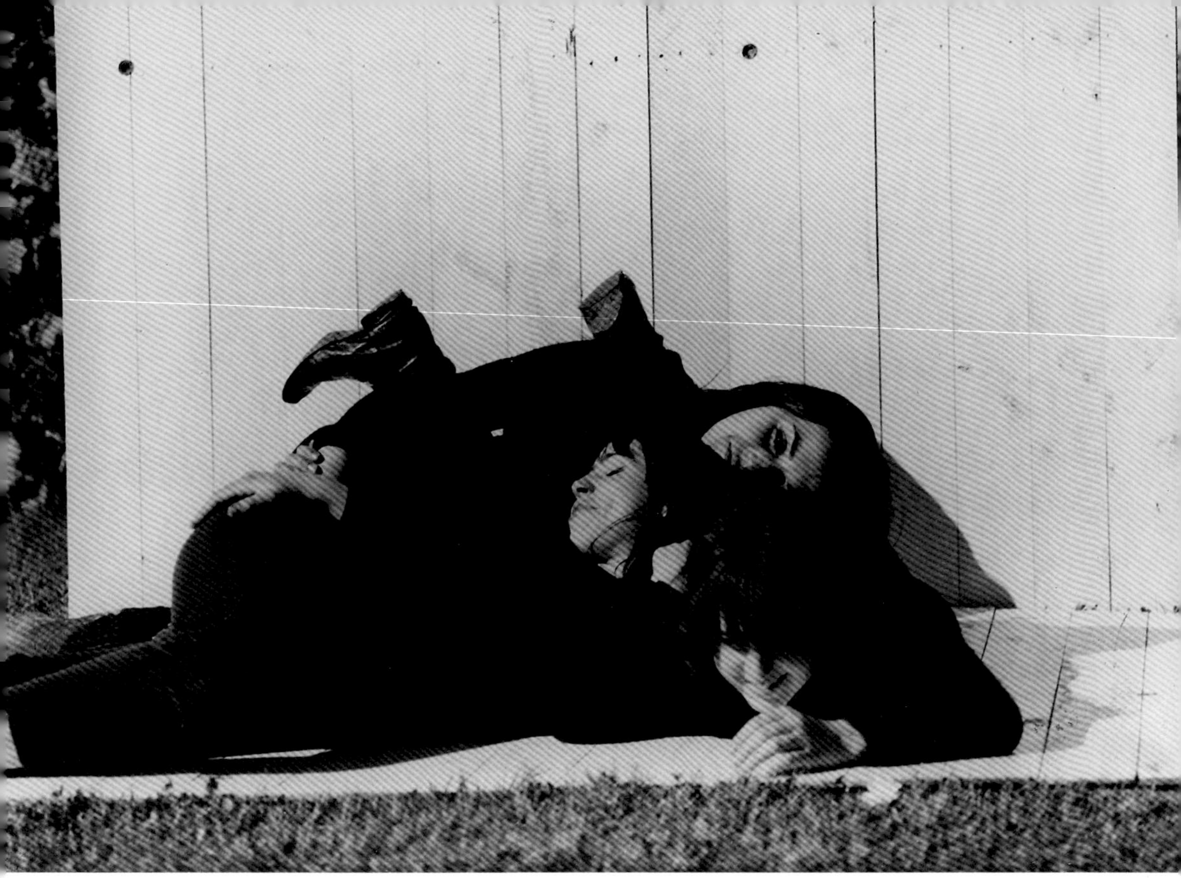

Cecilia and Tribu No friends, performing
Nudo de tres, Con cón, Chile, 1970

HUMAN KNOT

The quipu embraced me, and I began seeing my girlfriends' bodies joined as one in a knot.

I was a student in London when the military coup in Chile occurred.
I began my *Journal of Objects for the Chilean Resistance*, made of debris
picked up from London streets.

Quipu objects emerged among the ruins of what had been destroyed.

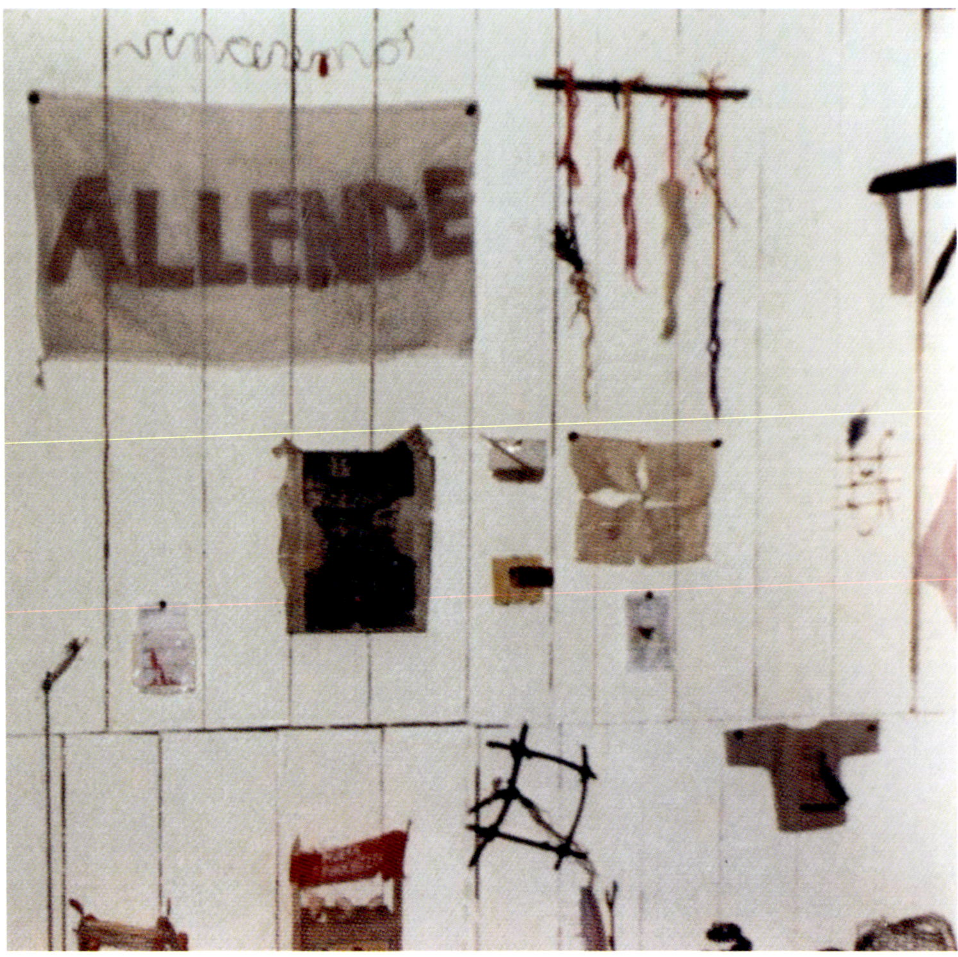

Precarios: Journal of Objects for the Chilean Resistance, Arts Meeting Place, London, 1974

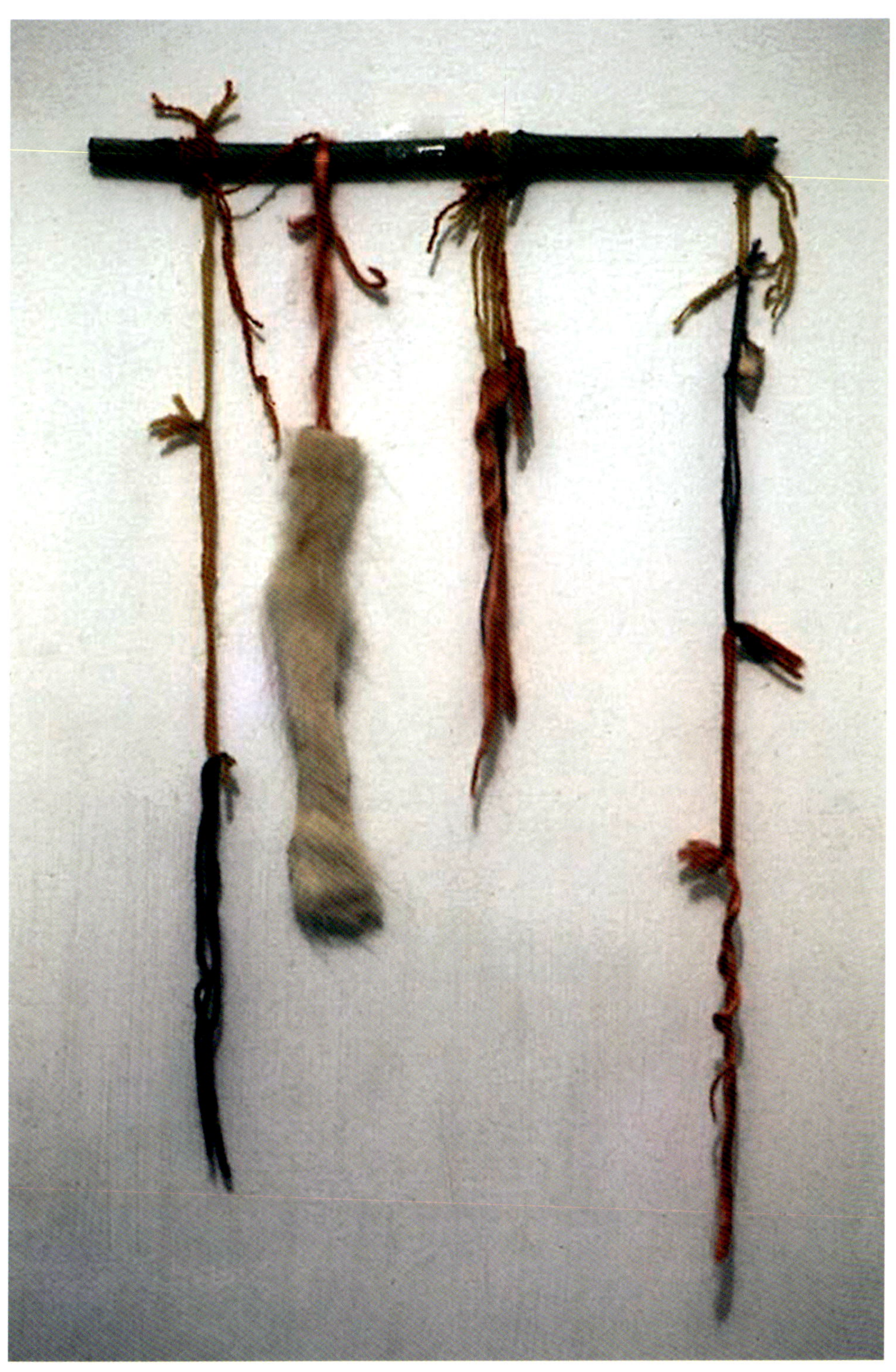

Precarios: Journal of Objects for the Chilean Resistance, Arts Meeting Place, London, 1974

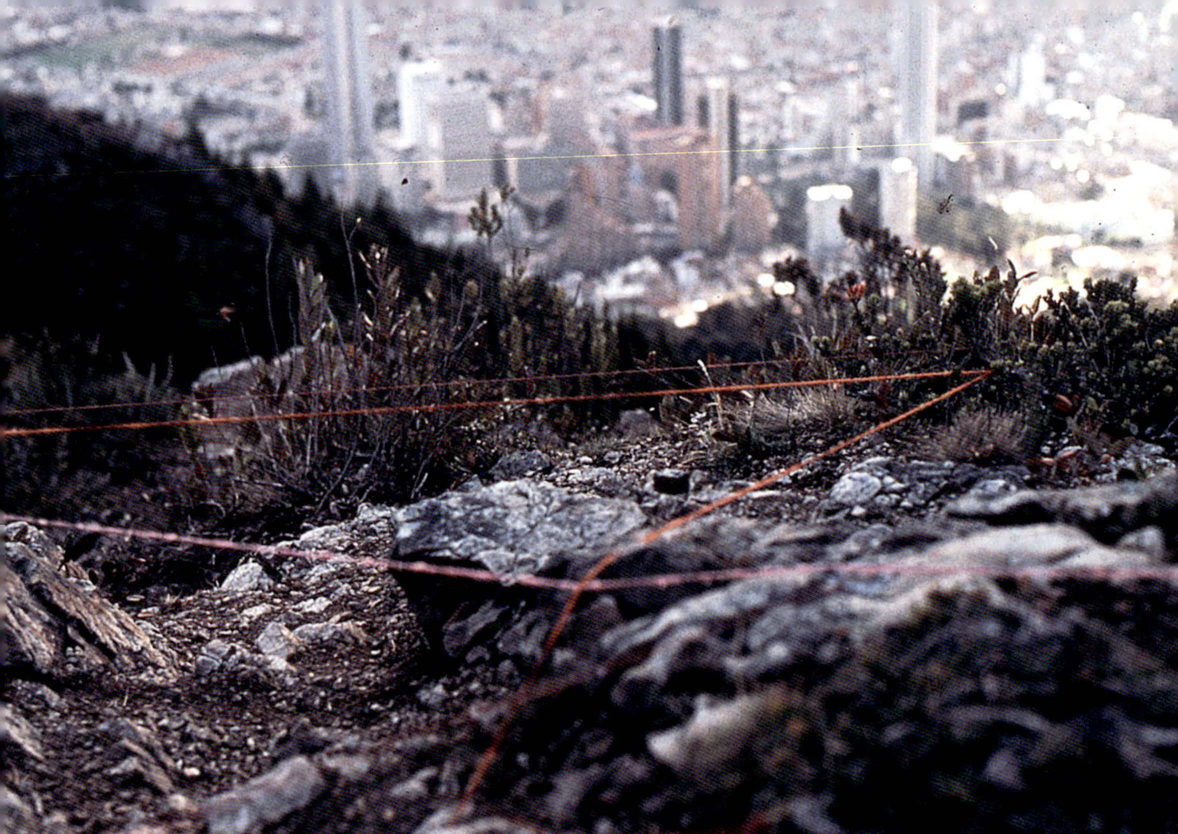

Sendero Chibcha 1981, ritual performance, Bogotá

SENDERO CHIBCHA

Returning to the Andes mountains, I settled in Bogotá, one of the few
places not under a dictatorship at the time.

> The Kogi say: 'The sun spins the thread of life around the world,
> the earth is a loom where the sun weaves the night and the day.'

> Poetry inhabits
> certain places
> where the cliffs
> need only a signal
> to bring them alive.

> Two or three lines
> A mark
> And silence begins
> To speak.

SIDEWALK FORESTS

Arriving in New York after leaving Bogotá, I felt the earth breathing
through the pavement cracks. Quipu wove the sidewalk forests.

Sidewalk Forests, New York, 1981

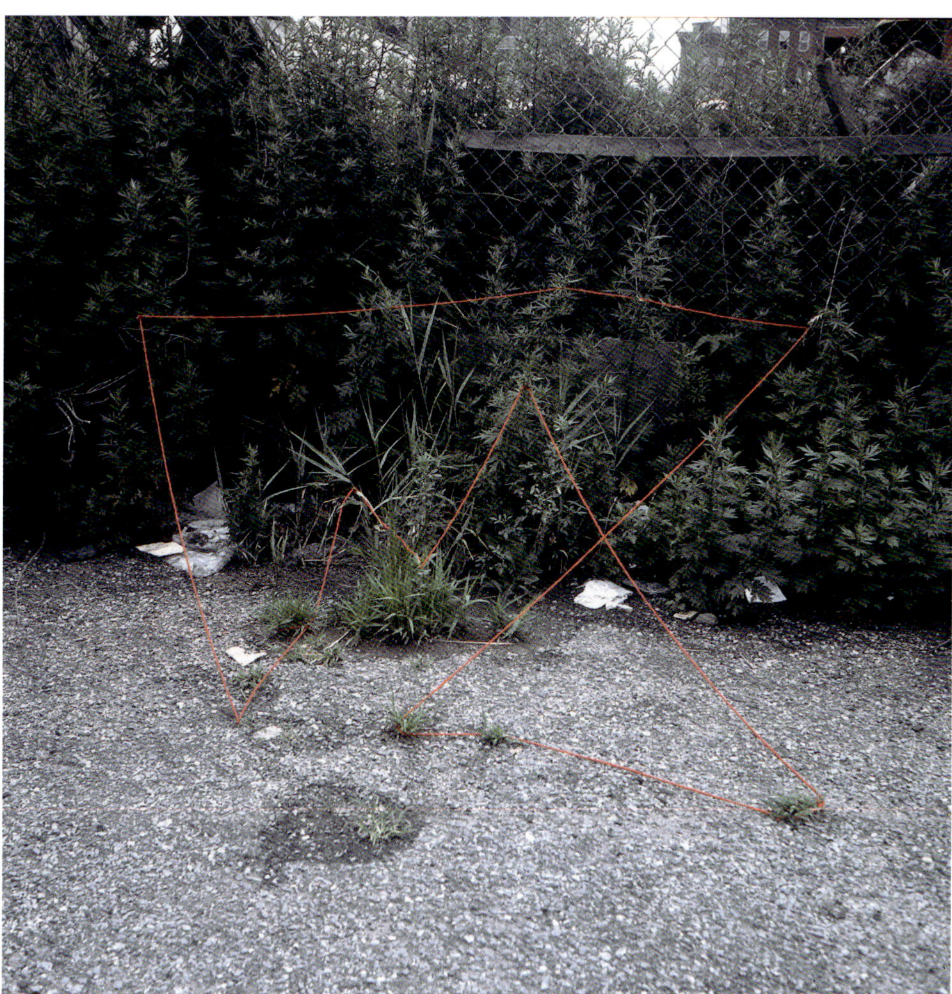

ANTIVERO

In Chile, quipu wove above and below the water.

Before being polluted, the river wants to be heard.

Antivero 1981, ritual performance, Colchagua, Chile

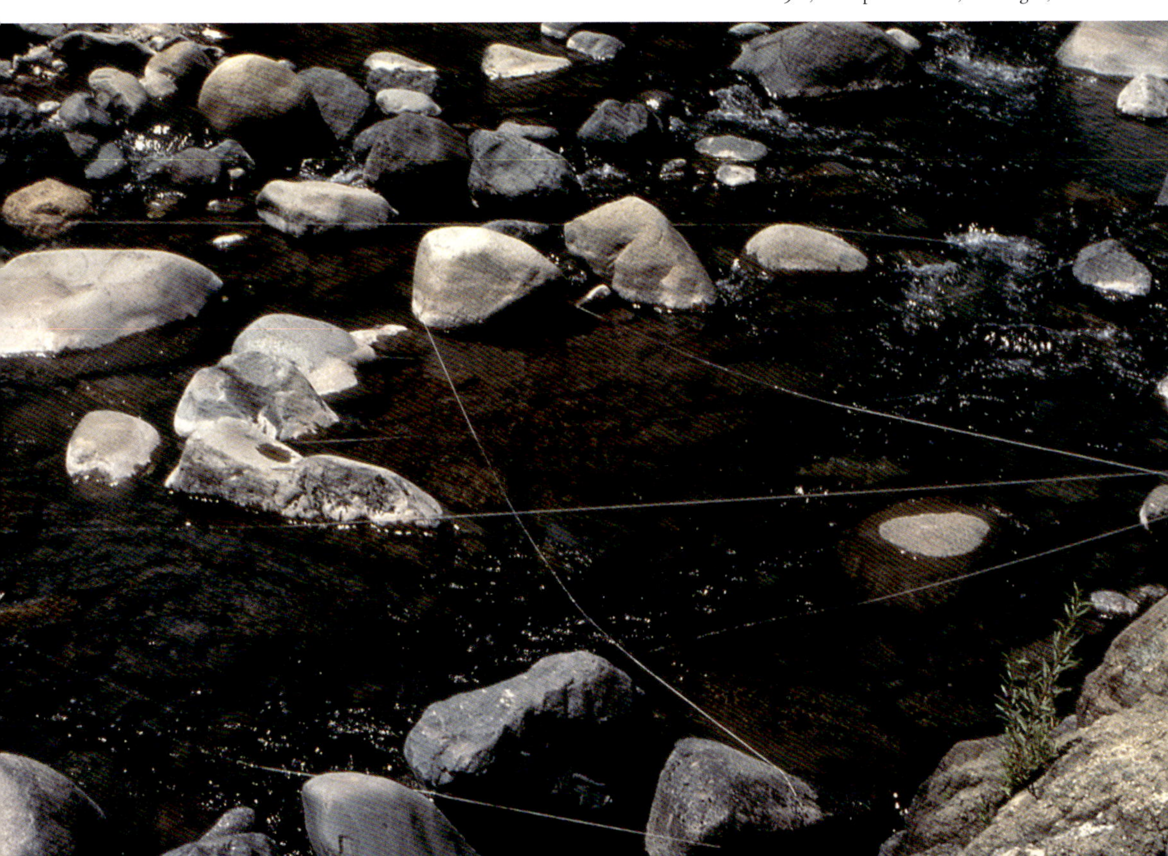

STREET WEAVINGS

In New York, I encountered a quipu bibliography, gathering centuries
of studies of the 'talking knots' destroyed by European colonisation.
Reading unleashed other forms of imagination that joined and differed
from the knowledge created by thousands of Andean hands for five
thousand years, including mine. From the tension between the two, new
forms emerged.

Collister Street 1994, ritual performance, Manhattan, New York

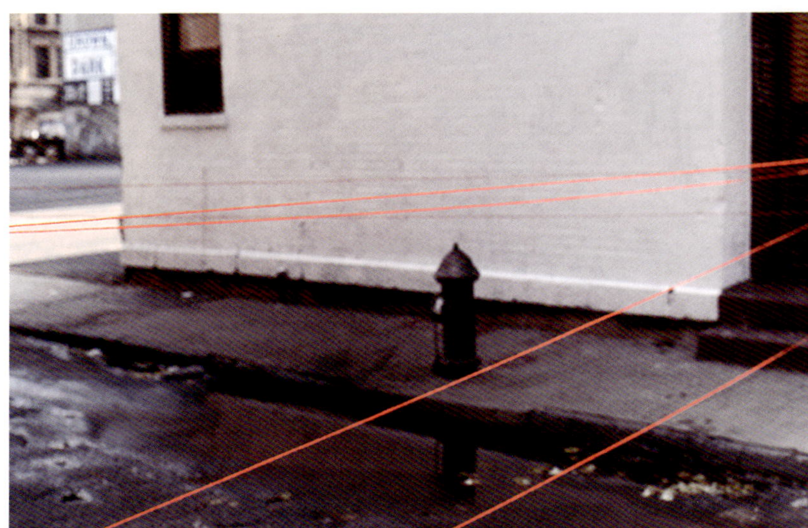

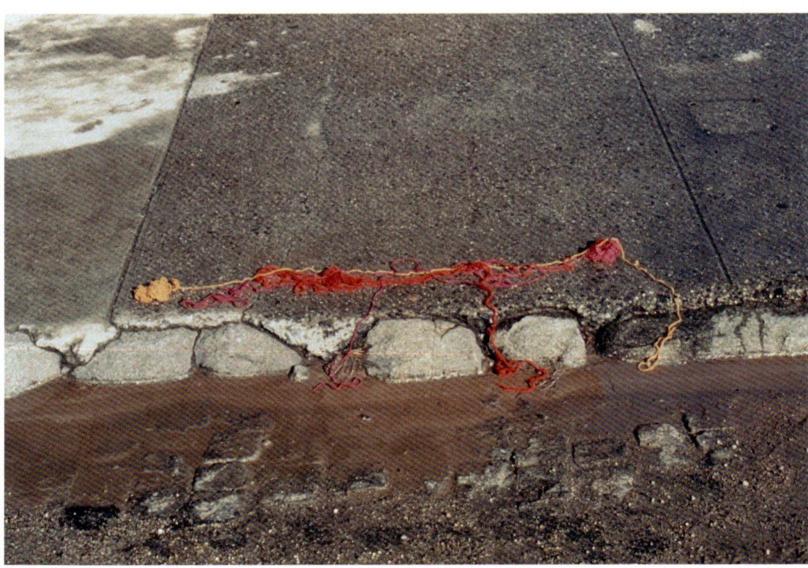

Quipu in the Gutter 1989, ritual performance,
Beach Stree, New York

Ceque

Thread Suns
"there are
still songs to be sung on the other side
of mankind"

—Paul Celan

The ceque is not a line, it is an instant, a gaze,

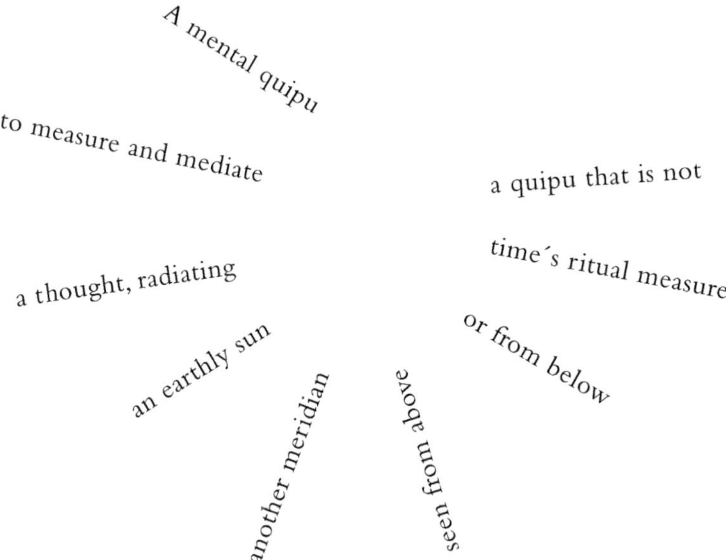

QUIPU-CEQUE

Before colonisation, quipu worked from the perspective of the knot's
'eye', observing how we are interconnected, 'tied' in mutual evolution
and change.

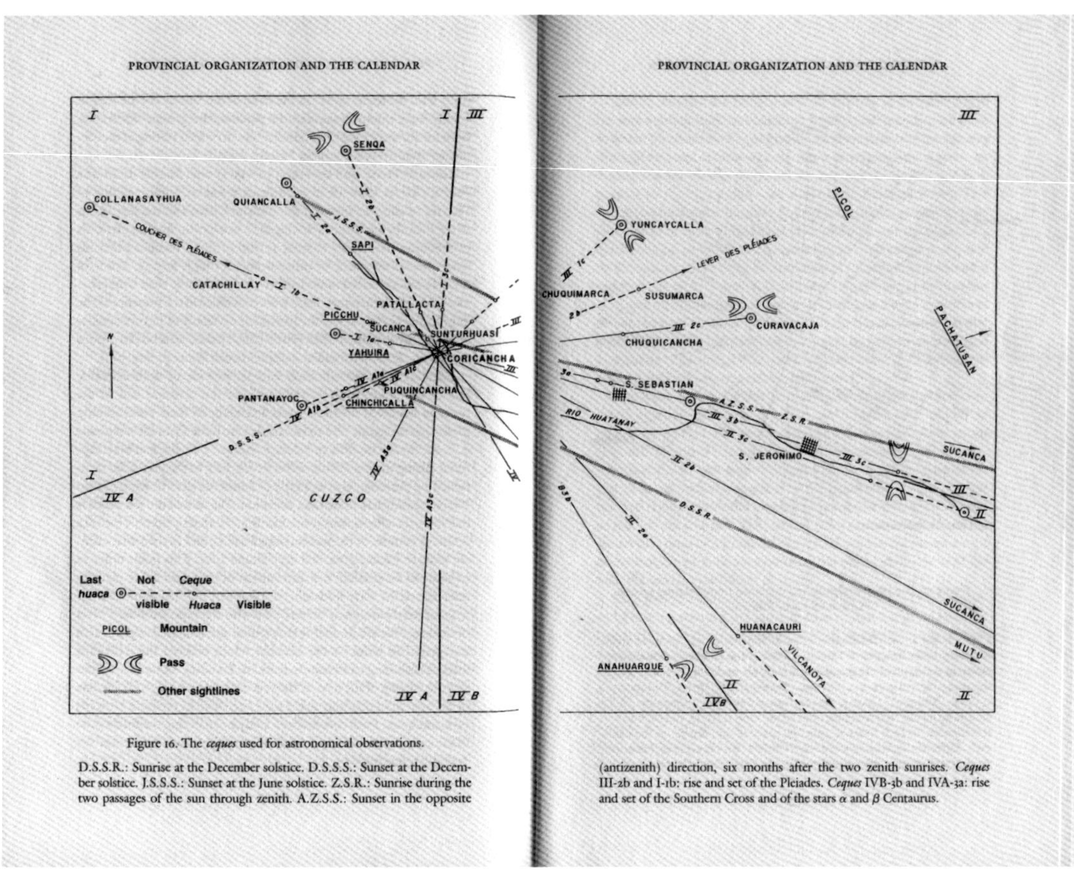

Figure 16. The *ceques* used for astronomical observations.

D.S.S.R.: Sunrise at the December solstice. D.S.S.S.: Sunset at the December solstice. J.S.S.S.: Sunset at the June solstice. Z.S.R.: Sunrise during the two passages of the sun through zenith. A.Z.S.S.: Sunset in the opposite (antizenith) direction, six months after the two zenith sunrises. *Ceques* III-2b and I-1b: rise and set of the Pleiades. *Ceques* IVB-3b and IVA-3a: rise and set of the Southern Cross and of the stars α and β Centaurus.

Ceque diagram for astronomical observation, from Tom R. Zuidema, *Inca Civilisation in Cuzco*, Austin 1990, pp.70–1

The quipu-ceque system of virtual sightlines to the horizon used the wakas (sacred sites) as 'knots' to organise the responsibilities of each community in caring for water and land, connecting to the source of life in the cosmos, and the source of water in the mountains, situating the social body in relation to the cosmic scale and the magna scale of the Andean landscape.

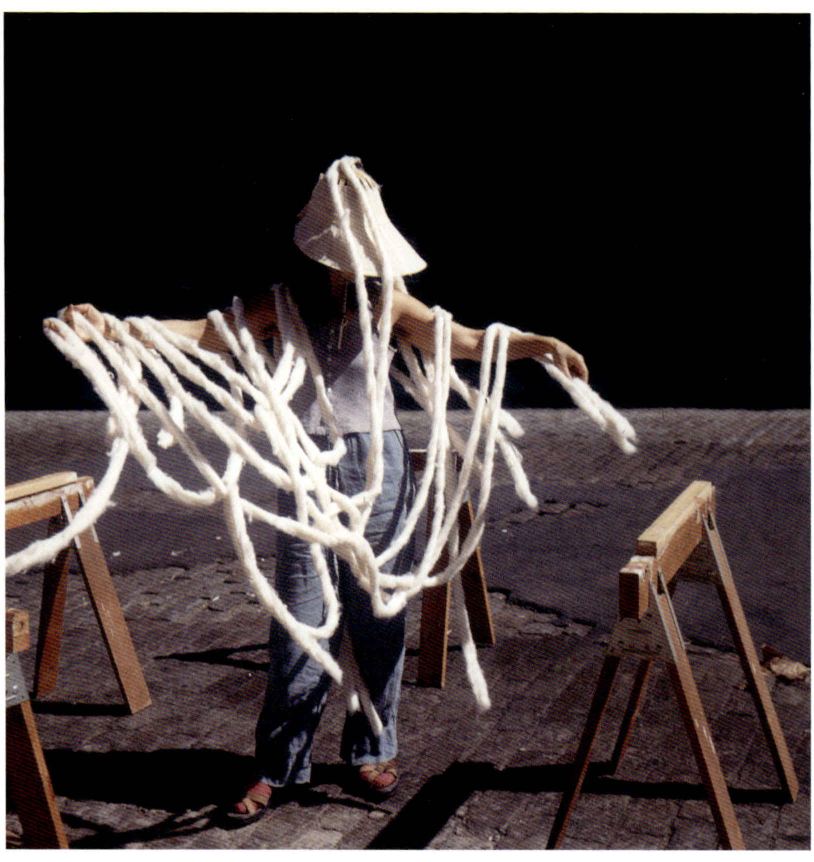

Cloud-Net 1998, street performance, New York

CLOUD-NET

In 1998 I was asked to create a travelling installation that would change
from place to place, and yet always be the same. I was inspired by the
American Museum of Natural History's Hall of Biodiversity, dedicated
to the Sixth Mass Extinction brought about by human activity.

> *In pushing other species to extinction, humanity is busy sawing off the limb on
> which it is perched*
>
> —PAUL EHRLICH

> *Today, we face losing 30,000 species a year ... the fastest mass extinction in
> Earth's 4.5-billion-year history. This time, however, it is mainly the result of
> human activity, not natural phenomena.*
>
> —THE HALL OF BIODIVERSITY WEBSITE, AMERICAN MUSEUM
> OF NATURAL HISTORY, NEW YORK

Meditating on extinction, I saw the image of a cloud basket cooling the
Earth, protecting it from our violence, the heat we create warming the
atmosphere.

I imagined a basket of unspun wool, the material of the ancient offerings
to the life force in Lake Titicaca, symbolising the cosmic gas where
galaxies are born. Nothing holds it together, except the fibres' desire to
be with one another.

I extended my arm and reached for 'Savitri', the long poem by Sri
Aurobindo, where I found these lines:

> *We who are vessels of a deathless force*
> *messengers of the incommunicable*
> *one day shall change the suffering earth*
> *Delight shall sleep in the cloud-net of her hair*
> *And in her body a music of griefless things shall weave*

Nur Al-Jerrahi says: 'In a new future civilisation all life forms will be
more precious than our own.'

Cloud-Net, Hallwalls, Buffalo, NY 1998

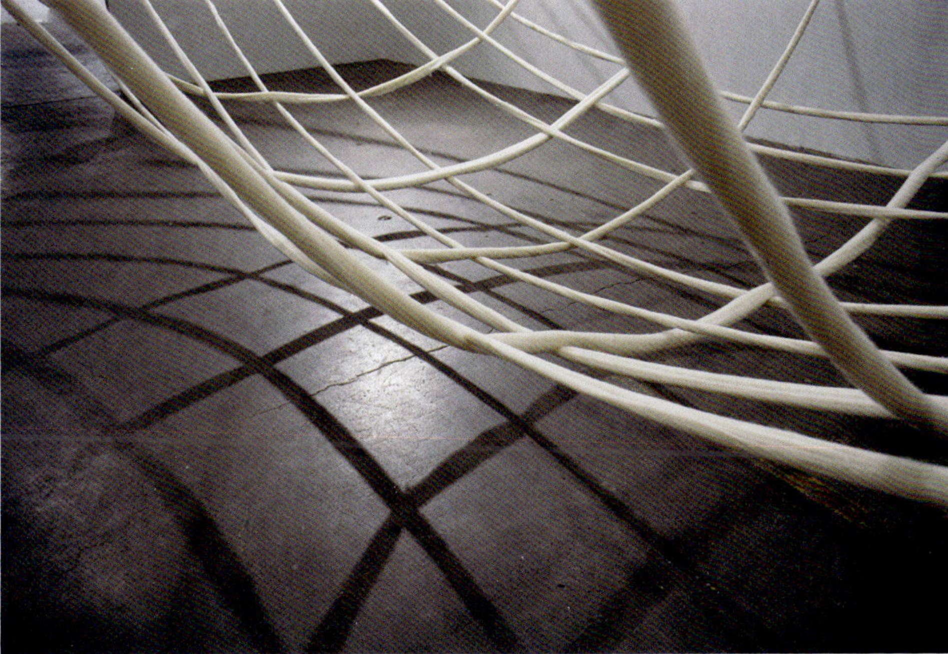

TYING

Sometime in the late 1980s and 1990s I began tying the audience or
tying myself to the audience, creating living quipu performances, as if
words and threads needed each other to be complete.

I loosely tied people's hands and feet. I remember tying the foot of the
poet Juan Calzadilla in Caracas, or Águeda Pizarro in New York, and
other poets in Chile, imagining new forms of connectivity with earth.

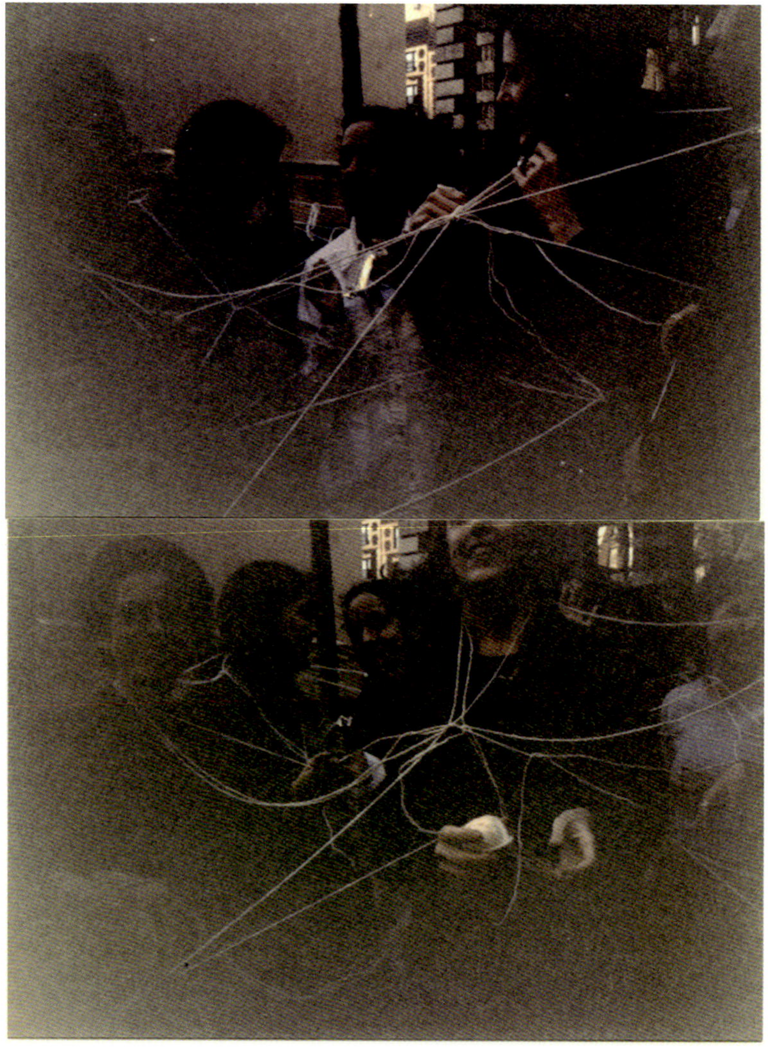

Tying a People's Knot 1999, Barnard College,
New York

QUIPU SEMIYO

Then, quipu (or I) began tying seeds, mourning the native seeds going
extinct and the erased memory of the disappeared prisoners of the
dictatorship.

    quipu
        I seed

    writing in air
            quipu I seed

    the seed is the thread
            the thread is the seed

    the bone is a seed
            where are they?

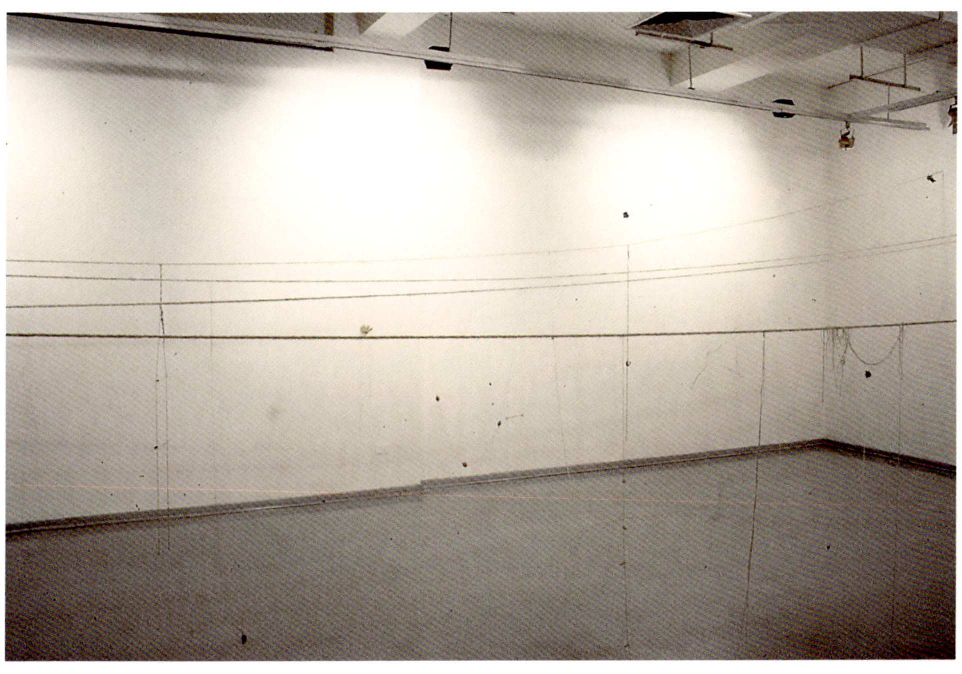

Quipu Semiyo 2000, Galería Gabriela Mistral,
Santiago

RED COIL

Honouring Gloria Anzaldúa, and the ancient, coiled snake associated
with women, and the fertility of water, rivers and oceans, I brought the
coils to the Hudson River.

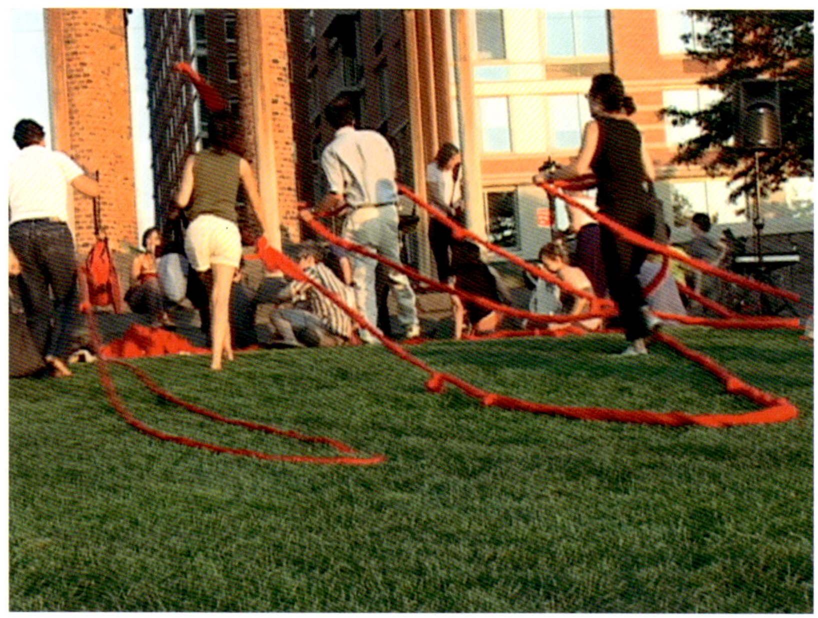

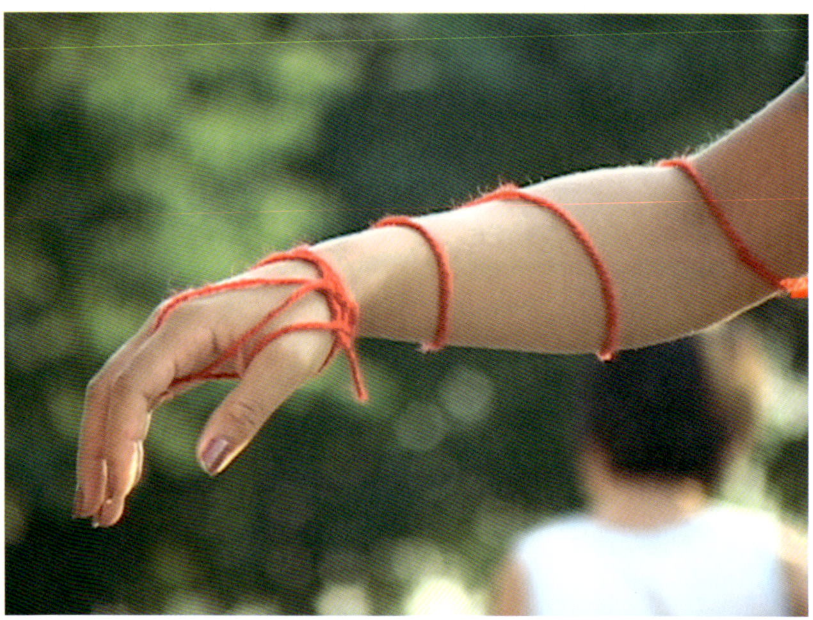

Red Coil, four performances by Cecilia Vicuña
and Jane Rigler at the Sitelines Festival, Battery
Park City, New York, 25 August 2005

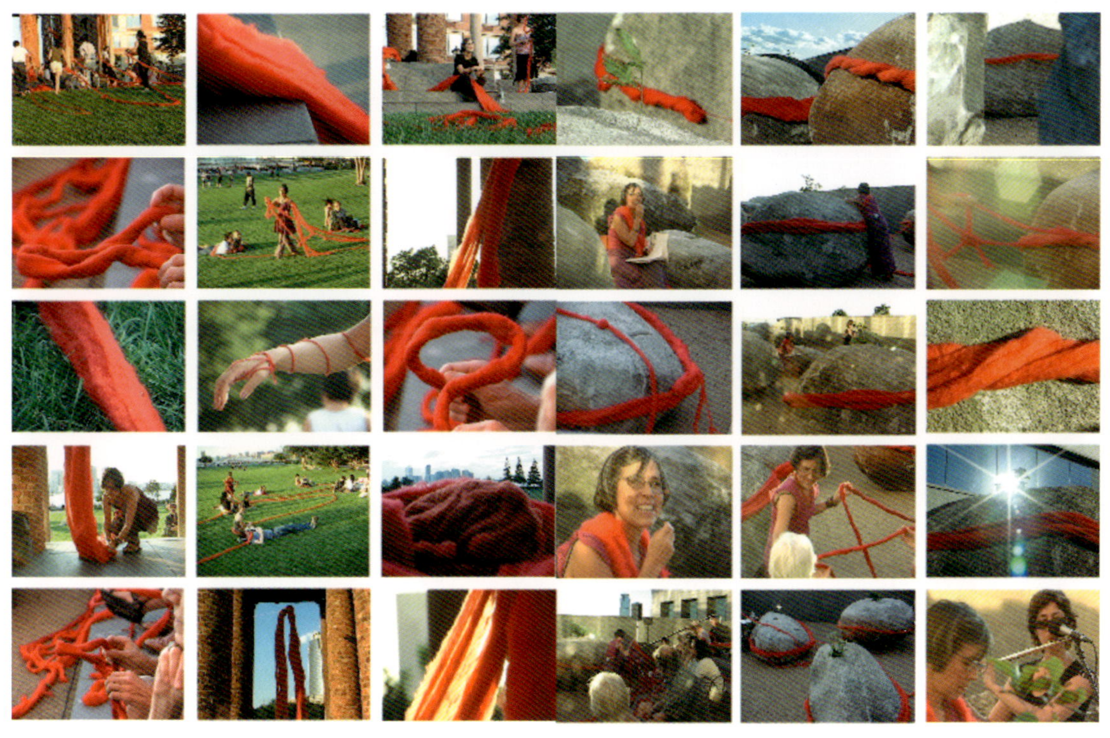

We are in a liquid crystalline state ... our blood is a liquid crystal in movement
—PHILIP S. CALLAHAN

Being human is being permeable ... we are a permeable membrane
—A.H. ALMAAS

When we make a memory connection, that's who we are, the connected self.
—JAMES O'HERN

QUIPU MENSTRUAL

With global warming, Andean glaciers were disappearing, but their slow death was ignored. The Chilean government continued selling them to foreign mining interests.

On election day, 15 January 2006, I climbed to the foot of the glacier facing Santiago to place my vote:

A menstrual quipu to ask President Michelle Bachelet to repeal the sale of the glaciers and safeguard water.

QUIPU MENSTRUAL (from a letter to Michelle Bachelet)

On election day
I climbed the mountain
to make an offering:

A menstrual quipu.

I climbed the condor's shadow
spinning a solar thread.

'Re

    member

        (it said)

re

   cord

The union of water
and blood.'

'The glacier's thirst.'

15 JANUARY 2006

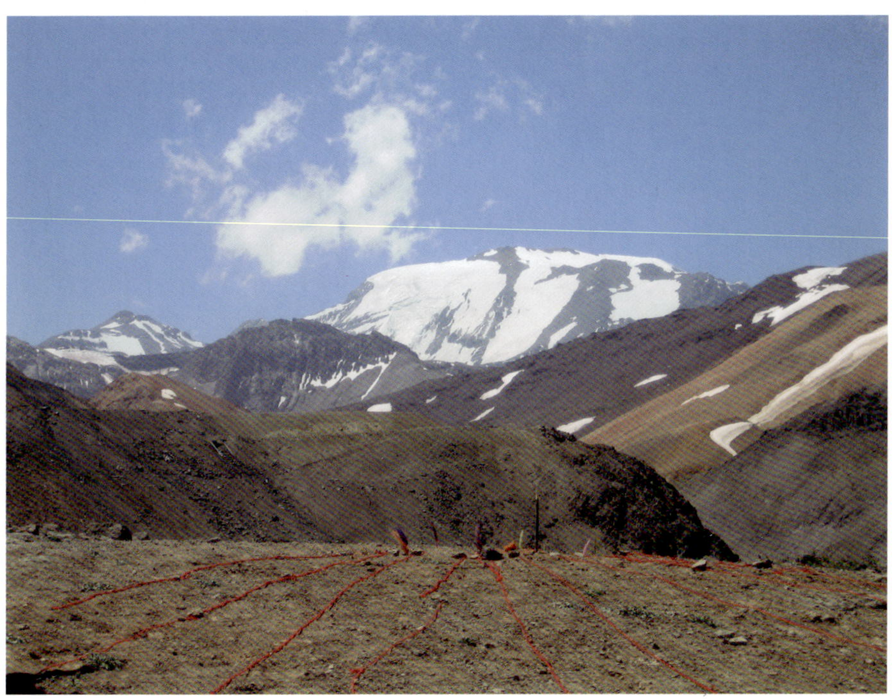

Menstrual Quipu (The Blood of the Glaciers), Chile, 2006

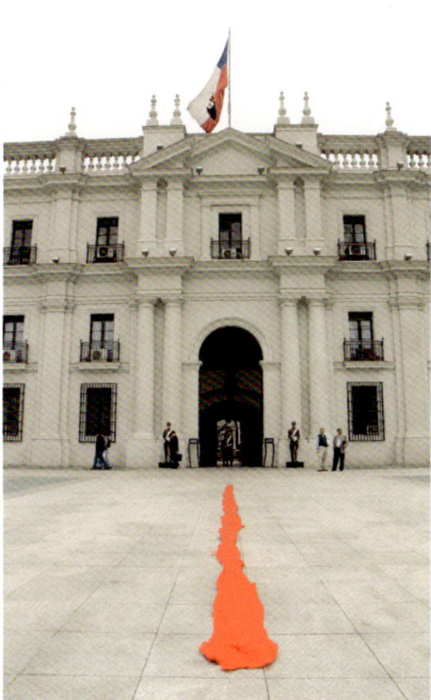

Quipu Menstrual (The Blood of the Glaciers), Palacio de La Moneda, Santiago, 2006

My plea was not heard, so I placed my quipu at the door of the presidential palace in Santiago.

The dictatorship privatised water, and the rivers and the ocean began dying, yet even after military rule ended, the law was upheld by the democratic governments.

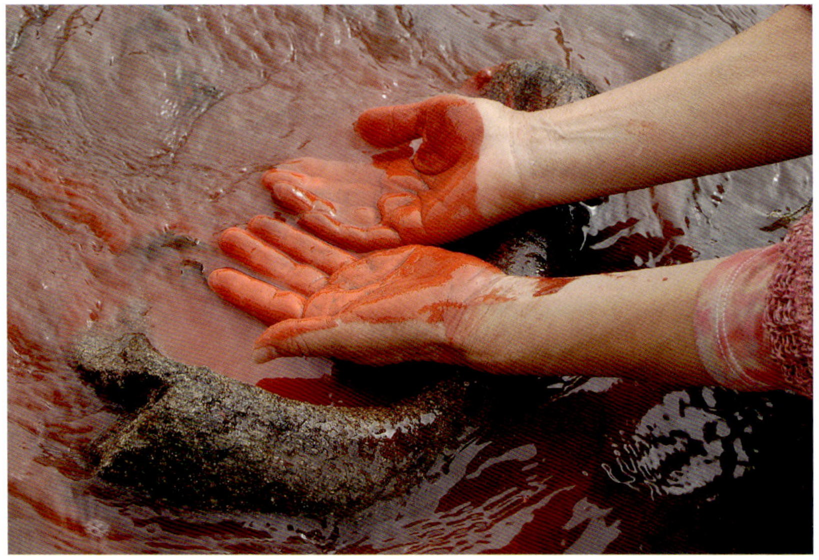

Kon Kon, offering to Kon, the Mother of the Sea, Con cón, Chile, 2006

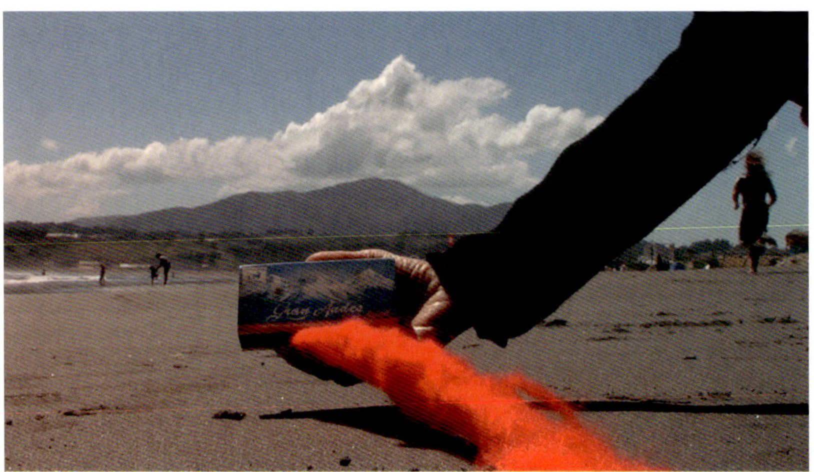

La Boca, the mouth of the Aconcagua River, Con cón, 2010

Returning to Con cón, the place of origin of my art, I created a time-based quipu, a film: *Kon Kon*, a documentary poem composed of one long fifty-four-minute film, and fourteen shorter films attached to it as quipu threads. *Kon Kon* pays homage to the fishermen's 'Torn Sound', a ritual sound-poetry-dance performance originating in pre-Columbian times, which continues to be performed and is now called 'baile chino'. The film also honours artists and poets in Con cón.

Kon Kon, time quipu diagram

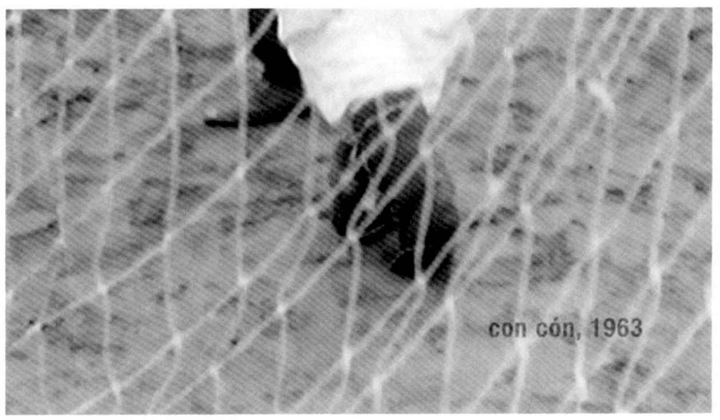

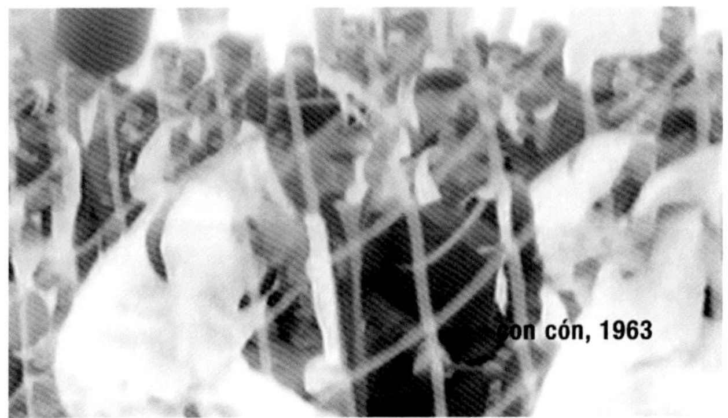

The fishermen's 'baile chino', Con cón, Chile, 1963

QUBIT

Reading about the qubit, a unit of quantum information in two states,
I thought: 'Like the quipu! Which is an object and a virtual construct,
existing in the knot, and the breath of the *quipucamayoc* (the one that
gives breath to the knot).' Bits of info, in the classical binary sense, are
1 or 0, yes or no. Qubits hold all the potential between zero and one.

> *A qubit is a two-state quantum-mechanical system, one of the simplest quantum
> systems displaying the peculiarity of quantum mechanics.*
>
> HTTPS://WWW.GEEKSFORGEEKS.ORG/DIFFERNCE-BETWEEN-BITS-
> AND-QUANTUM-BITS/

I imagined a quipu qubit performance, where we could all be in two
states, as ourselves, and as part of the quipu at once.

Quipu is a qubit
pure potential

Multiple states

Entangled atoms
in memory dimensions

States vector
in superposition

A double turning
on itself

QUBIT, CORNELL UNIVERSITY, 2008

The ancient Peruvians created the quipu (khipu) knot, nudo, an act of measurement, a writing in space.

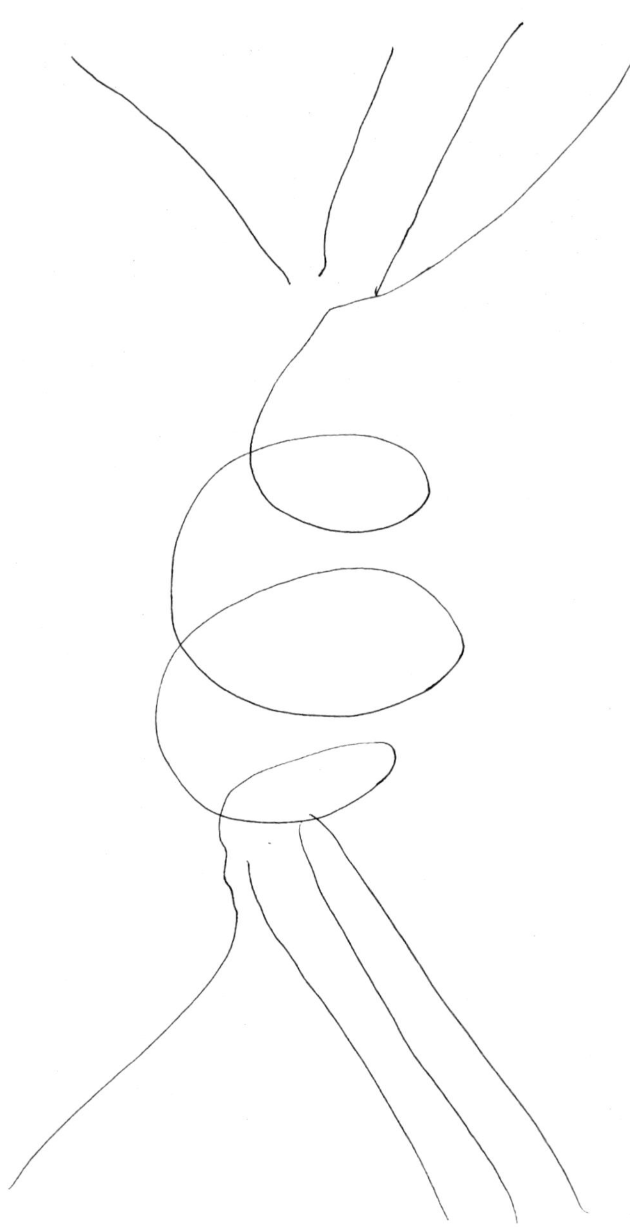

The Living Khipu Performance, Cornell University, 23 September 2008

QUIPU AUSTRAL

Associating the poetics of the *quipu-ceque* and the Aboriginal Songlines of Australia, I created the *Quipu Austral* on Cockatoo Island/Wareamah, a sacred site of the Eora People.

> *It is where the rivers join and is in the middle of where the sun rises and sets over the harbour. It is part of the milky way dreamtime stories …*
>
> —ISABEL COE

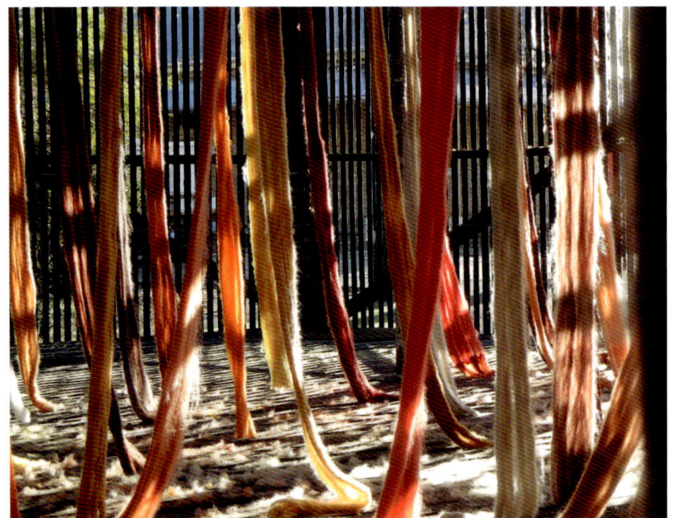

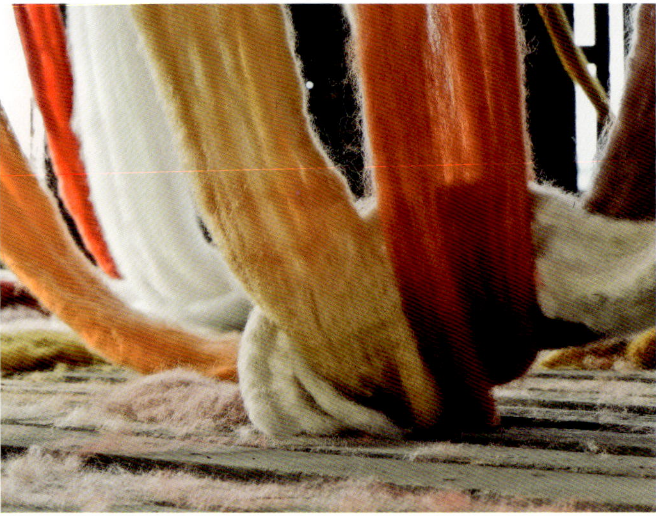

Quipu Austral, 12th Sydney Biennial, Sydney, 2012

QUIPU OF LIGHT

To weave
is to awake

The web of life
weaving itself

Cosmic

umbilical

cord

Tactile

numen

Womb's
filament

Stellar mouth

The cosmos

speaks in you.

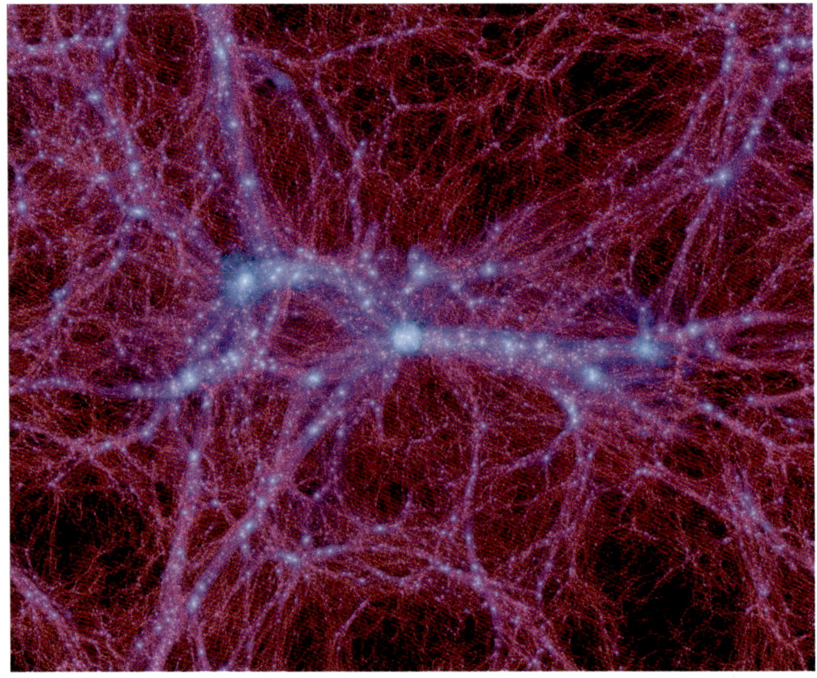

'Cosmic Thread', simulated view of the
interconnecting filaments between galaxies

*What we have discovered is evidence for the cosmic thread that connects us to
the vast expanse of the universe,' says Dr Stefan Keller of the Research School of
Astronomy and Astrophysics at ANU.*

*The filament of star clusters and small galaxies around the Milky Way is like
the umbilical cord that fed our galaxy during its youth.*

'COSMIC "UMBILICAL CORD" DISCOVERED', *TECH GURU DAILY*,
29 SEPT. 2011, HTTPS://TGDAILY.COM/SCIENCE/SPACE/COSMIC⁄
UMBILICAL⁄CORD⁄DISCOVERED/

*The quipumaker composed his recording by tracing figures in space … direct
construction – required tactile sensitivity … In fact, the overall aesthetic of
the quipu is related to the tactile: the manner of recording and the recording
itself are decidedly rhythmic: the first in the activity, the second in the effect
… anyone familiar with the activity of caressing will immediately see the
connection between touch and rhythm. In fact, tactile sensitivity begins in
the rhythmic pulsating environment of the unborn child far in advance of the
development of the other senses.*

—MARCIA AND ROBERT ASCHER, *CODE OF THE QUIPU: A STUDY
IN MEDIA, MATHEMATICS AND CULTURE*, ANN ARBOR 1981, P.61

QUIPU MAPOCHO

During the course of three years, I created *Quipu Mapocho*, a performance conceived as several knot-acts conducted throughout the course of the Mapocho River, from its birth at El Plomo Glacier to its mouth in Llolleo, Chile.

I was born at the edge of the Mapocho, a river made sacred by an ancient sacrifice. Its waters, now polluted by sewage and mining, gave life to the valley where the city of Santiago is situated.

Quipu Mapocho 2016–17, site-specific performative installation, Fío Mapocho, Chile

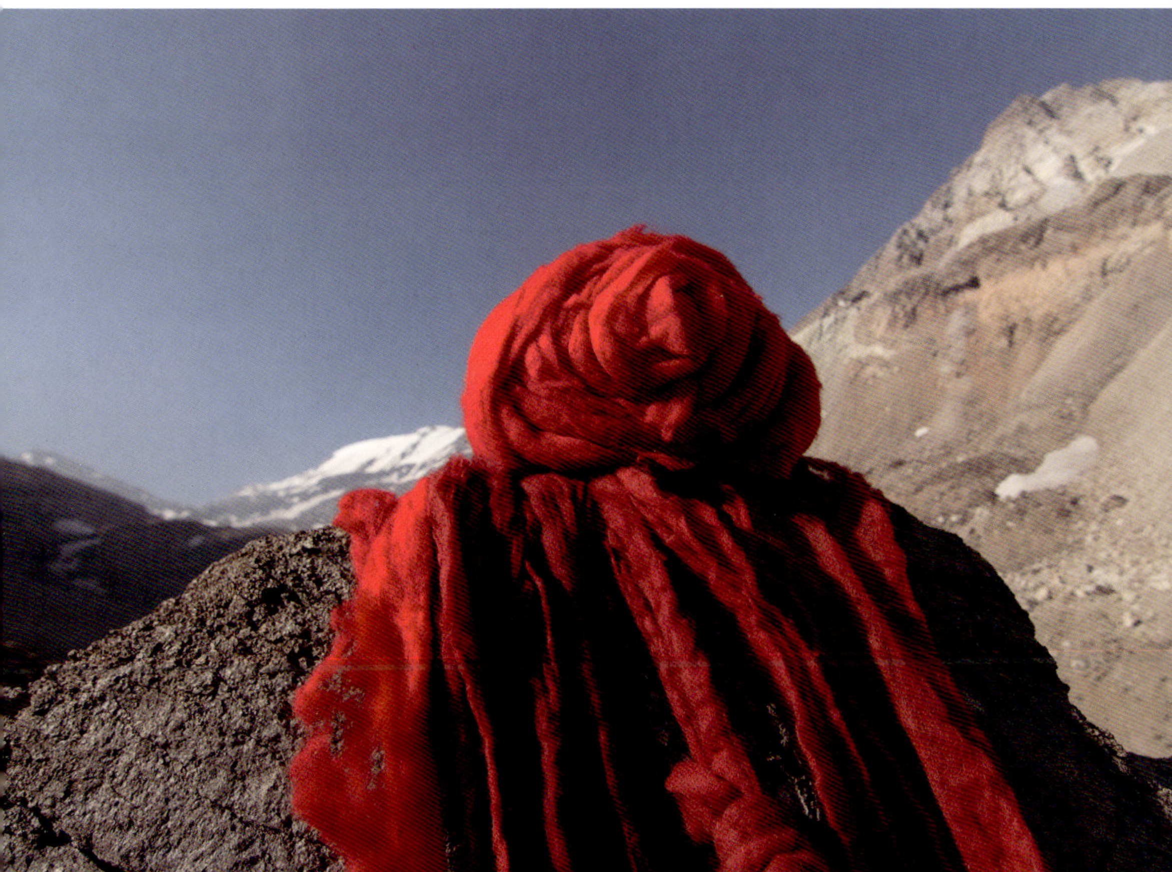

QUIPU WOMB

For documenta 14 in Athens and in Kassel, I created *Quipu Womb*,
a river of menstrual blood for us to remember who we really are,
vulnerable people depending on each other: a prayer for the continuity
of life, inspired by the commonality between the red knots ancient
Cretan women wore in their hair and waists and my own red quipus.
A double womb to give birth to a new reality, a culture of solidarity
on earth.

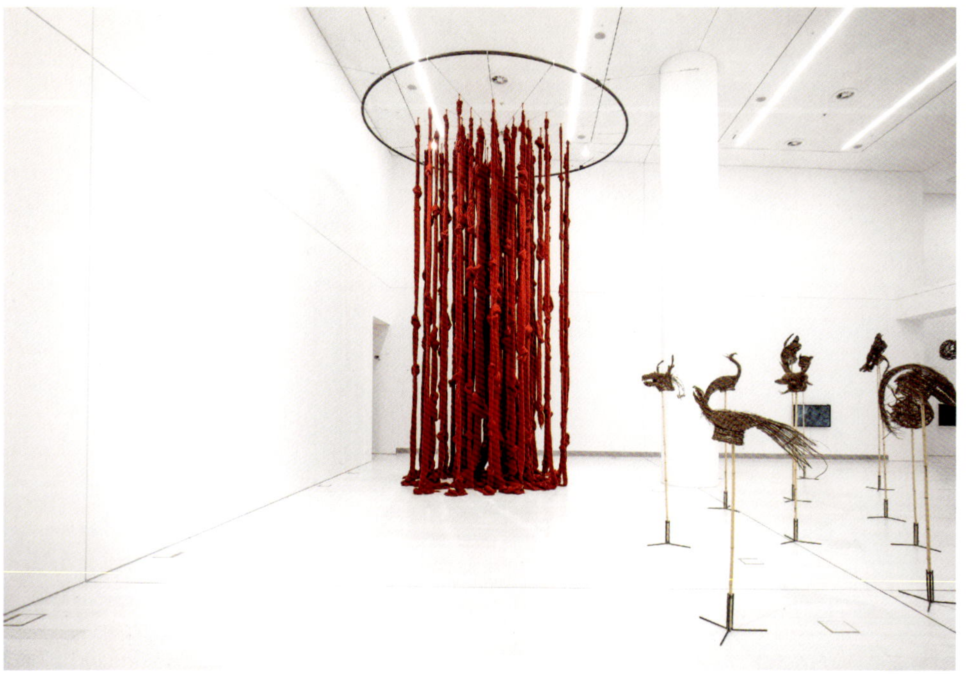

Quipu Womb, EMST Museum, Athens, documenta 14, 2017

*A 'quipoem', then, paying homage to the ancient, pre-Columbian art of
the quipu – a species of writing involving intricate knotting patterns. This
particular quipu consists of giant strands of untreated wool, sourced from a
local Greek provider, and dyed a startling crimson red in honor of a syncretic
religious tradition that – via the umbilical cord of menstrual symbolism –
connects Andean mother goddesses with the maritime mythologies of ancient
Greece.*

—DIETER ROELSTRATE, LABEL FOR *QUIPU WOMB* AT EMST MUSEUM,
ATHENS, DOCUMENTA 14

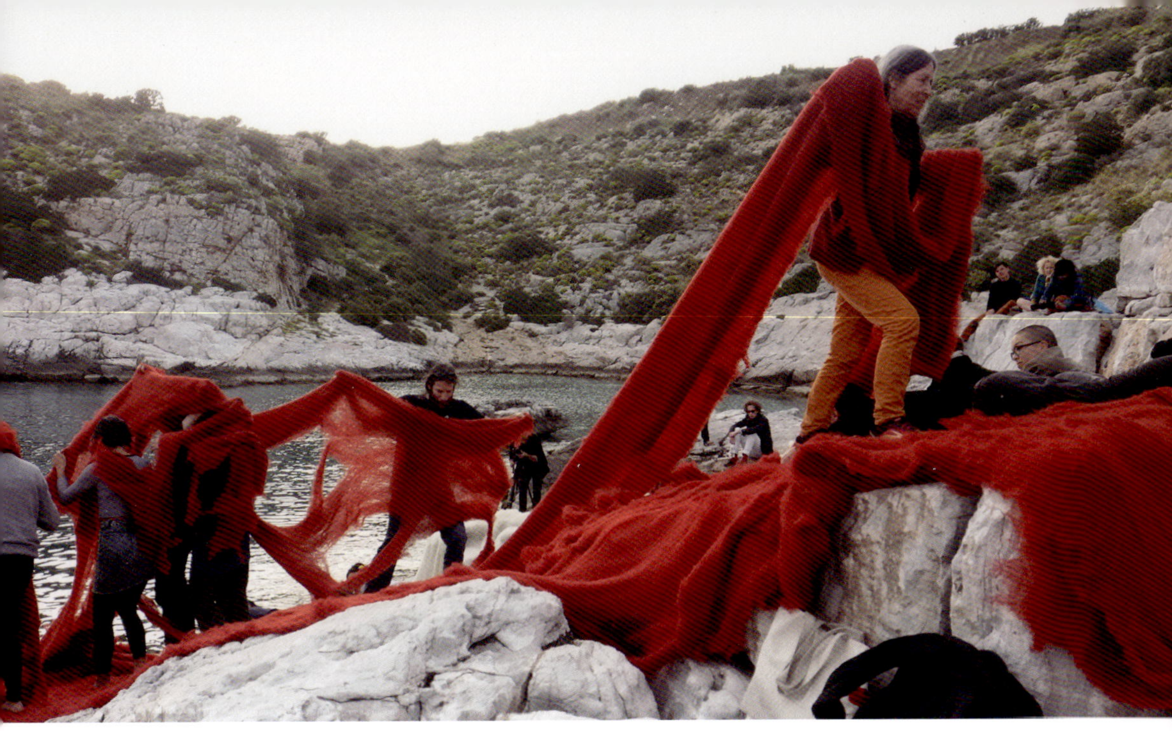

Beach Ritual (near Athens) 2017, documenta 14

After having done collective quipu rituals for many decades, the reference to a collective ritual performed in Inca times, involving a ball of red wool, came to me.

a very long cable ... woven in four colours, black, white, red and yellow, at the end of which there was a stout ball of red wool ... When they came to the square after making reverences to the huacas and the Ynka, they kept going round and round until they were the shape of a spiral shell. Then they dropped the huascar on the ground, and left it coiled up like a snake.

—CRISTOBAL DE MOLINA (CUSCO, C.1529–85). QUOTED IN WILLIAM CONKLIN, 'A KHIPU INFORMATION STRING THEORY', IN JEFFREY QUILTER AND GARY URTON (EDS.), *NARRATIVE THREADS: ACCOUNTING AND RECOUNTING IN ANDEAN KHIPU*, AUSTIN, TEXAS 2002, P.64

At the end of the dance, the moro urco rope was deposited in the Coricancha, the 'golden enclosure' that served as the Temple of the Sun, and the resting place of venerated ancestors. The objective of this ritual was to transmit the life force emanating from the ancestors (camac) to the people (camasca) via serpents.

—ARABEL FERNÁNDEZ LÓPEZ, 'SERPENT ORNAMENT A.D. 1450– 1532', (2020), METROPOLITAN MUSEUM OF ART, NEW YORK, WWW.METMUSEUM.ORG/ART/COLLECTION/SEARCH/316938, ACCESSED 14 AUG. 2022

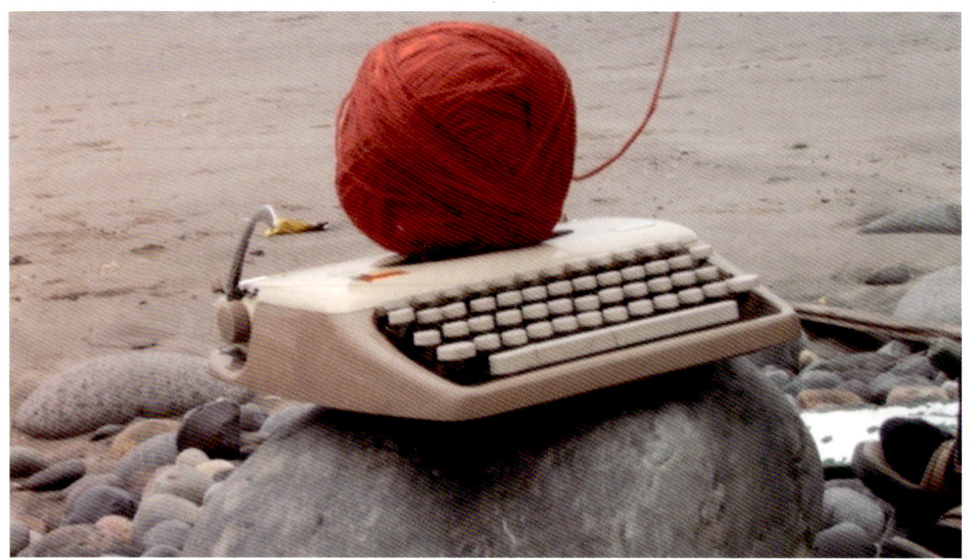

Kon Kon 2010, HD video, colour and sound,
53 min 55 sec, Spanish with English subtitles

Simultaneously, the evidence of the political use of quipu by current Andean communities was emerging. If during Inca times, quipus kept track of state affairs, in the post-Inca era – after European colonisation-, quipu became an iconic symbol dedicated to preserve rules of self-governance, and the relationship with the mountain deities on which the well-being of the community depends.

> *... when 'Indian' villages came to be part of an independent republic, cord keeping still carried on the Toledan vision of the cord master as 'a kind of moral policeman'*
>
> —BURNS 2004:11

Like many Andean villages, Tupicocha is a confederation of corporate kin groups (ayllu). In such a system, the core social contract is equitable contribution … The accounting of reciprocal duties, whether by khipus or (today) by ledgers, guarantees equity of contribution.

Villagers today disclaim any ability to decipher cords. They do, however, offer three ideas about what might be encoded on these cords. Kaha Wayi's ritualist, and a few other elders strongly attached to Kaha Wayi's sacred regimen, see them as the trace of interactions with the jirka, or divine mountains, perhaps records of sacrifices or encounters.

—FRANK SALOMON, CARRIE J. BREZINE, REYMUNDO CHAPA, AND VÍCTOR FALCÓN HUAYTA, 'KHIPU FROM COLONY TO REPUBLIC: THE RAPAZ PATRIMONY', IN ELIZABETH HILL BOONE AND GARY URTON (EDS.), *THEIR WAY OF WRITING, SCRIPTS, SIGNS, AND PICTOGRAPHIES IN PRE-COLUMBIAN AMERICA*, WASHINGTON, DC 2011, WWW.ACADEMIA.EDU/7057172/KHIPU_FROM_COLONY_TO_REPUBLIC, ACCESSED 14 AUG. 2022

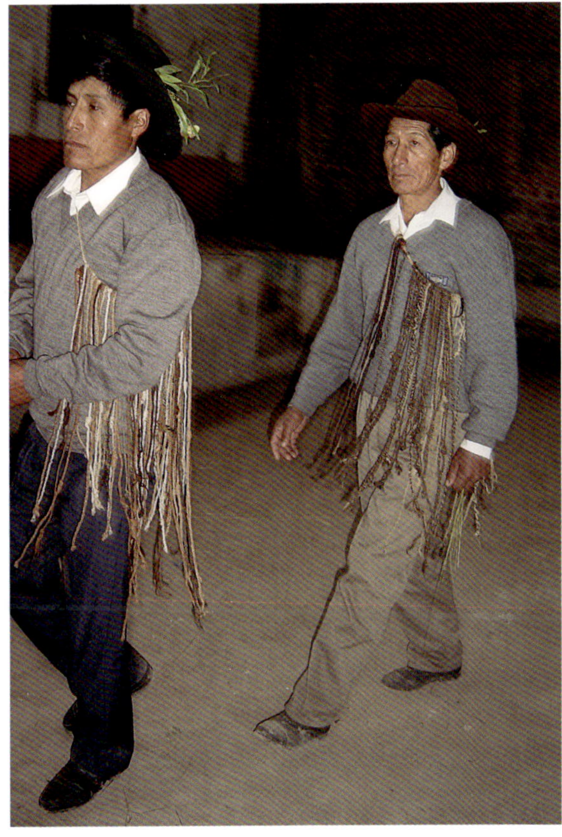

Investiture of new presidents of ayllus in Tupicocha, Huarochiri province, 2005

BURNT QUIPU

Mourning the loss endured by people, land and animals around the world, in the forest fires in California, the Amazon, the Boreal Forest, Africa, Australia, and the temperate forests in Chile, I created *Burnt Quipu* as a prayer for us to change our destructive ways.

Burnt Quipu, created in situ at the Berkeley Art Museum and Pacific Film Archive (BAMPFA), University of California, as ash from nearby fires rained on the museum: for the exhibition *Cecilia Vicuña, About to Happen*, 2018

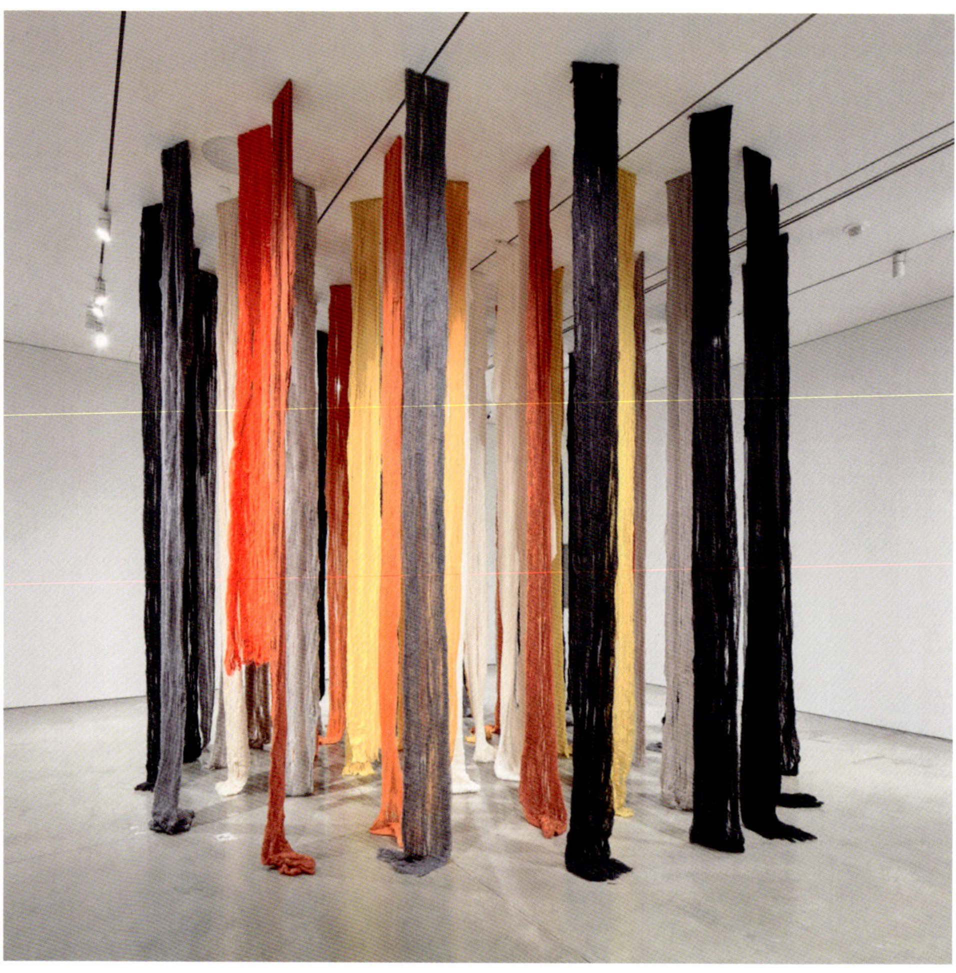

QUIPU WOMB

Joining the Tate collection, *Quipu Womb* shared space with Joseph
Beuys's installation *Lightning with Stag in its Glare* 1958–85, a pairing of
two realities that bring forth a common view of society as a work of art,
and a common concern for modern society inclining towards ecological
disaster.

Quipu Womb (The Story of the Red Thread, Athens) 2017,
installed alongside Joseph Beuys, *Lightning with Stag
in its Glare* 1958–85, Tate Modern, 2020,

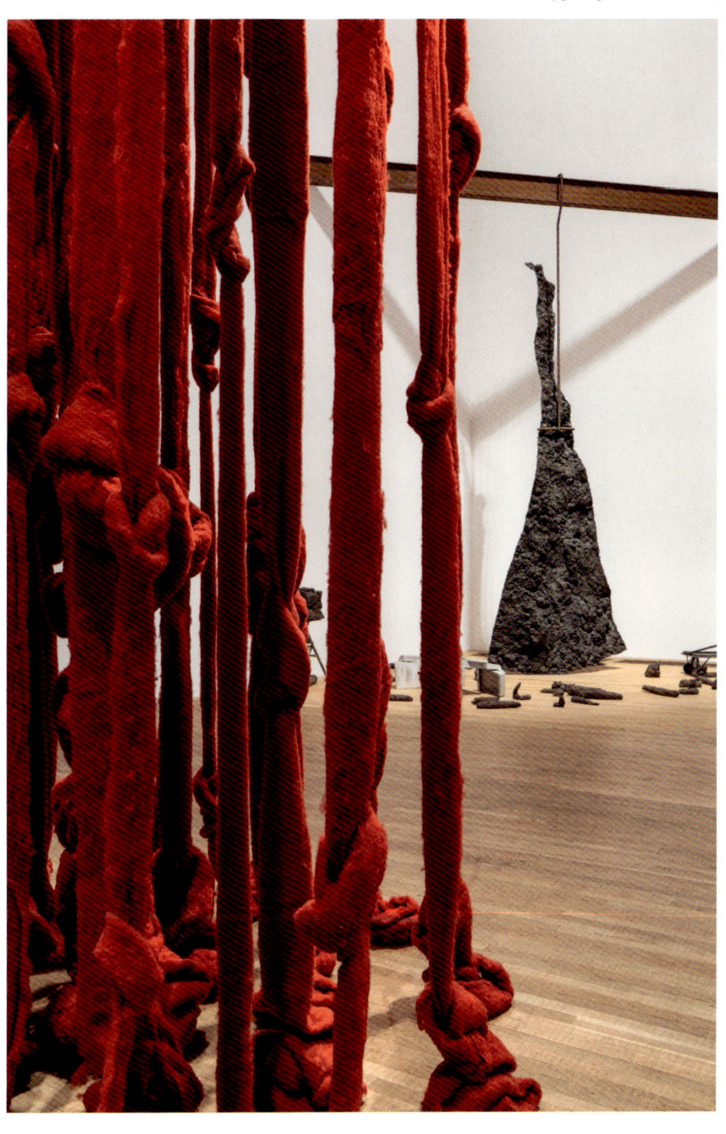

QUIPU LAVA

The *Quipu Lava* was performed on 7 February 2022 at the foot of
the volcanoes Popocatépetl and Iztaccíhuatl, which gave life to the
valley where Mexico City now exists, within the *Espacio Escultórico*
– a collective sculpture created in the 1960s in the lava field at the
Universidad Autónoma de México, where my retrospective exhibition
Veroír el Fracaso Iluminado, curated by Miguel Lopez, was on view.
The performance of *Quipu Lava* was dedicated to the girls and women
who have been victims of violence.

Quipu Lava, performance, Espacio Escultórico,
MUAC, Mexico City, 7 February 2020
Below: still from the video
Right: photo documentation of the performance

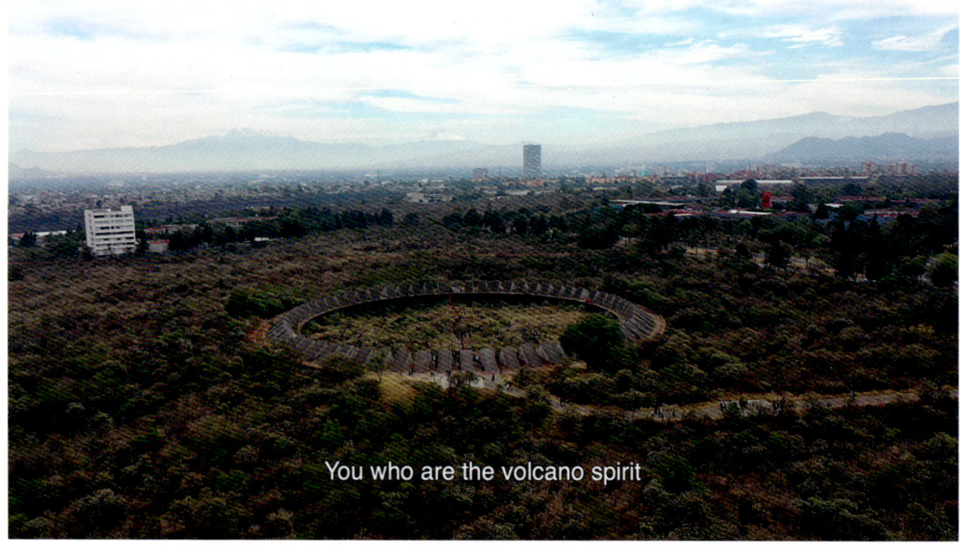

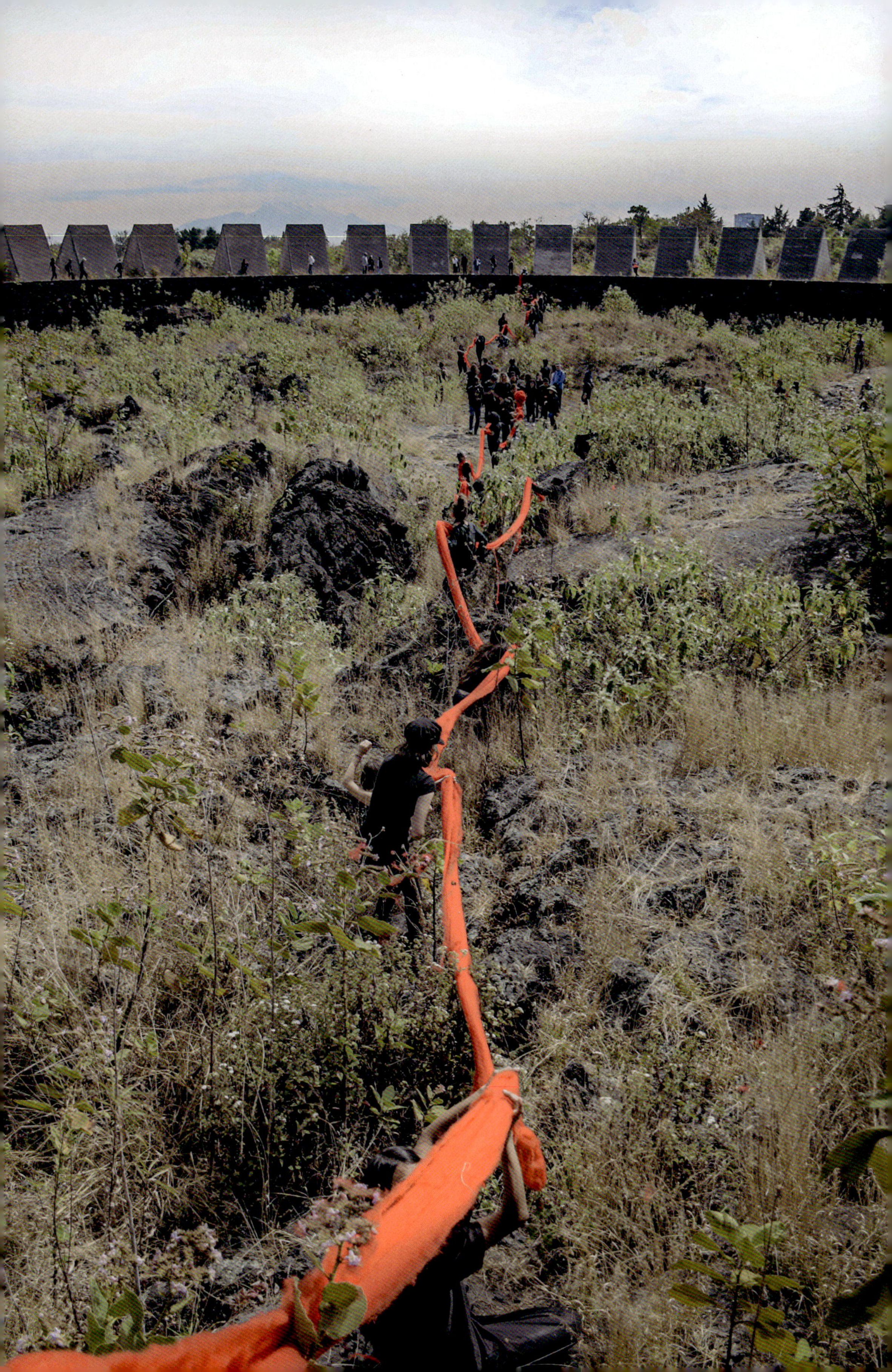

NAUFRAGA

Paying homage to the ancient fishermen of the Venice lagoon, and the struggle of the people of Venice to save their city from being taken over by foreign investors, I created a quipu from the lagoon's debris.

NAUfraga, 2022, site specific installation for the 59th International Art Exhibition – Venice Biennale, *The Milk of Dreams*, Central Pavilion, Venice Biennale 2022

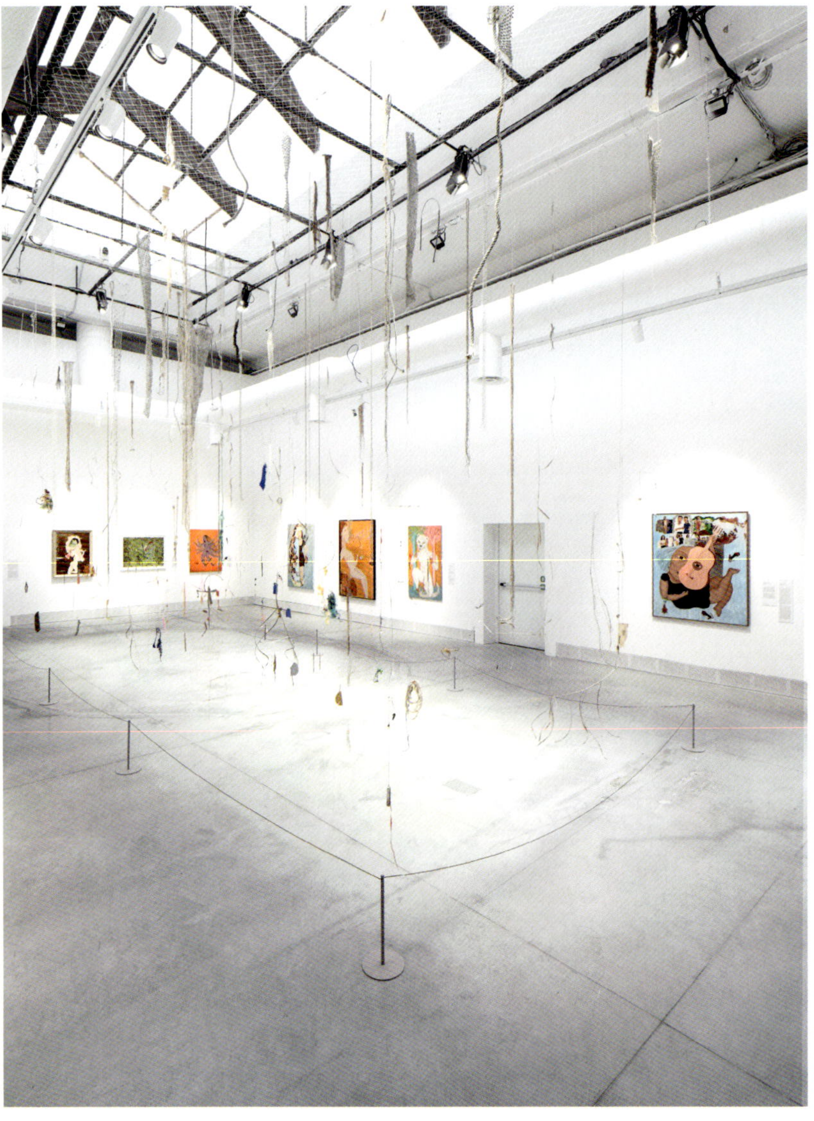

NAUFRAGA

A work dedicated to the Venice lagoon.

Naufraga, from navis (ship) + frangere (to break).

We are breaking our ship sinking Venice and other lands.

Fraga, is the root of 'fragile' and 'failure': Our failure to care for Earth.

Naufraga journeys to the memory of the lagoon, its grasses and the stories held by the cords twined by its first peoples.

May the rustle of its twigs move our hearts to care for Her, our Earth ship.

EXTERMINATION QUIPU

Quipu is coming back into the world, in art and poetry, information theory and quantum knots, creating wondrous collective effects.

… the method of making quantum states pulse to a shared rhythm could … be leveraged to synchronize remote nodes in a quantum communication network

—CHRISTOPHER CROCKETT, 'A SHARED QUANTUM RHYTHM', *PHYSICS*, 1 JULY 2020, PHYSICS.APS.ORG/ARTICLES/V13/S87, ACCESSED 15 AUG. 2022

Extermination Quipu, Guggenheim Museum, New York, 2022

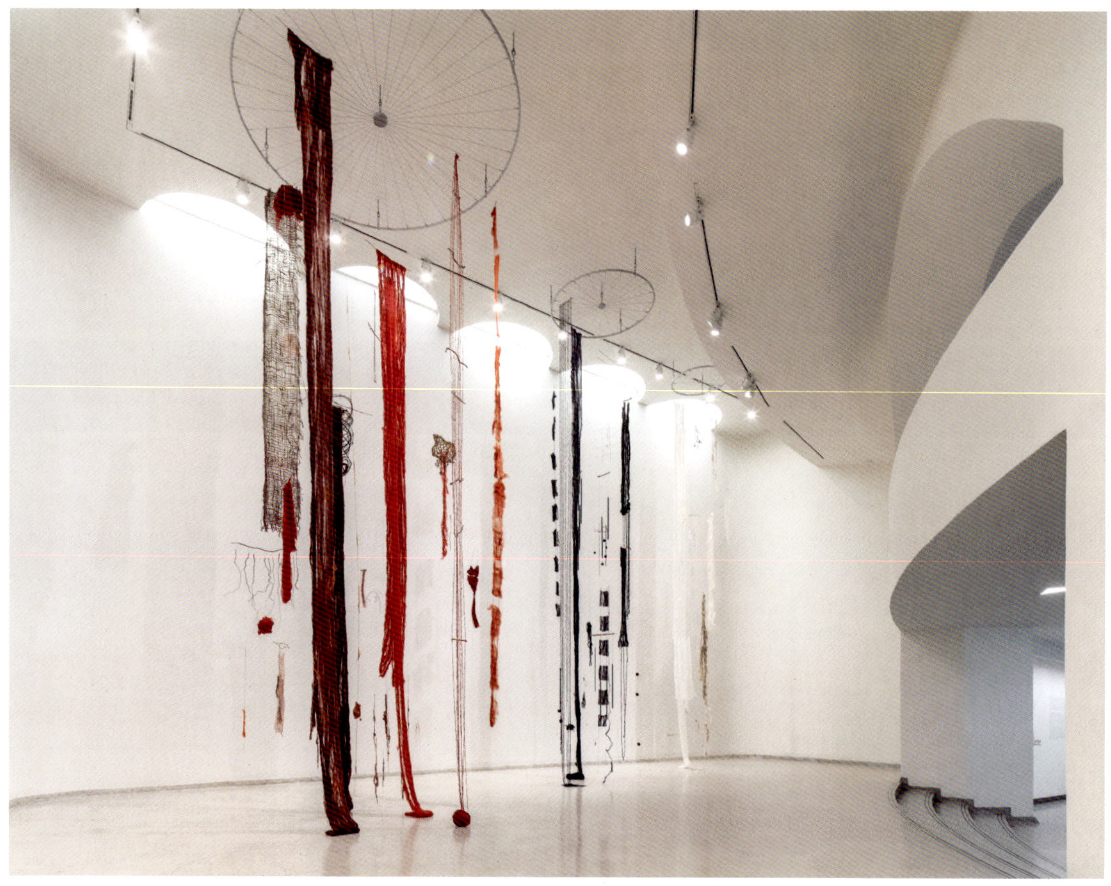

On 28 February 2017, the Nobel Prize-winning physicist Frank Wilczek published a memorable article in *Quanta*, expressing a new vision of quipu:

> *Computing with anyons exploits their ability to map their knotted histories into (observable) quantum-mechanical amplitudes. We move anyons around in clever ways and then access the tangled history of their motion. Topological quantum computing is, therefore, a form of computing with knots. As such, it is a modernization of quipu, the Incan technology for computation and encryption.*

—FRANK WILCZEK, 'INSIDE THE KNOTTY WORLD OF "ANYON" PARTICLES', *QUANTA*, 28 FEB. 2017, WWW.QUANTAMAGAZINE. ORG/HOW-ANYON-PARTICLES-EMERGE-FROM-QUANTUM- KNOTS-20170228, ACCESSED 15 AUG. 2022

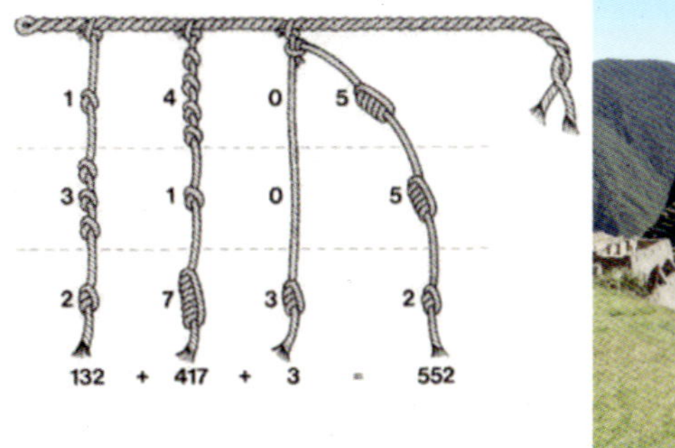

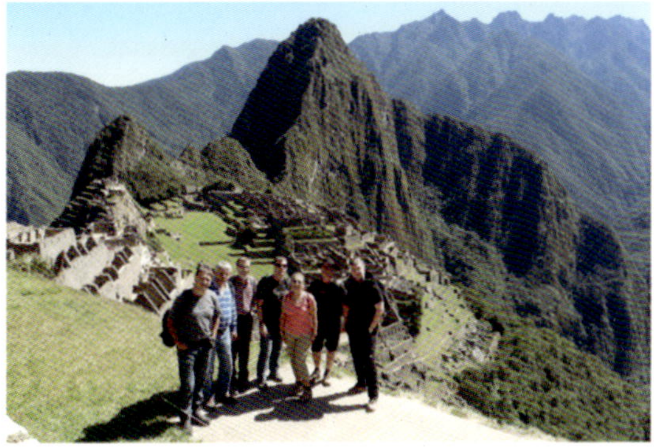

In a later article, Wilczek expanded on the links between quipu and quantum physics theory:

> *Several ancient Andean civilizations, including the Inca, developed a versatile and nonverbal method to record and process information that served them well for many centuries. Quipus are formed from a sequence of colored strings containing knots. Each of the strings is tied at one end to a common cord, so that when the cord is suspended the strings hang down and can be scanned easily. The colors of the strings and the placement of the knots might convey an accounting ledger, a historical chronicle, or a military roster. In the quantum world, one might imagine using braids to represent information in a similar manner. Anyons empower such an approach, because the wave functions of multi-anyon systems store memories of the braids formed by their world-lines.*

—FRANK WILCZEK, 'QUANTA OF THE THIRD KIND', *INFERENCE*, VOL.6, NO.3, NOV. 2021, INFERENCE-REVIEW.COM/ARTICLE/ QUANTA-OF-THE-THIRD-KIND, ACCESSED 15 AUG. 2022

quipu exterminio

We
are

can we ack

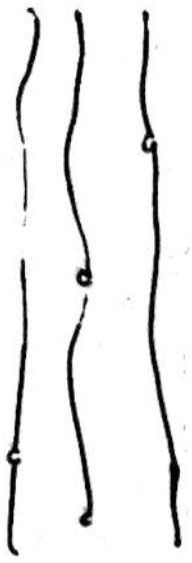

now

ledge

ex

termi

nation

?

all

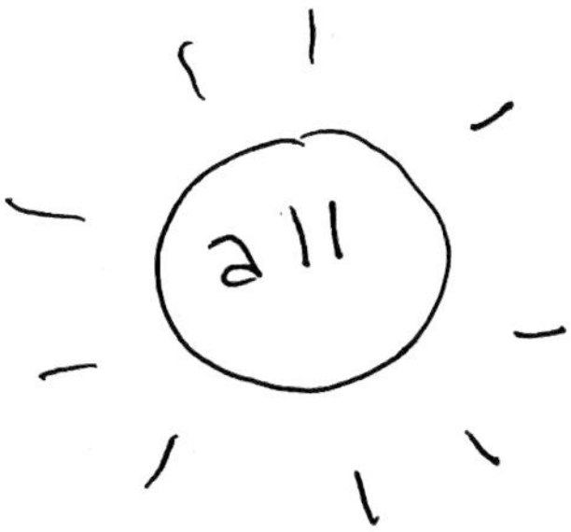

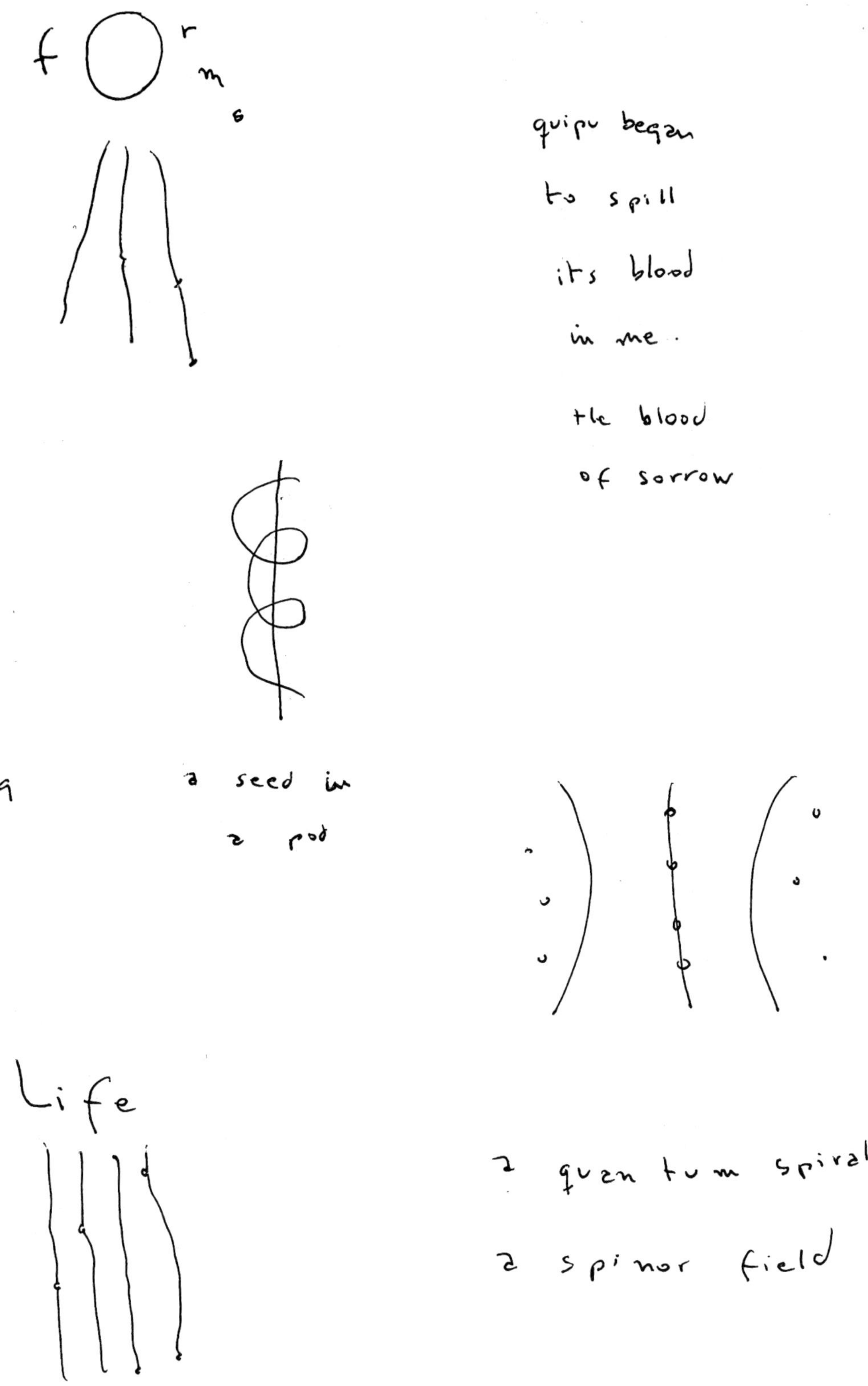

forms
quipu began
to spill
its blood
in me.
the blood
of sorrow
a seed in
a pod
t i n g
Life
a quantum spiral
a spinor field

the blood
of the
glaciers
of the
earth

the
people
murdered
for
profit

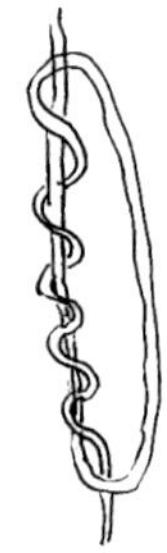

quiet
is the
speaker
of blood

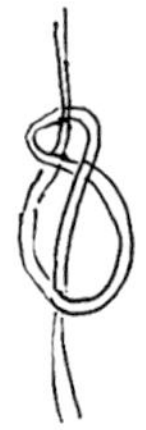

the extinction of life

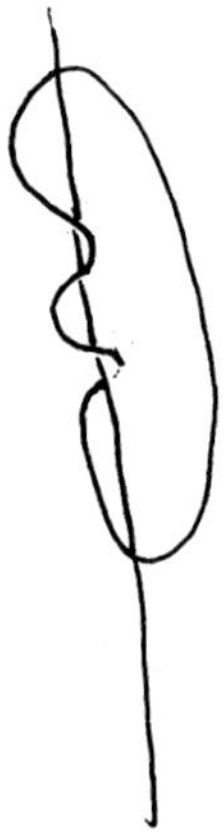

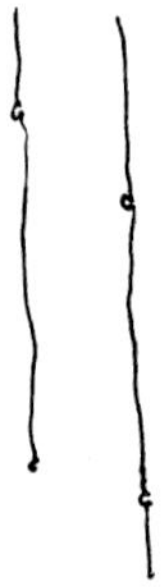

each knot

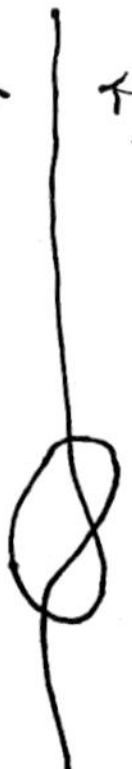

marking a loss

a wound

"Weaving is the birth of Light"

Lezama Lima

maximun fragility
against maximum power

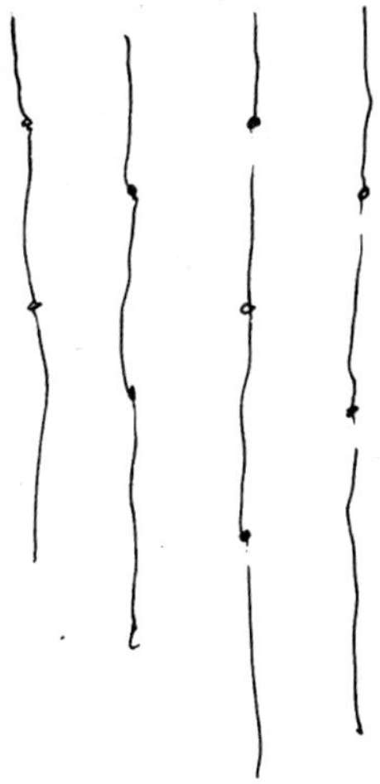

"the weak force

per forms

natural Al

chemy

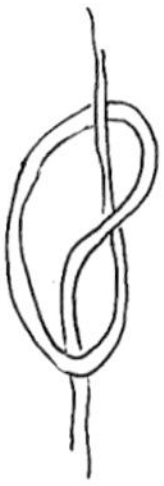

the

quipu

Spin

S

its

magnetic

f   f
  o   o
 r   r
c   c
          e
e
f   e
 o   u
  r   i
   c   c
    e   o
        r
      e   r

weaves
atoms

into

mole cu les"

Frank Wilczek

In April 2022 the *Wall Street Journal* published Wilczek's article 'A Quantum Leap, With Strings Attached':

> *The Inca system of quipu – tying a series of knots to record information – is providing a surprising model to modern physics and quantum computing … The basic letters of quipu are knots made in strings[,] a trick similar to how differentiated cells apply epigenetic variation to the four-letter codes of DNA … In traditional quipu, each string is independent … They can be wound around one another, producing braids … There are certain particles, called anyons, whose quantum behavior keeps track of the braid that their world-lines form. The anyon world-lines form a quantum quipu … The result could be a topological quantum computer ready to take on otherwise intractable computational challenges, while evoking how the Inca recorded what they knew.*
>
> —FRANCK WILCZEK, 'A QUANTUM LEAP, WITH STRINGS ATTACHED', *WALL STREET JOURNAL*, 14 APRIL 2022, WWW.WSJ.COM/ARTICLES/A-QUANTUM-LEAP-WITH-STRINGS-ATTACHED-11649960549, ACCESSED 15 AUG. 2022

With the confluence of quantum quipus and the Webb Telescope's 'time machine', spanning across 13.5 billion years of cosmic history, a 'Quipu of time' may be emerging as new states of matter come to the fore, highlighting the qualities of interactions as did the quipu long ago.

> *When the ancient Incas wanted to archive tax and census records, they used a device made up of a number of strings called a quipu, which encoded the data in knots. Fast-forward several hundred years, and physicists are on their way to*

Skyscraper Quipu 2006, New York

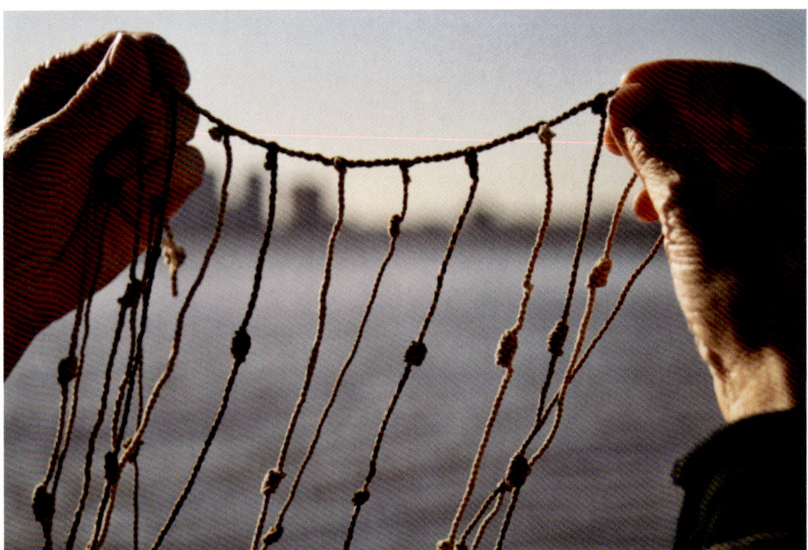

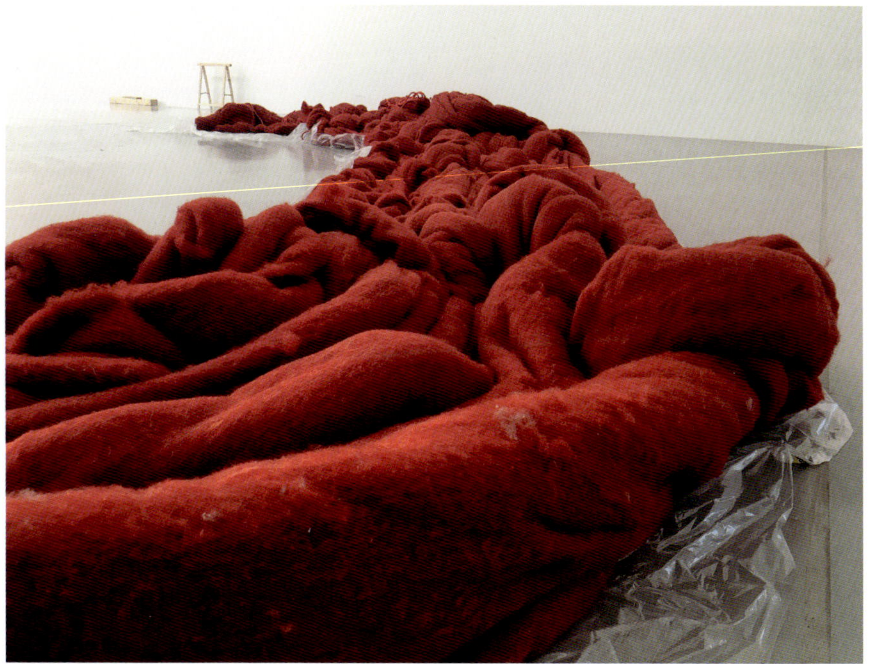

developing a far more sophisticated modern equivalent. Their 'quipu' is a new phase of matter created within a quantum computer, their strings are atoms, and the knots are generated by patterns of laser pulses that effectively open up a second dimension of time ...

These materials display order not on the basis of how their constituents are arranged—like the regular spacing of atoms in a crystal—but on their dynamic motions and interactions ... In a quantum computer that exploits topology, information is not encoded locally in the state of each qubit but is woven across the material globally. It's like a knot that's hard to undo—like quipu.

—ZEEYA MERALI, 26 JULY 2022, *SCIENTIFIC AMERICAN*
HTTPS://WWW.SCIENTIFICAMERICAN.COM/ARTICLE/NEW-PHASE-OF-MATTER-OPENS-PORTAL-TO-EXTRA-TIME-DIMENSION/

Adding to the new knowledge in knot theory and topology is the recent discovery of knotted quantum twists:

As physicists delve deeper into the quantum realm, they are discovering an infinitesimally small world composed of a strange and surprising array of links, knots and winding. Some quantum materials exhibit magnetic whirls called skyrmions – unique configurations described as 'subatomic hurricanes.' Others host a form of superconductivity that twists into vortices.

—PRINCETON UNIVERSITY, 'ELECTRONS IN A CRYSTAL FOUND TO EXHIBIT LINKED AND KNOTTED QUANTUM TWISTS', *PHYS.ORG*, 20 MAY 2022, PHYS.ORG/NEWS/2022-05-ELECTRONS-CRYSTAL-LINKED-QUANTUM.HTML, ACCESSED 15 AUG. 2022

BRAIN FOREST QUIPU

The *Brain Forest Quipu* at Tate Modern's Turbine Hall mourns the dead forests of the world, connecting communities struggling to preserve them across the globe in collective acts of awareness and love to realise the quipu's dream of the interconnectedness of all, to each other and the cosmos.

As we come to the close of this book, the Webb Telescope connects us to the birth of the universe, reminding us of ancestors who created the quipu five thousand years ago, knotting themselves metaphorically to the stars and the dark cloud constellations between them, the intergalactic dust where life and water are born.

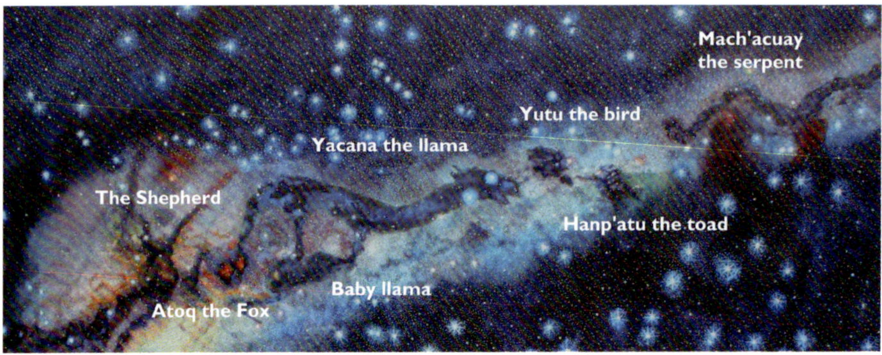

One of the most important dark cloud constellations was Yacana – the llama, which rises above Cusco, the ancient capital city of the Incas, in November: https://futurism.com/the-dark-constellations-of-the-incas

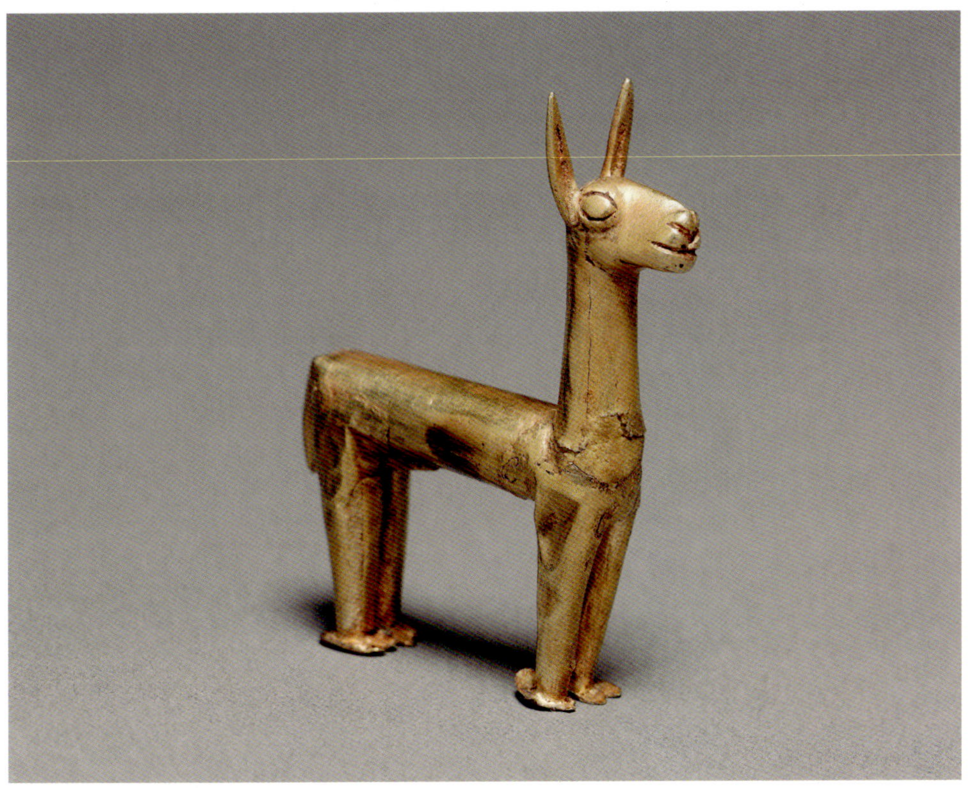

The llama also featured in pre-Inca mythology, in the oral tradition of the
Huarochirí in Peru's mountainous north-east. A llama dreams of an approaching
flood and warns its owner and their family. They take heed and, with the llama,
ascend Willka Qutu, the region's highest mountain, where they find many other
animals gathered. Soon, the waters rise, leaving only Willka Qutu's summit
unsubmerged. When they descend, they alone must repopulate the empty world.
https://www.historytoday.com/archive/foundations/gold-llama

Perhaps we are not at an end, but at the beginning of a new time.

Long ago, I wrote: 'The true performance is that of our species on
Earth: the way we cause suffering to others, the way we warm the
atmosphere or cause other species to disappear.'

To change course, we must see our collective responsibility to create
a different cultural memory.

A Quichua word says it: *riparana*, to repair injustice or harm by
becoming aware.

APPENDIX

Quipu / khipu: 'knot' in Quechua

*Quipu is the Spanish spelling and the most common spelling in
English is khipu. In most Quechua varieties, the term is kipu. https://
en.wikipedia.org/wiki/Quipu

*In the Andes people did not write, they wove meaning into textiles and knotted
cords. Five thousand years ago they created the quipu (knot), a poem in space, a
way to remember, involving the body and the cosmos at once. A tactile, spatial
metaphor for the union of all. The quipu, and its virtual counterpart, the
ceque (a system of sightlines connecting all communities in the Andes), were
banished after the [European] Conquest. Quipus were burnt, but the vision of
interconnectivity, a poetic resistance endures underground.*

Cecilia Vicuña, 'Quipus', http://www.ceciliavicuna.com/quipus,
accessed 15 Aug. 2022

ACKNOWLEDGEMENTS

I thank the many authors, artists, scientists and curators who have
participated in the quipu field of knowledge, expanding its potential for
the future. All of them are the co-authors of these thoughts. I especially
thank my partner, the poet James O'Hern, who senses along with me
each one of its dimensions slowly coming forth.

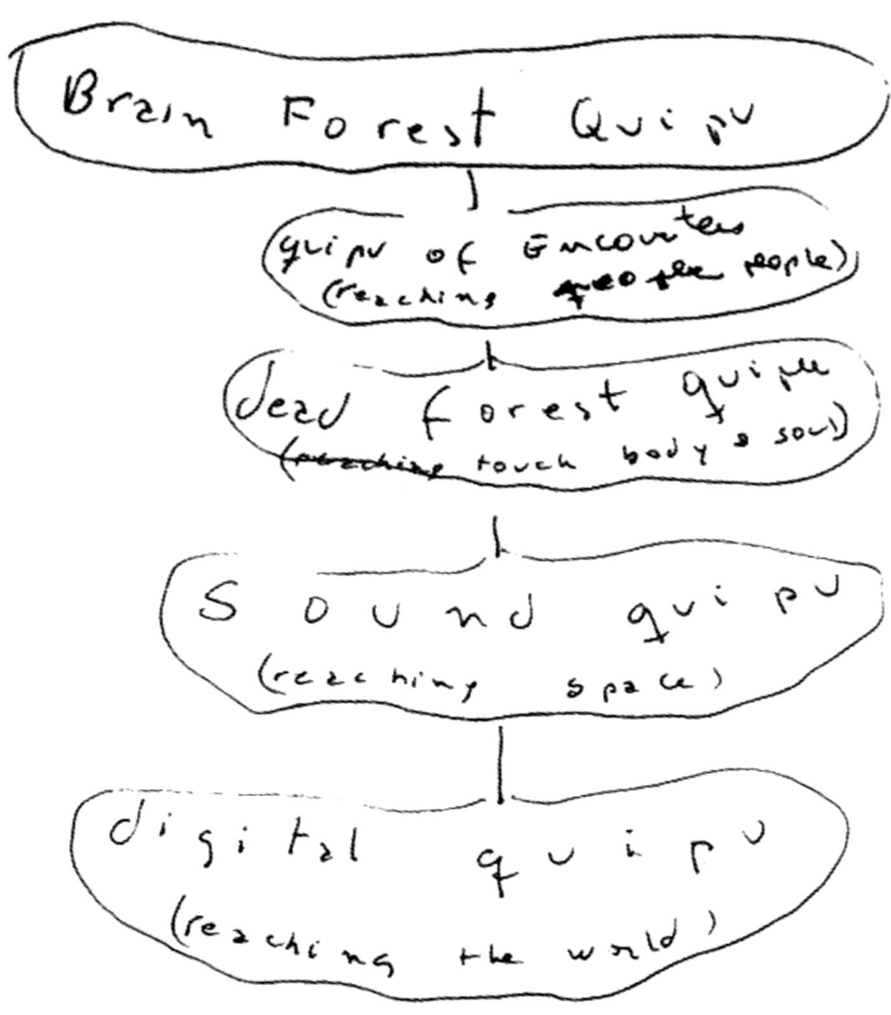

Four quipus 2022, ink drawing

Cecilia Vicuña: Biography

Born 1948 in Santiago, Chile
Lives and works in New York
1971 MFA, National School of Fine Arts, University
of Chile, Santiago
1973 Slade School of Fine Art, University College
London, London

SELECTED SOLO EXHIBITIONS

2023
Cecilia Vicuña: Soñar el agua, Museo Nacional de Bellas
Artes, Santiago, Chile
Cecilia Vicuña: Flower Mundo Quipu, Museum of
Contemporary Art, Tucson
2022
Hyundai Commission: Cecilia Vicuña, Tate Modern,
London
Spin Spin Triangulene, Solomon R. Guggenheim
Museum, New York
Veroír el fracaso iluminado, Museo de Arte Miguel Urrutia
(MAMU), Bogotá
2021
Cecilia Vicuña: Veroír el fracaso iluminado, Centro de Arte
Dos de Mayo (CA2M), Madrid
Quipu Girok, Lehmann Maupin, Seoul
2020
Cecilia Vicuña: Veroír el fracaso iluminado, Museo
Universitario de Arte Contemporáneo (MUAC), Mexico
City
Cecilia Vicuña is on our mind, CCA Wattis Institute for
Contemporary Arts, San Francisco
2019
Minga del Cielo Oscuro, Centro Cultural de España,
CCE, Santiago
Cecilia Vicuña: Seehearing the Enlightened Failure, Witte de
With Center for Contemporary Art, Rotterdam
Cecilia Vicuña: About to Happen, Henry Art Gallery,
Seattle, WA; Institute of Contemporary Art,
Philadelphia, PA; Museum of Contemporary Art North
Miami, Miami
Cecilia Vicuña: Lo Precario | The Precarious, Wexner
Center for the Arts, Columbus
2018
Cecilia Vicuña: About to Happen, Berkeley Art Museum
and Pacific Film Archive (BAMPFA), Berkeley

Quipu Desaparecido, Brooklyn Museum, New York;
Museum of Fine Arts, Boston, Boston
Cecilia Vicuña: La India Contaminada, Lehmann Maupin,
New York
Cecilia Vicuña: PALABRARmas, Neubauer Collegium,
University of Chicago, Chicago
2017
Cecilia Vicuña: About to Happen, Contemporary Arts
Center, New Orleans
2015
Cecilia Vicuña: The Origin of Weaving, Poetry Foundation,
Chicago
2014
Artists for Democracy: El Archivo de Cecilia Vicuña, Museo
de la Memoria y los Derechos Humanos, Santiago;
Museo Nacional de Bellas Artes, Santiago
2013
Cecilia Vicuña, England & Co, London
2012
Aural, Galería Patricia Ready, Santiago
2009
Water Writing: Anthological Exhibition, 1966–2009,
Institute for Women & Art, Rutgers University,
New Brunswick
Noche de las Especies: la mar herida nos mira, El Gran
Vidrio, pensamiento ocular, Consejo Nacional de la
Cultura y las Artes, Valparaíso
2008
Parti Si Pasión, Metales Pesados, Santiago
2007
Otoño: Reconstrucción Documental, Museo Nacional de
Bellas Artes, Santiago
2002
Thread Mansion, Boulder Museum of Contemporary Art,
Boulder
2001
Book No Book, Woodland Pattern Book Center,
Milwaukee
2000
Se mi ya, Galería Gabriela Mistral, Ministerio de
Educación, Santiago
1998
Cloud-Net, Hallwalls Contemporary Arts Center,
Buffalo, NY; DiverseWorks ArtSpace, Houston, TX;
Art in General, New York
1997
K'isa, University Art Gallery, University of
Massachusetts at Dartmouth, New Bedford

1996
Precario, Inverleith House, Royal Botanic Gardens,
Edinburgh
1994
Ceq'e Fragments, Center for Contemporary Arts, Santa Fe
Hilumbres Allqa, Kanaal Art Foundation, Kortrijk
1992
El Ande Futuro, BAMPFA, Berkeley
1990
Precarious, Exit Art Gallery, New York
1977
Homenaje a Vietnam, Fundación Gilberto Alzate
Avendaño, Bogotá
1974
A Journal of Objects: 400 precarious objects, Arts Meeting
Place, London
1973
Pain Things & Explanations, Institute of Contemporary
Arts, London
1971
Pinturas, Poemas y Explicaciones, Museo Nacional de
Bellas Artes, Santiago
Otoño, Museo Nacional de Bellas Artes, Santiago

SELECTED GROUP EXHIBITIONS

2022
Life Between Buildings, MoMA PS1, New York
The Milk of Dreams, 59th International Art Exhibition,
Venice Biennale, Venice
2021
Artist and Society, Tate Modern, London
Bodies of Water, 13th Shanghai Biennale, Shanghai
Minds Rising, Spirits Tuning, 13th Gwangju Biennale,
Gwangju
And if I devoted my life to one of its feathers?, Kunsthalle
Wien, Vienna
The Space Between Classrooms, Swiss Institute, New York
2020
Witch Hunt, Kunsthal Charlottenborg, Copenhagen
Rewrite the World, Glassell School of Art, Museum of
Fine Arts Houston, Houston
More, More, More, Tank Shanghai, Shanghai
2019
A Year in Art: 1973, Tate Modern, London
An Emphasis on Resistance: 2019 CIFO Grants &
Commissions Program Exhibition, El Museo del Barrio,
New York

Contemporary Art: Five Propositions, Museum of Fine Arts
Boston, Boston
Collaboration for a Dark Sky, Centro Cultural de España,
Santiago
Artistic License: Six Takes on the Guggenheim Collection,
Solomon R. Guggenheim Museum, New York
2018
Radical Women: Latin American Art, 1960–1985,
Brooklyn Museum, New York; Pinacoteca de São Paulo,
São Paulo
2017
Radical Women: Latin American Art, 1960–1985,
Hammer Museum, Los Angeles
documenta 14, Athens, Greece; Kassel
Movimientos de Tierra, Museo Nacional de Bellas
Artes, Santiago
La timidité des cimes, Fonds Régional d'Art Contemporain
de Lorraine, Metz
2016
Embodied Absence: Chilean Art of the 1970s Now,
Carpenter Center for the Visual Arts, Harvard
University, Cambridge
Una imagen llamada palabra, Centro Nacional de Arte
Contemporáneo, Cerrillos
La emergencia del pop: Irreverencia y calle en Chile, Museo
de la Solidaridad Salvador Allende, Santiago
A Kingdom of Hours, Gasworks, London
2015
Agitprop!, Brooklyn Museum, New York
*Ausencia Encarnada: Efimeralidad y Colectividad en el Arte
Chileano de los Años Setenta*, Museo de la Solidaridad
Salvador Allende, Santiago
2014
Really Useful Knowledge, Museo Nacional Centro de Arte
Reina Sofía, Madrid, Spain; Ashkal Alwan, Cairo, Egypt
artevida (corpo), Casa França-Brasil, Rio de Janeiro,
Brazil
artevida (política), Museu de Arte Moderna do Rio de
Janeiro, Rio de Janeiro
2013
Les Immémoriales, Fonds Régional d'Art Contemporain
de Lorraine, Metz
2012
all our relations, 18th Biennale of Sydney, Sydney
2011
Dance/Draw, Institute of Contemporary Art / Boston,
Boston
re.act.feminism #2 – a performing archive, Centro Cultural
Montehermoso Kulturunea, Vitoria-Gasteiz; Galerija

Miroslav Kraljević, Zagreb; Wyspa Institute for Art,
Gdansk; Museum of Contemporary Art, Roskilde;
Tallinn Art Hall, Tallinn; Fundació Antoni Tàpies,
Barcelona; Academy of Arts, Berlin
Chile años 70 y 80: Memoria y experimentalidad, Museo de
Arte Contemporáneo, Universidad de Chile, Santiago
   2010
On Line: Drawing Through the Twentieth Century, The
Museum of Modern Art, New York
   2009
*Subversive Practices: Art under Conditions of Political
Repression 60s–80s*, Württembergischer Kunstverein,
Stuttgart
   2007
WACK!: Art and the Feminist Revolution, The Museum of
Contemporary Art (MOCA), Los Angeles
   2006
Multiplicación, Museo de Arte Contemporáneo, Santiago
Del otro lado, Centro Cultural Palacio de La Moneda,
Santiago
   2005
*Gabinete de lectura: Artes visuales, Chilenas contemporáneas
1971–2005*, Museo Nacional de Bellas Artes, Santiago
   2004
*Fishing in International Waters: New Acquisitions from
the Latin American Collection*, Blanton Museum of Art,
University of Texas at Austin, Austin
   2002
DIS SOLVING: Threads of Water and Light, The Drawing
Center, New York
   2001
Abstraction: The American-Indian Paradigm, Palais des
Beaux-Arts, Brussels, Belgium; Institut Valencià d'Arte
Modern, Valencia
Antagonismos: Casos de estudio, Museu d'Art
Contemporani de Barcelona, Barcelona
Agitación como ritual cotidiano, Cartografías del deseo,
Museo Nacional Centro de Arte Reina Sofía, Madrid
   2000
Quotidiana, Castello di Rivoli, Turin
Transferencia y Densidad, Museo Nacional de Bellas
Artes, Santiago
   1998
IV Bienal de Barro de América, Museo Alejandro Otero,
Caracas
   1997
Whitney Biennial, Whitney Museum of American Art,
New York
Inside the Visible: An Elliptical Traverse of Twentieth Century

Art in, of, and from the Feminine, The Art Gallery of
Western Australia, Perth
   1996
*Inside the Visible: An Elliptical Traverse of Twentieth
Century Art in, of, and from the Feminine*, Institute of
Contemporary Arts / Boston, Boston; Whitechapel Art
Gallery, London
   1992
*America: The Bride of the Sun – 500 Years of Latin
American Art and the Low Countries*, Antwerp Royal
Museum of Fine Arts, Antwerp
   1991
*Efecto de Viaje: Trece Artistas Chilenos Residentes en Nueva
York*, Museo Nacional de Bellas Artes, Santiago
   1990
The Decade Show: Frameworks of Identity in the 1980s,
New Museum, New York
   1988
The Debt, Exit Art Gallery, New York
   1987
Latin American Artists in New York since 1970, Archer
M. Huntington Gallery, University of Texas at Austin,
Austin
   1986
2nd Havana Biennial, Havana
   1983
Chilenas, Kunstamtes Kreuzberg, Berlin
   1982
Women of the Americas, Center for Inter-American
Relations, New York
   1981
Video from Latin America, The Museum of Modern Art,
New York
Ikon & Logos, The Alternative Museum, New York
4th Medellín Biennial, Medellín
Bienal de Arte INBO, Cochabamba
   1974
Arts Festival For Democracy in Chile, Royal College of Art,
London
7 Artists, The British Council Students Centre, London
   1973
East London Open, Whitechapel Art Gallery, London
   1972
Pintura Instintiva Chilena, Museo Nacional de Bellas
Artes, Santiago

HONORS AND DISTINCTIONS

2022
Golden Lion for Lifetime Achievement, Venice
Biennale, Venice
2019
Premio Velázquez de Artes Plásticas, Spanish Ministry
of Culture, Madrid
Herb Alpert Award in the Arts, Santa Monica
2014
SLAS Spring 2014 Scholar in Residence, Pratt
Institute, New York
2011
Sello de Excelencia, Consejo Nacional de la Cultura
y las Artes, Santiago
2009
Estelle Lebowitz Visiting Artist in Residence,
Rutgers University, New Brunswick
1999
Anonymous Was a Woman Award, New York
1997
The Andy Warhol Foundation Award, New York
1996
The Fund for Poetry Award, New York
Pollock-Krasner Foundation Grant, New York
1992
Arts International Award, Lila Wallace-Reader's
Digest Fund, New York
1985
Human Rights Exile Award, Fund for Free
Expression, New York
1972
British Council Scholarship, London

POETRY VOLUMES

2022
Cecilia Vicuña, *Libro Venado*, Buenos Aires
Cecilia Vicuña, *Sudor de Futuro*, Viña del Mar
2020
Cecilia Vicuña, *Cruz del Sur*, Santiago
2018
Cecilia Vicuña, *AMAzone palabrarmas, 1977–1978*,
trans. James O'Hern, Chicago
2017
Cecilia Vicuña, et al., *Read Thread: The Story of the Red
Thread*, Berlin

Cecilia Vicuña, *New and Selected Poems of Cecilia
Vicuña*, ed. Rosa Alcalá, Berkeley
2015
Cecilia Vicuña, *Kuntur Ko*, Santiago
2013
Cecilia Vicuña, *El Zen Surado: 1965–1972*, Santiago
2012
Cecilia Vicuña, *Chanccani Quipu*, New York
Cecilia Vicuña, *Spit Temple: The Selected Performances
of Cecilia Vicuña*, ed. and trans. by Rosa Alcalá,
Brooklyn, New York
2011
Cecilia Vicuña, *beforehand*, Brooklyn, New York
Cecilia Vicuña, *Saborami*, 2nd edn, Oakland and
Philadelphia
2010
Cecilia Vicuña, *Soy Yos: Antología, 1966–2006*,
Santiago
2007
Cecilia Vicuña, *Sabor a Mí*, Santiago
2005
Cecilia Vicuña, *Palabrarmas*, Santiago
2004
Cecilia Vicuña, *I tu*, Buenos Aires
2002
Cecilia Vicuña, *Instan*, Berkeley
2001
Cecilia Vicuña, *El Templo*, trans. Rosa Alcalá, Bristol
1996
Cecilia Vicuña, *Palabre e hilo / Word & Thread*, trans.
Rosa Alcalá, Edinburgh
Cecilia Vicuña, *PALABRARmas /
WURDWAPPINschaw*, trans. Edwin Morgan,
Edinburgh
1992
Cecilia Vicuña, *Unravelling Words & Weaving Water*,
ed. Eliot Weinberger, trans. Eliot Weinberger and
Suzanne Jill Levine, Saint Paul
1990
Cecilia Vicuña, *La Wik'uña*. Santiago
1986
Cecilia Vicuña, *Samara*, Roldanillo
1984
Cecilia Vicuña, *PALABRARmas*. Buenos Aires
1983
Cecilia Vicuña, *Luxumei, o, el Traspié de la Doctrina:
Poemas 1966–1972*, Mexico City
Cecilia Vicuña, *Precario / Precarious*, trans. Anne
Twitty, New York

1979

Cecilia Vicuña, *Siete Poemas*, Bogotá

1973

Cecilia Vicuña, *Saborami*, trans. Felipe Ehrenberg, Collumpton, UK

BOOKS IN COLLABORATION

2018

Camila Marambio and Cecilia Vicuña, *Slow Down Fast, A Toda Raja* (conversation), Berlin

SELECTED EDITED VOLUMES

2020

Cecilia Vicuña et al., *Minga del Cielo Oscuro*, Santiago

2009

Cecilia Vicuña and Ernesto Livon-Grosman (eds.), *The Oxford Book of Latin American Poetry*, Oxford

1998

Cecilia Vicuña (ed.), *Ül: Four Mapuche Poets: An Anthology*, New York and Pittsburgh

SELECTED MONOGRAPHS AND PUBLICATIONS

2019

Cecilia Vicuña: Seehearing the Enlightened Failure, exh. cat., Witte de With Center for Contemporary Arts, Rotterdam

2017

Cecilia Vicuña: About to Happen, exh. cat., Contemporary Arts Center, Los Angeles

2015

Meredith Gardner Clark (ed.), *Vicuñiana: El Arte y la Poesía de Cecilia Vicuña*, un Diálogo Sur/Norte, Santiago

2013

Cecilia Vicuña, exh. cat., England & Co, London

2012

Cecilia Vicuña, 1966–2012: Obras, exh. cat., Galería Patricia Ready, Santiago

2000

Cecilia Vicuña: Semi Ya, exh. cat., Galería Gabriela Mistral, Santiago

1998

Cecilia Vicuña: Cloud-Net, exh. cat., Art in General, New York

1997

Catherine de Zegher (ed.), *The Precarious: The Art and Poetry of Cecilia Vicuña*, Hanover

PUBLIC COLLECTIONS

Berkeley Art Museum and Pacific Film Archive (BAMPFA), Berkeley, CA

Blanton Museum of Art, University of Texas at Austin, Austin, TX

Cisneros Fontanals Art Foundation, Miami, FL

Cranford Collection, London

EMDASH Foundation, Berlin

Fonds Régional d'Art Contemporain de Lorraine, Metz

KADIST, Paris and San Francisco CA

Museo de Arte Contemporáneo, Santiago

Museo de Arte Latinoamericano de Buenos Aires (MALBA), Buenos Aires

Museo de Arte de Lima (MALI), Lima

Museo Nacional Centro de Arte Reina Sofía, Madrid

Museum of Contemporary Art San Diego (MCASD), San Diego, CA

Museum of Fine Arts, Boston, MA

The Museum of Modern Art, New York, NY

Museo Nacional de Bellas Artes, Santiago

National Portrait Gallery, Smithsonian Institution, Washington, D.C.

Pérez Art Museum Miami (PAMM), Miami, FL

Philadelphia Museum of Art, Philadelphia

Princeton University Art Museum, Princeton, NJ

Solomon R. Guggenheim Museum, New York

Tate, London

Climate Impact Report

Introduction

Tate declared a climate and ecological emergency in July 2019, recognising the unique role art and art museums can play in creating fundamental societal change. Through reduction activities, Tate are committed to reducing their carbon emissions by 50 per cent by 2023 from the baseline year of 2007/8 and are working towards a net zero target in 2030. This analysis supports Tate's pledge to educate patrons and raise awareness of the climate and ecological emergency through collaboration and communicating programme impacts.

Greenhouse Gas Emissions

The greenhouse gas emissions associated with this commission were estimated using the framework of the World Resource Institute's Greenhouse Gas Protocol. Calculations utilise emission factors sourced from the United Kingdom's 'Greenhouse Gas Reporting: Conversion Factors 2022' data, as well as other factors from a variety of lifecycle assessment studies. Data included in this review is reported in units of tonnes of carbon dioxide equivalents, or tonnes CO_2e. Carbon dioxide equivalents by mass are the standard used for calculating greenhouse gas emissions, as different greenhouse gases affect the climate with different intensity.

How Much is 1 tonne of CO_2e?

Tonnes CO_2e is the primary unit of measure for greenhouse gas emissions, so it is important to contextualise its meaning in terms of everyday activities. The examples below have been calculated using the UK GHG Conversion Factors 2022 data set.

1 tonne of CO_2e is equivalent to the GHG emissions from:

- Driving an average petrol car 5,800 km
- Recharging an electric vehicle 129 times
- Flying from London to Edinburgh 7.5 times

Assumptions

This review follows the framework of the World Resource Institute's Greenhouse Gas Protocol, in which emissions are analysed for direct, indirect and supply chain sources. Each emissions category is titled using common terminology and provides the relevant categorisation within Greenhouse

Gas Protocol guidance. This analysis uses the best available information sourced from staff, suppliers, government entities, and research bodies to estimate the carbon footprint of this work to provide viewers with the information to consider the impact of this commission, and to more acutely understand how their lifestyle impacts the planet. Most emission factors used in this analysis are from the 'UK Greenhouse Gas Reporting: Conversion Factors 2022', while additional factors have been sourced from scientific journals and research.

As most of the coordination of this display is associated with acquiring goods and services from third parties, the data available is not fully comprehensive. At the time of publication, the project was not able to accurately include visitor travel, transportation of materials to Tate Modern, emissions associated with installation, staff commutes, related events, among other areas.

Carbon Footprint Summary

The estimated carbon footprint of this commission, assuming that the work will be transported back to New York by cargo vessel, is 47.9 tonnes CO2e. For comparison, the emissions from all Tate facilities were reported as 9,367 tonnes CO2e for 2020/21 annual accounts reporting.

In terms of relative impacts, artwork material sourcing travel is the most significant emitting activity followed by business travel, catalogues, and electricity consumption of the commission. More detailed information is provided by the emitting category below.

Artwork Materials

Scope 3, Category 1: Purchased Goods and Services

All materials have a carbon footprint based on primary resource production, transportation, processing, and more. This analysis utilises emission factors from the United Kingdom in parallel with lifecycle assessment factors for more unique products such as hemp or cotton in order to estimate the carbon emissions associated with this commissioned work.

To reduce associated climate and sustainability impacts, the materials for this artwork have been selected by the artist and curation team with a preference for materials that are organic, plastic-free, non-toxic, and from vendors local to the United Kingdom.

This section of analysis accounts for 'Cradle-to-Gate' emissions, which include primary material extraction, primary processing, manufacturing, and transportation for each material on a weight basis. In total, the cradle-to-gate emissions associated with the materials used for the artwork amounts to approximately 27.7 tonnes CO2e. Over 3,500 kg of engineered steel was used in the creation of this work and is the largest contributor to these emissions. This underlying structure provides the framework upon which the material elements were placed and was manufactured to conform with strict safety and engineering specifications. The other largest contributors to the materials carbon footprint are the hemp and fabrics based on the quantity of materials required to develop a commission on this scale.

Business Travel

Scope 3, Category 6: Business Travel
Scope 3, Category 3: Fuel & Energy-Related Activities

Emissions resulting from travel are often one of the largest sources of greenhouse gas emissions for art exhibitions, primarily as a result of the frequent air travel required in the coordination of a display. At the time of publication, 8 flights, 8 train rides, and 5 vehicle rides have been accounted for, with 10 more flights anticipated in support of the commission. Through expanded use of teleconference tools, Tate and the artist have reduced the amount of travel required in comparison to prior commissions.

By the end of this commission, the artist and support staff will have travelled over 60,000 km by plane, 5,000 km by rail, and 100 km by vehicle, resulting in an estimated 17.4 tonnes CO2e of greenhouse gases emitted. This estimate also includes the emissions associated with the lifecycle of fuel and electricity consumed to enable travel - described by the term 'Well-To-Tank' (WTT).

Note that this impact only accounts for the personnel directly involved in this commission and does not include an estimate for emissions associated with patrons travelling to Tate Modern to view the commission. Visitor emissions are commonly the largest source of emissions related to an art institution's carbon footprint.

Catalogue Printing and End Use
Scope 3, Category 1: Purchased Goods and Services / Category 12: End of Life Treatment of Sold Products

1,500 copies of this catalogue have been printed, requiring approximately 735 kg of paper. These catalogues were printed using a Heidelberg Druckmaschinen industrial printer, which draws on average 133.5 kilowatts of power. When considering the cradle-to-gate emissions for the paper and the emissions from the consumed electricity (including considerations for the lifecycle of that electricity), the catalogues have an estimated carbon footprint of 1.1 tonnes CO2e.

The UK Department for Environment, Food and Rural Affairs (DEFRA) estimates that 80% of paper in the UK is recycled while 20% is sent to landfill. Using these percentages as a guide, we estimate that the end use of these catalogues if they are discarded to recycling and landfill will result in emissions of approximately 0.2 tonnes CO2e. According to DEFRA factors, the landfilling of paper products emits 49 times more carbon than when the paper is recycled, so please consider this information when managing this catalogue.

Artwork Energy Consumption
Scope 2: Indirect Emissions from Supplied Electricity

Consumption of electricity results in the emissions of greenhouse gases from power generation. This section considers the electricity consumed exclusively associated with the commission and does not include lighting fixtures that are routinely used.

The audio system supplementing the artwork draws about 1,600 watts of power. The AV equipment is anticipated to operate for 12 hours per day over the course of the 187-day commission display, which will amount to approximately 3,600 kilowatt-hours of electricity consumed, resulting in 0.9 tonnes CO2e of GHG emissions. This figure includes the emissions associated with fuel consumption in generation as well as losses through transmission and distribution.

Considerations for the Close of Commission
At the time of publication, a decision was made that after the close of the commission in 2023 the materials composing the artwork would be retained and returned to New York City by sea. This section analyses the case in which the artwork returns to New York City.

Transport
Scope 3, Category 9: Downstream Transportation & Distribution

After the close of the commission, the work will be transported back to New York. It will move by heavy goods vehicle to the Port of Tilbury, where it will disembark on a cargo vessel bound for the Port of New York. Another heavy goods vehicle will pick up the work and transport it to a storage facility. In total, this shipping process will result in an estimated 0.7 tonnes CO2e of GHG emissions.

Shipping the work by freight vessel was chosen as an alternative to air freight, as it has a significantly lower impact due to the gained efficiency of moving goods in bulk at a slower pace. By shipping the work via freight vessel, an estimated 31.1 tonnes CO2e of emissions will be avoided.

In Support of Climate Action
This report was produced in partnership with the US-based consultancy, Co2Action. Co2Action focuses on helping clients demystify the quantitative aspects of sustainability and climate change, and supports clients in developing educational programs, greenhouse gas inventories, and roadmaps for emissions reduction.

www.Co2Action.us

Copyright Credits

Photographic Credits

Unless stated otherwise all images are courtesy the artist and Lehmann Maupin, New York, Hong Kong, Seoul and London
Photo: Johanna Arnold, courtesy the artist and BAMPFA p.108
Photo: Claudio Bertoni p.79
Photo: M. Boylan-Kolchin / Millennium-II Simulation p.102
Photo: Jorge Brantmayer p.62 top
© Trustees of the British Museum p.58 left
Courtesy La Biennale di Venezia and Lehmann Maupin, New York, Hong Kong, Seoul, and London. Photo: Marco Cappelletti p.68 bottom
Photo: Rachel Dedman p.9
Photo DiverseWorks, Houston, TX, Kim Thompson p.45 top
Photo: John Dugger Archive, courtesy England & Co Gallery, London p.65 top
Photo: England & Co Gallery, London pp.63, 67
Photo by Natalia Figueroa p.105
Heritage Image Partnership Ltd / Alamy Stock Photo p.123
Photo: Matthew Hermann p.39
Photo: James O'Hern pp.94–5
Photo: Eva Herzog p.112
Photo: Geoffrey Jones pp.92–3
Photo by Kenneth Lu p.122
Photo: Oscar Monsalve p.82
Photo: Catalina Mejia Moreno: second-year M-Arch students (Spatial Practices, Central Saint Martins UAL), Tate Modern, 13 October 2022; students Elise Blackmore, Zhongyang Chen, Samuel Fraquelli, Emilia Kepista, Emily Llumigusin, Joy Matashi, Sabina Shaybazyan, Adam Stanford; tutor Catalina Mejia Moreno pp.158–9
Photo: Juan Pablo Murrugarra p.56 bottom
Courtesy Museo Nacional de Bellas Artes, Santiago p.60
Photo: César Paternosto pp.31, 46, 85 bottom, 88
Photo: Lucía Pérez p.106
Photo: Pilar Polanco p.96 bottom
Photo: Mario Ruiz p.69
Photograph by Frank Salomon p.107
Photo: Charles Stiffler p.89
Tate: Sonal Bakrania pp.2–3, 6, 16, 54 bottom, 152–3, 160; Lucy Dawkins pp.12–15; Matt Greenwood pp.4, 5, 8, 10, 20, 135–51, 154–7; Joe Humphrys pp.11, 109
Photo: Antonia Taulis, 2021, courtesy of the artist p.69 top
Photo: Kim Thompson p.45 top
Photo: Mathias Voelzke pp.22, 41, 54 top, 68 middle, 104
Wesleyan University Press p.86
Photo: Catherine Wood p.7

Production Credits

Cecilia Vicuña
Brain Forest Quipu 2022
Multi-media installation consisting of multiple quipus

Brain Forest Quipu

2 sculptures
Plant and animal fibres (unspun wool, cotton Tape, cotton Gauze, cotton rope, hemp rope, jute net, twine, recycled packing paper and carboard, khadi paper, Bamboo sticks, plant fibres), with clay paint, resin, and paint, and mudlarked bones, pipes, sticks, glass, and ceramic from the River Thames, hung from two steel structures
Approximately 27 metres × 7 metres

INSTALLATION TEAM:
Lead Production Coordinator: Edward Oliver
Materials Research & Development Maker & Coordinator: Soraia Salim Samju
Material Research & Development Maker: Louise Bennetts
Community Participants & Makers: Siomara Giraldo Bedoya, Patricia Bidi, Soraya Fernandez D.F., and María Eugenia CH.
Makers and installers: Gino Saccone, Giacomo Layet, Veronica Arino, Claire Pritchard, Ali Forbes, Gusty Ferro Lopes, Tom Gould, Calum Stevens, Chris Hewson, Joseph Morris-Doherty, Sam Reason, Ralph Parks, Juan Gimenez-Zapiola, Miranda Samuels, and Anthony Kleanthous
Technical designers and project coordinators: Mark Torrens, Piers Saxby-Candy, Ashley Elliott, Robin Baker-Gibbs, Maria Martin, Tony Martin and Elliot Hepworth
Structural Engineers: Peter Laidler and Alastair Barnard, Anton Sawicki, Jonathan Jackson, Ellie Moore, Bastien Delechelle

Sound Quipu

4 stereo tracks of approximately 8 hours each, containing 168 sound files from 23 contributors and one archive (played from within the Dead Forest Quipu, 2 stereo tracks on each of the 2 quipus); and one 8-hour quadraphonic sound file (played underneath the Turbine Hall bridge)

Concept by Cecilia Vicuña
Directed by Ricardo Gallo

Designed and arranged by Ricardo Gallo and Ariel Bustamante
with contributions from:
Benjamin Calais, Yao Chunyang, Diego Espinosa, Julián Gallo (with samples from the town of Santa María de Timbiquí, Colombia), Ricardo Gallo, Tomoko Hojo, Germán Lázaro, lololol (a.k.a. Sheryl Cheung), André Magalhães (Aldeia Multiétnica, Brazil), Claudio Mercado (Museo Chileno de Arte Precolombino's Sonic Archive), Teto Ocampo, Julie Patton, José Pérez de Arce, Bernardo Rozo and Ariel Bustamante, Paulo Santos, Urian Sarmiento, Samita Sinha, Jonathan Skinner, Benjamim Taubkin, Juan Manuel Toro, Paola Torres Nuñez del Prado & The People of Tupicocha, Cecilia Vicuña, Wei Wei (a.k.a. VAVABOND) and archival recordings of Pygmy people from Middle-Congo and Gabon recorded by Gilbert Rouget

External Project Researcher: Miranda Samuels
For detailed information on each sound contribution see the Tate website

Digital Quipu

Video, colour, subtitled, looped
Concept by Cecilia Vicuña
Material collated by Cecilia Vicuña and Miranda Samuels (External Project Researcher)
with contributions from the following environmental and Indigenous-led organisations:
Amazon Watch, Indigenous Climate Action (ICA), Global Witness, Karen Environmental and Social Action Network (KESAN), Project Sepik and Save the Sepik campaign, If Not Us Then Who?, and Survival International

Featuring Indigenous land and water defenders across Brazil, Ecuador, Paraguay, Democratic Republic of Congo, Tanzania, Kenya, India, Myanmar, The Philippines, Papua New Guinea, and the United States of America, including peoples of the following Indigenous communities: Munduruku; Kayapó; Xokleng; Huni Kui; Xikrin; Guajajara; Xakriabá; Yanomami; Awá; Waorani; Sarayaku; Ayoreo-Totobiegosode; Walikale; Twa; Maasai; Sengwer; Gond; Oraon; Chenchu; Karen Indigenous peoples; T'boli; Sepik peoples; Ojibwe; Ponca Pa'tha'ta

More videos added throughout the exhibition. For more detailed information visit the Tate website
Installed under the Turbine Hall staircase, on Levels 2 and 4 of Natalie Bell Building, and every half hour on information screens on Levels 0 and 1

Quipu of Encounters: Rituals and Assemblies

Performance-ritual with multiple participants
Conceptualised by Cecilia Vicuña in the context of the Hyundai Commission at Tate Modern and her exhibition Spin Spin Triangulene at the Solomon R. Guggenheim Museum, New York, and developed in collaboration with artists, musicians, activists, scientists and poets

Presented at Tate Modern, Friday 14 October 2022

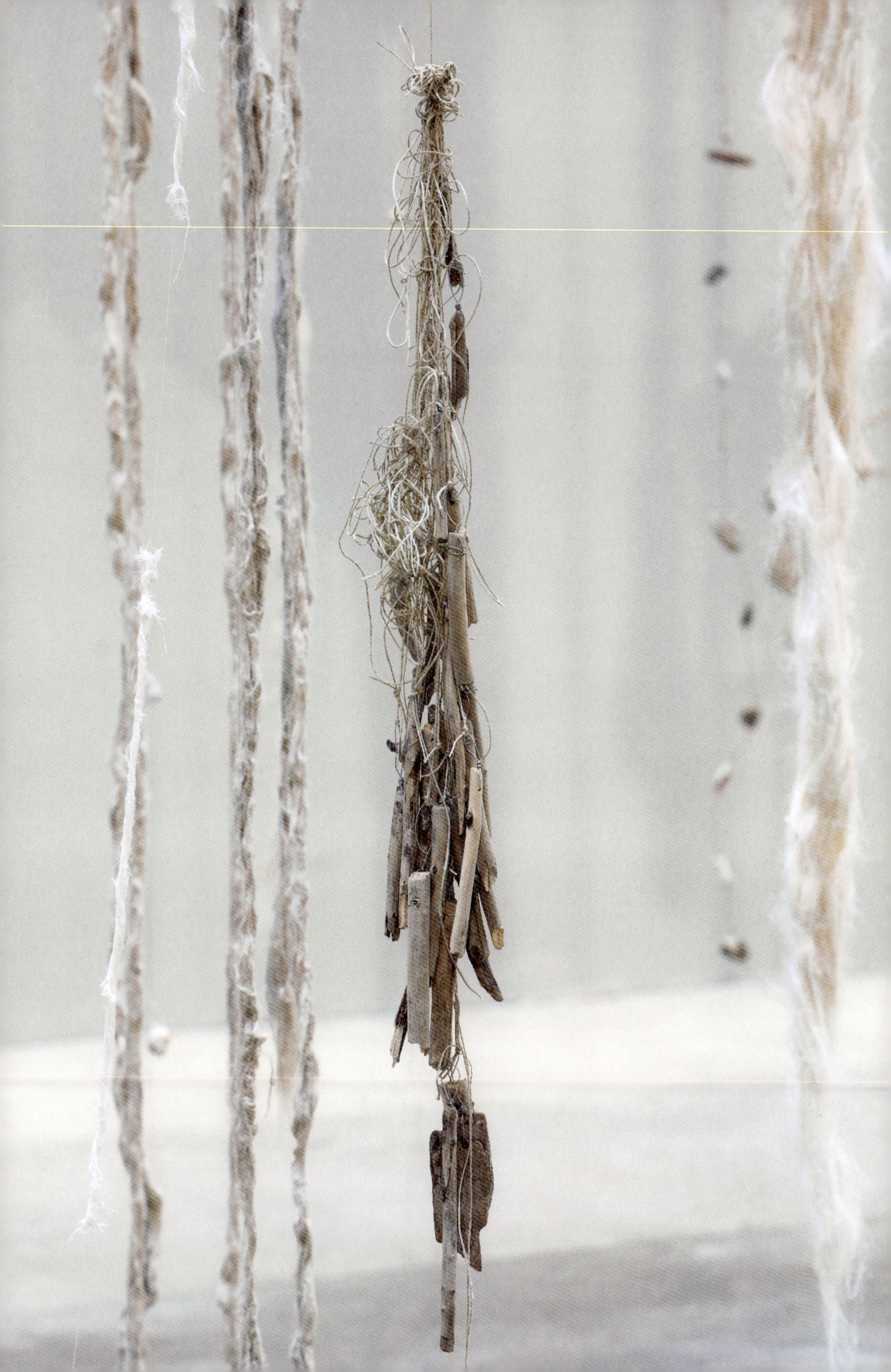

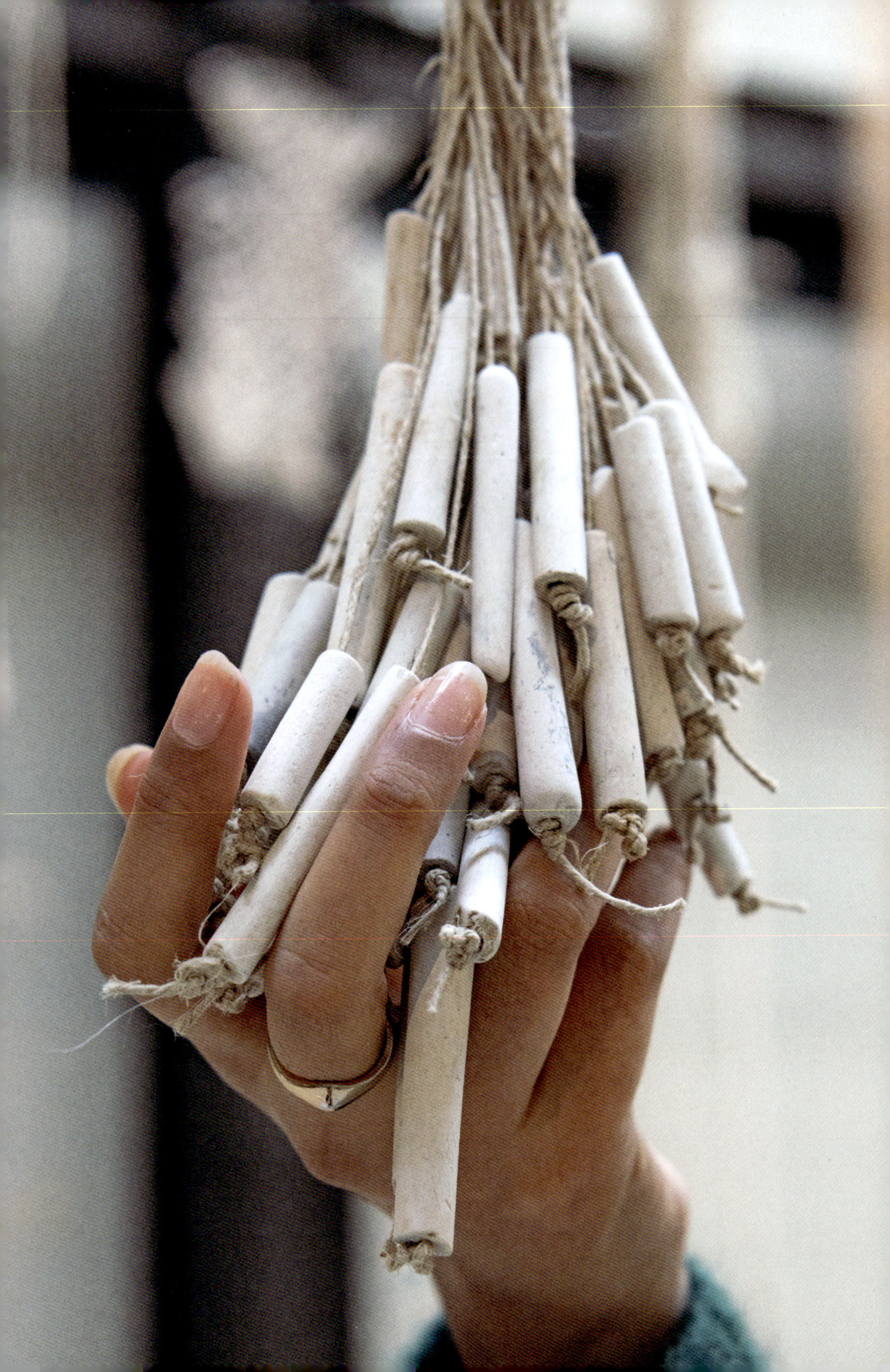

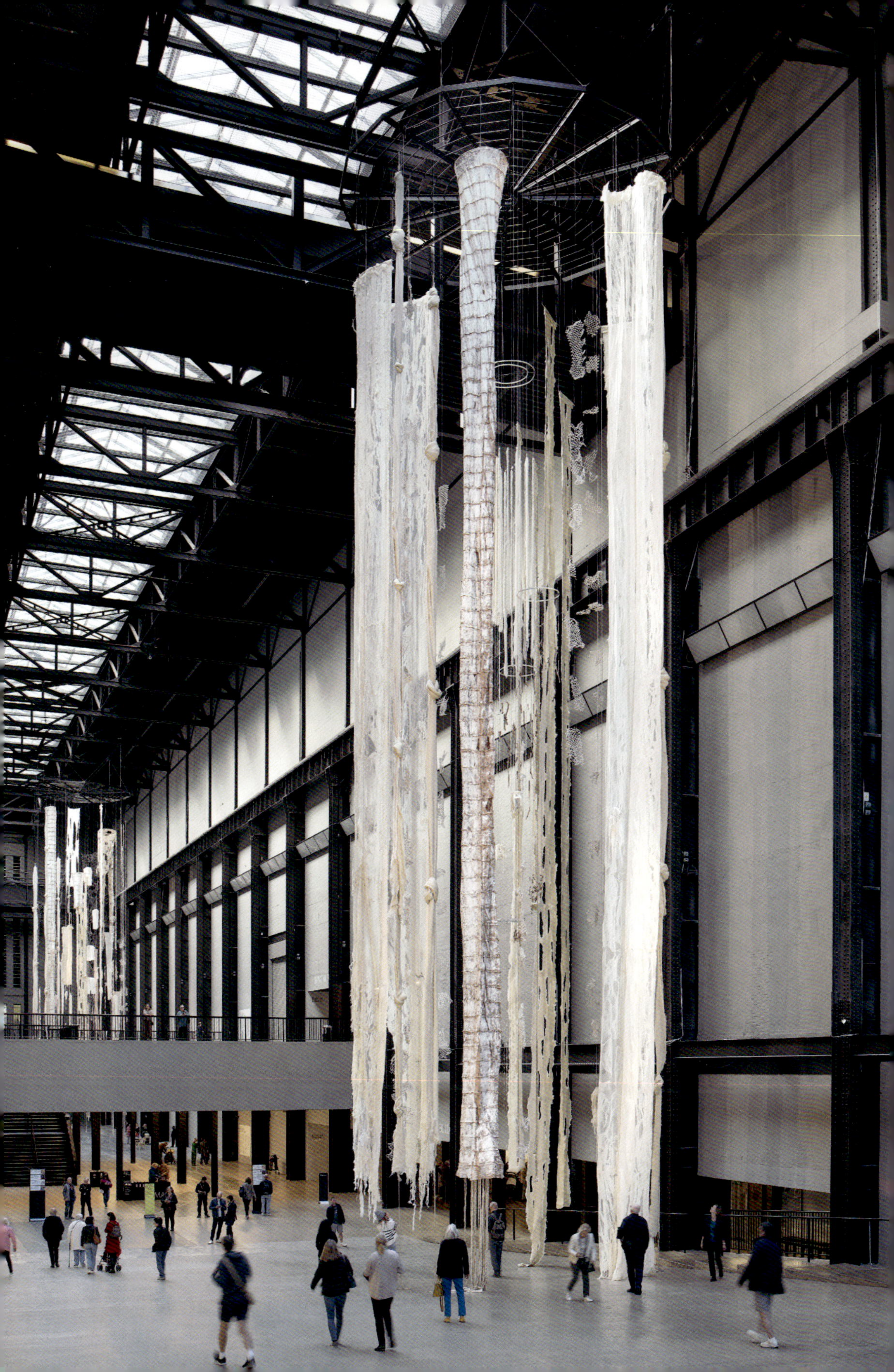

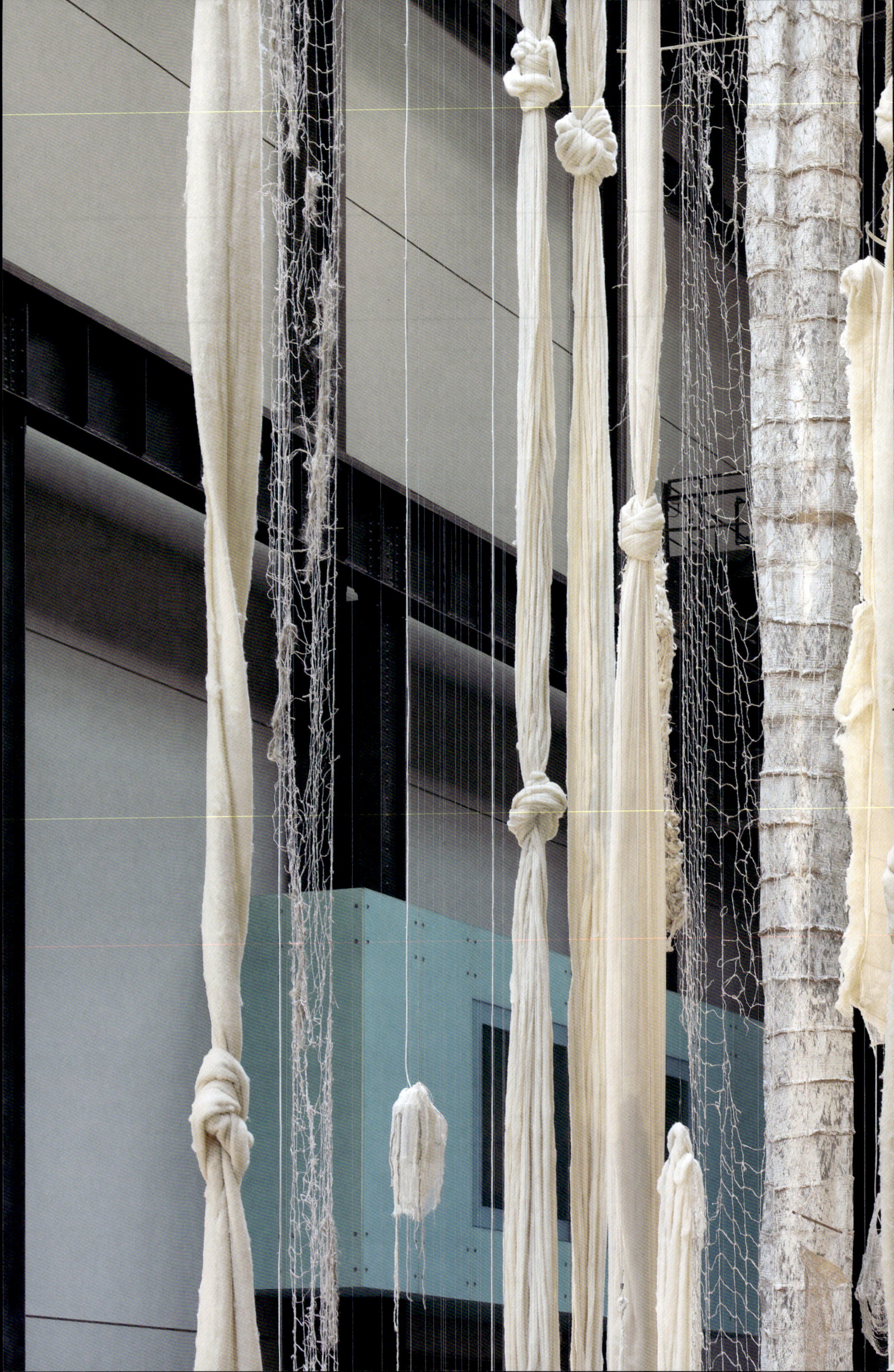

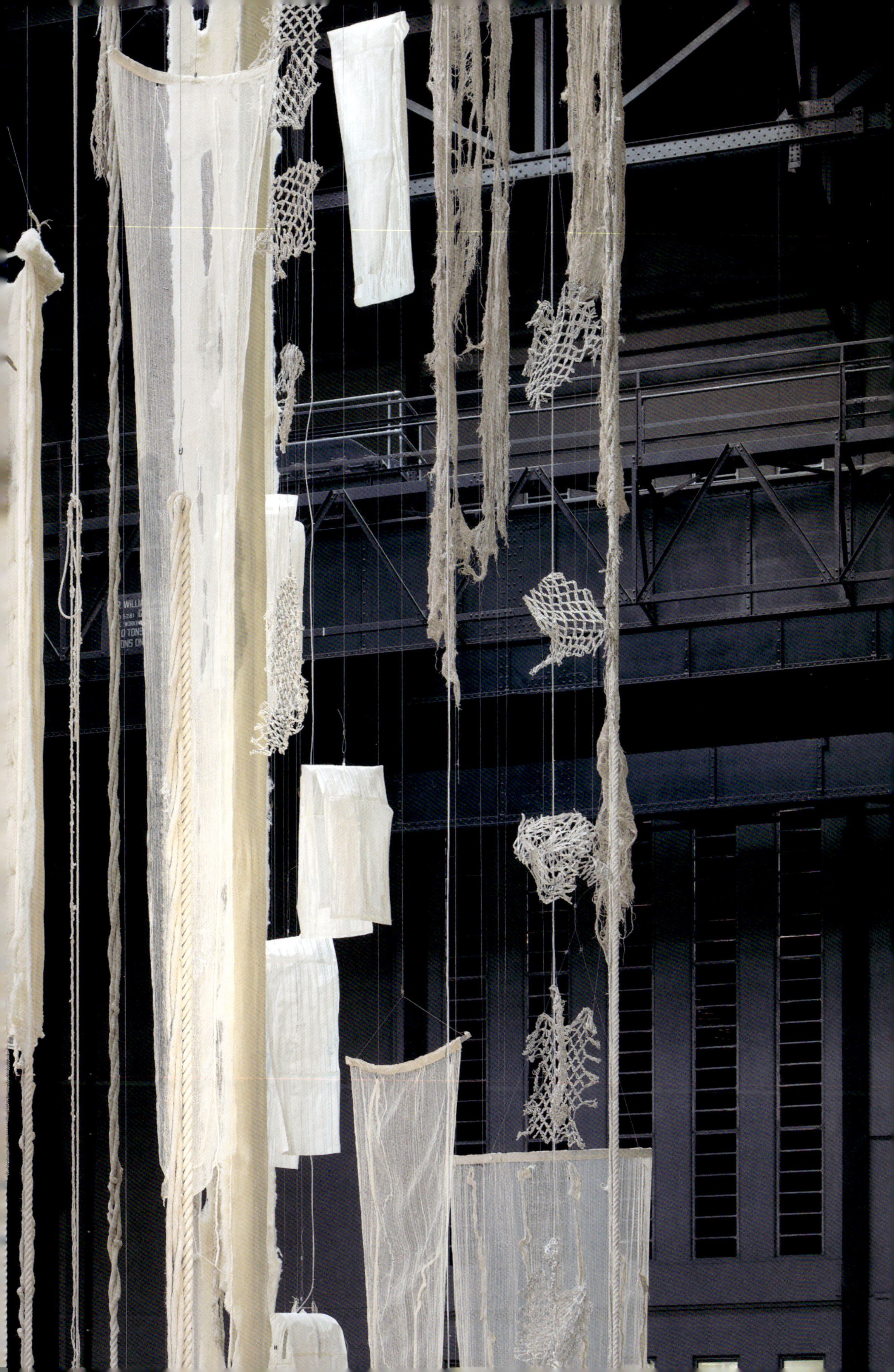
WILLIA
WORKING
TONS

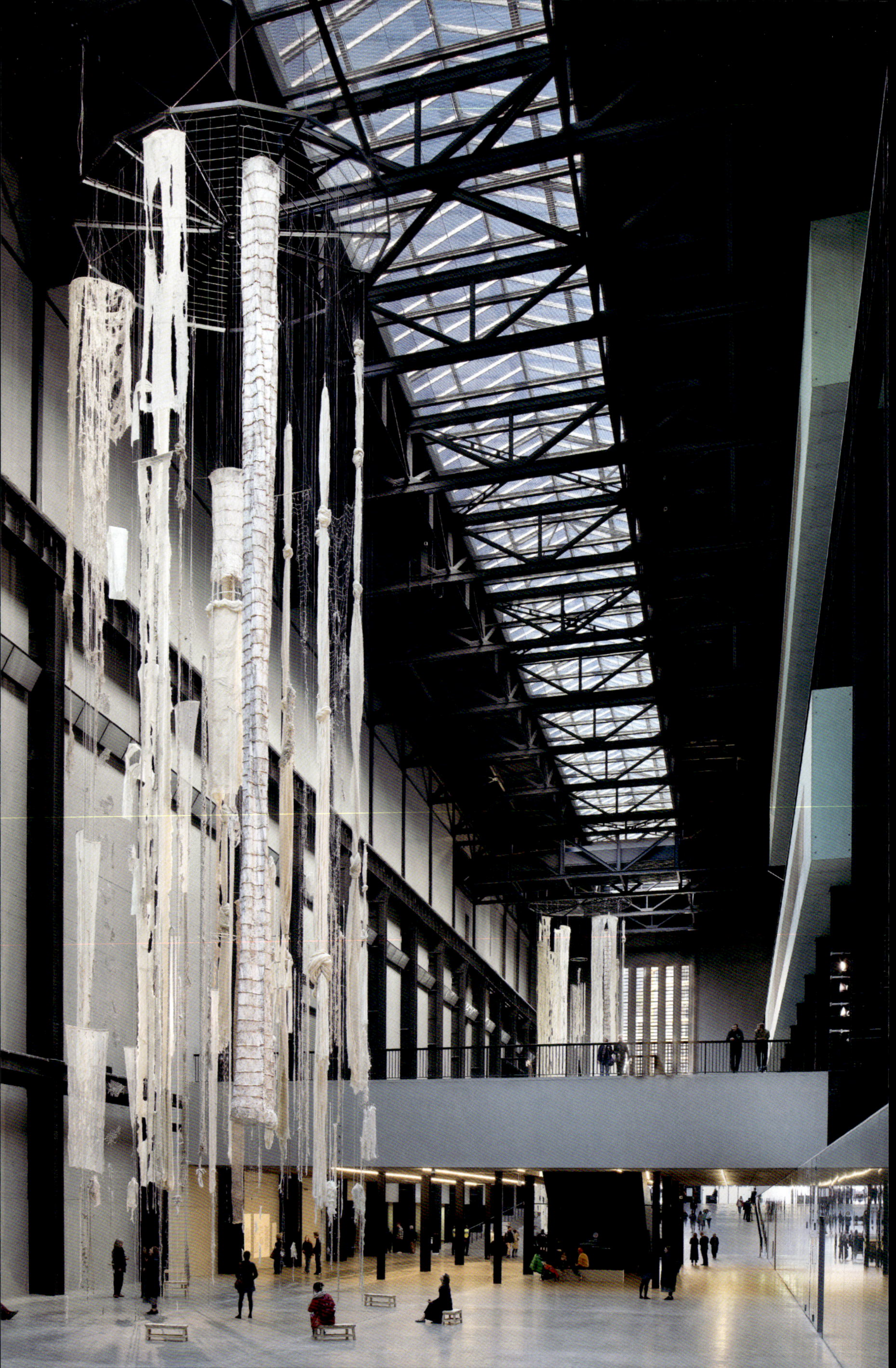

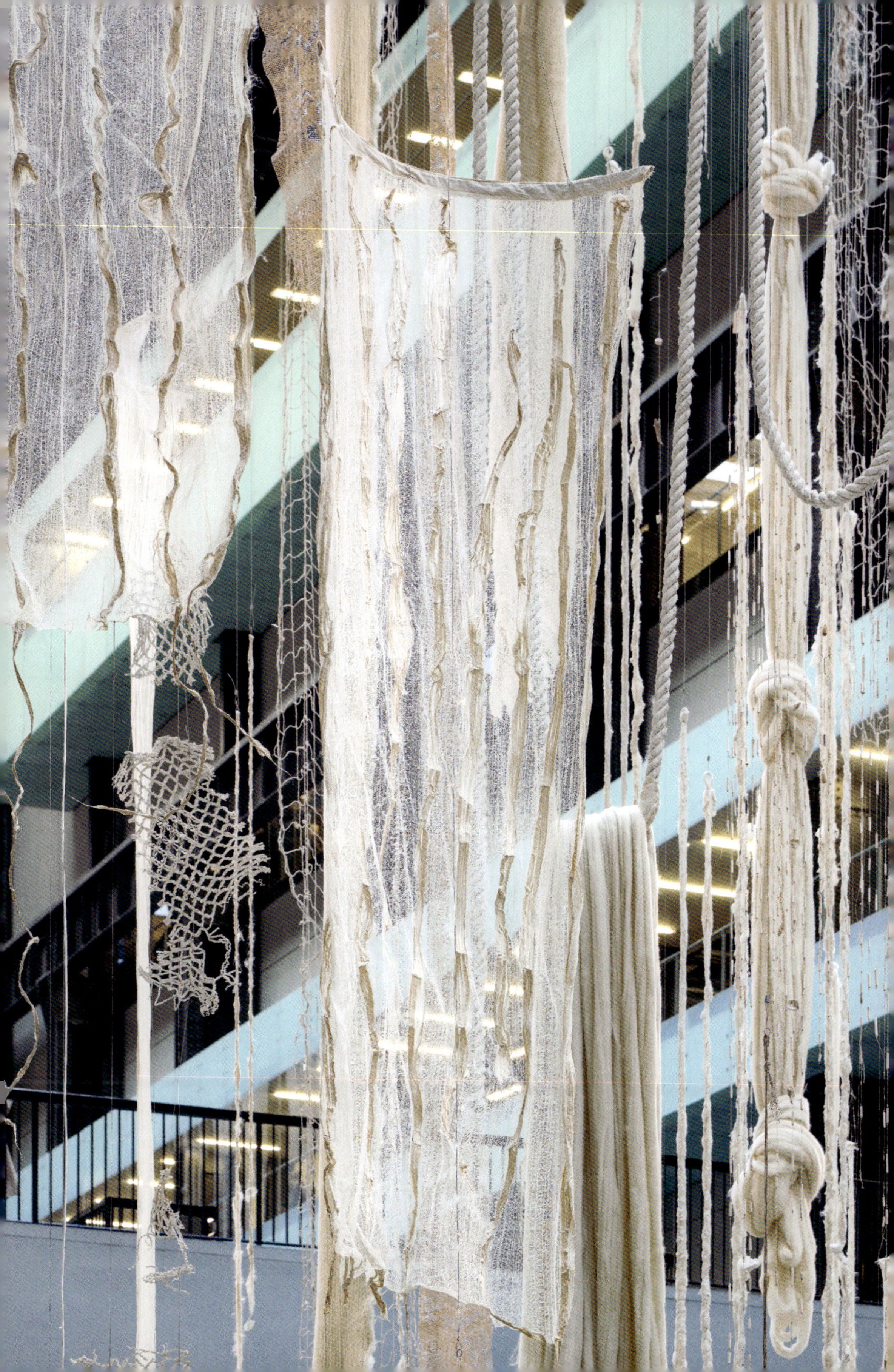

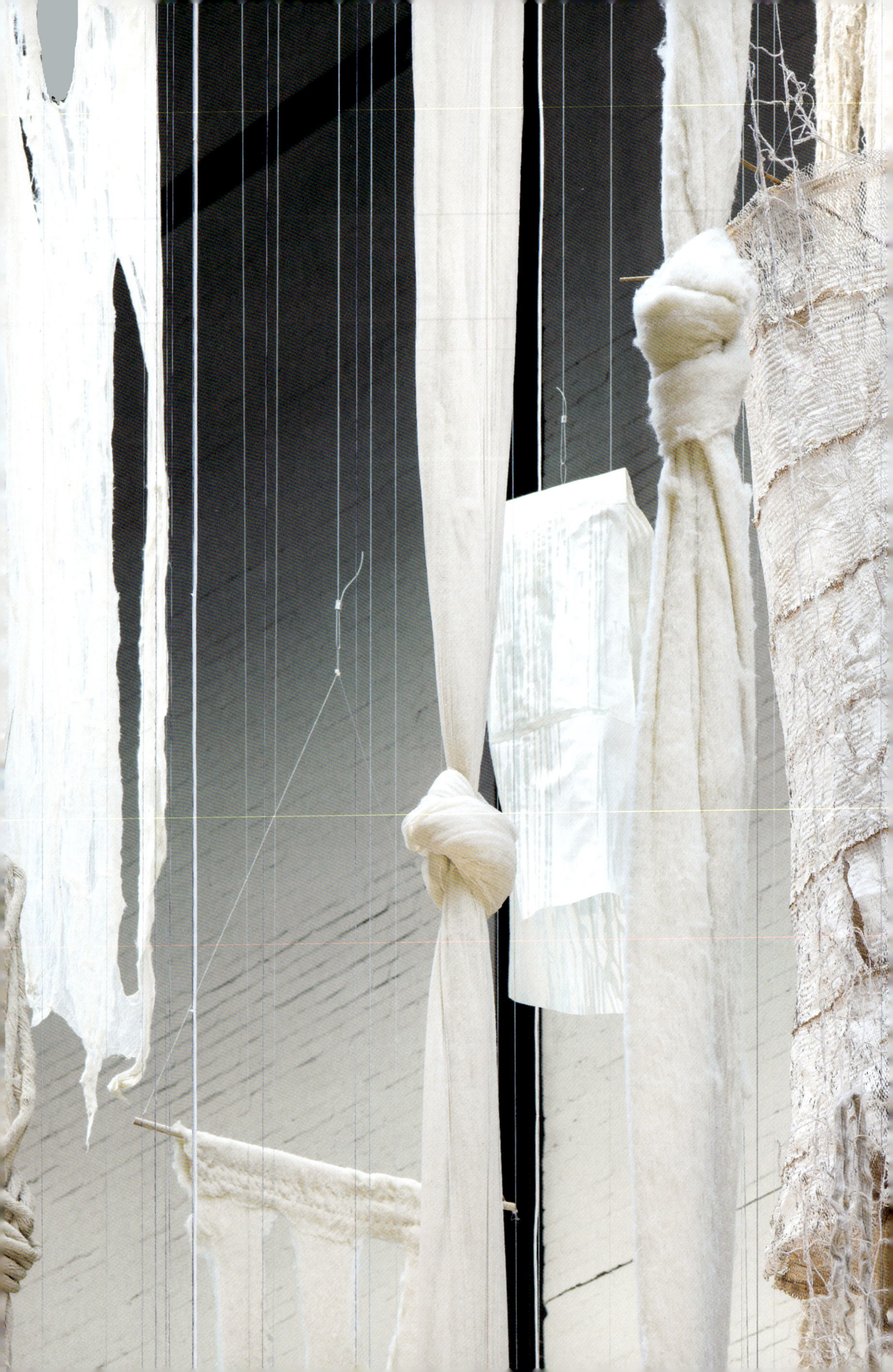

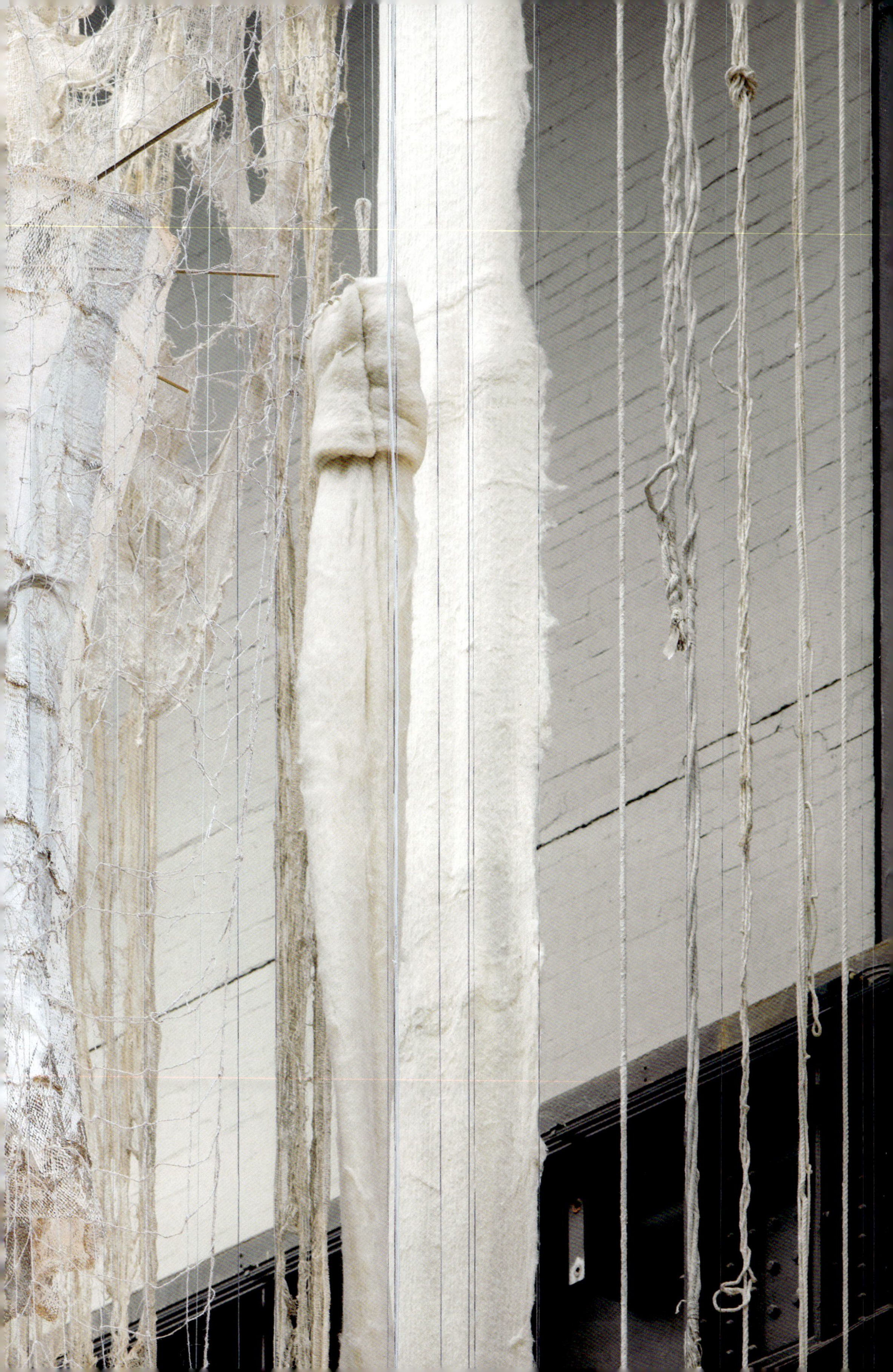

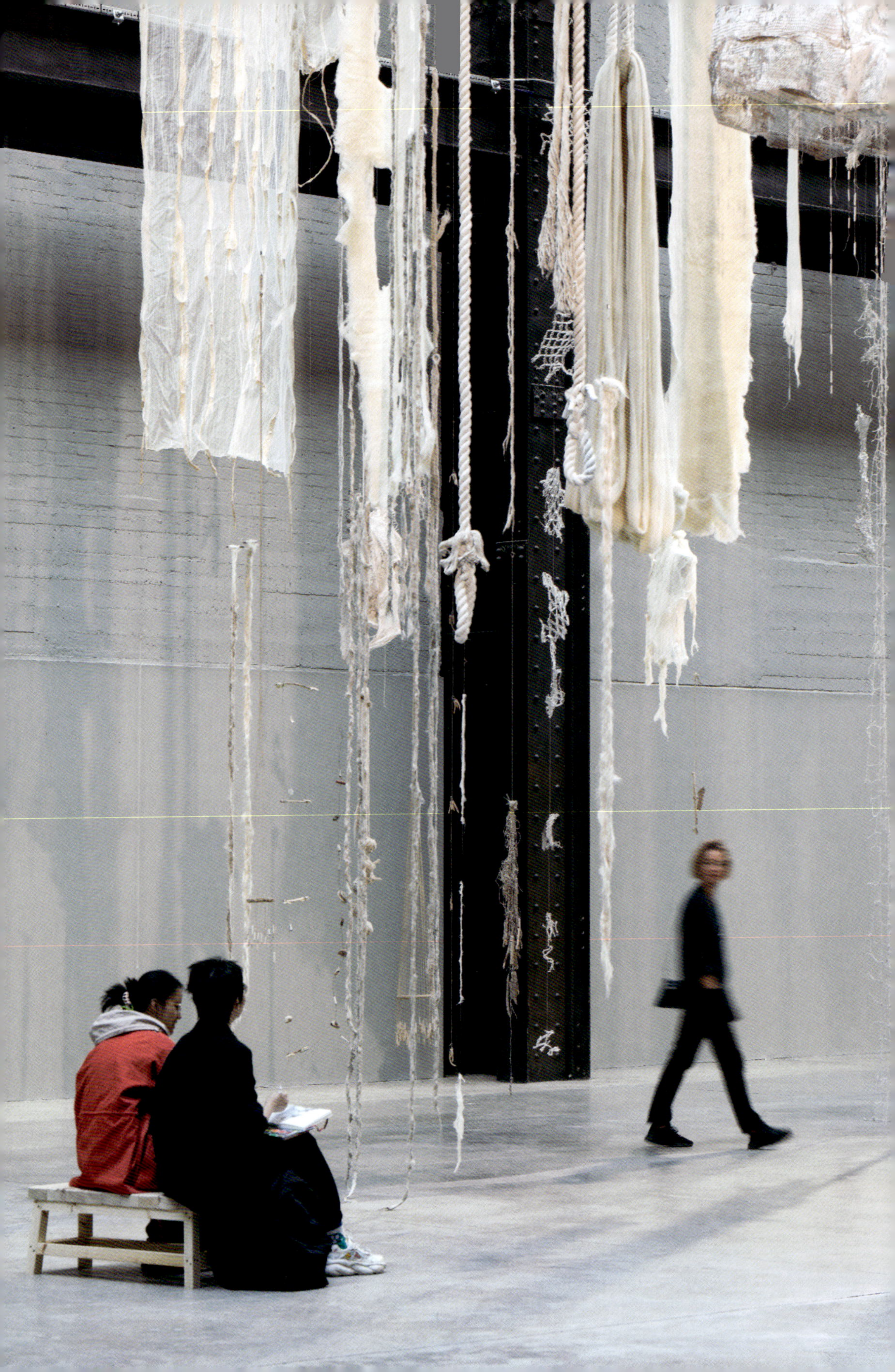

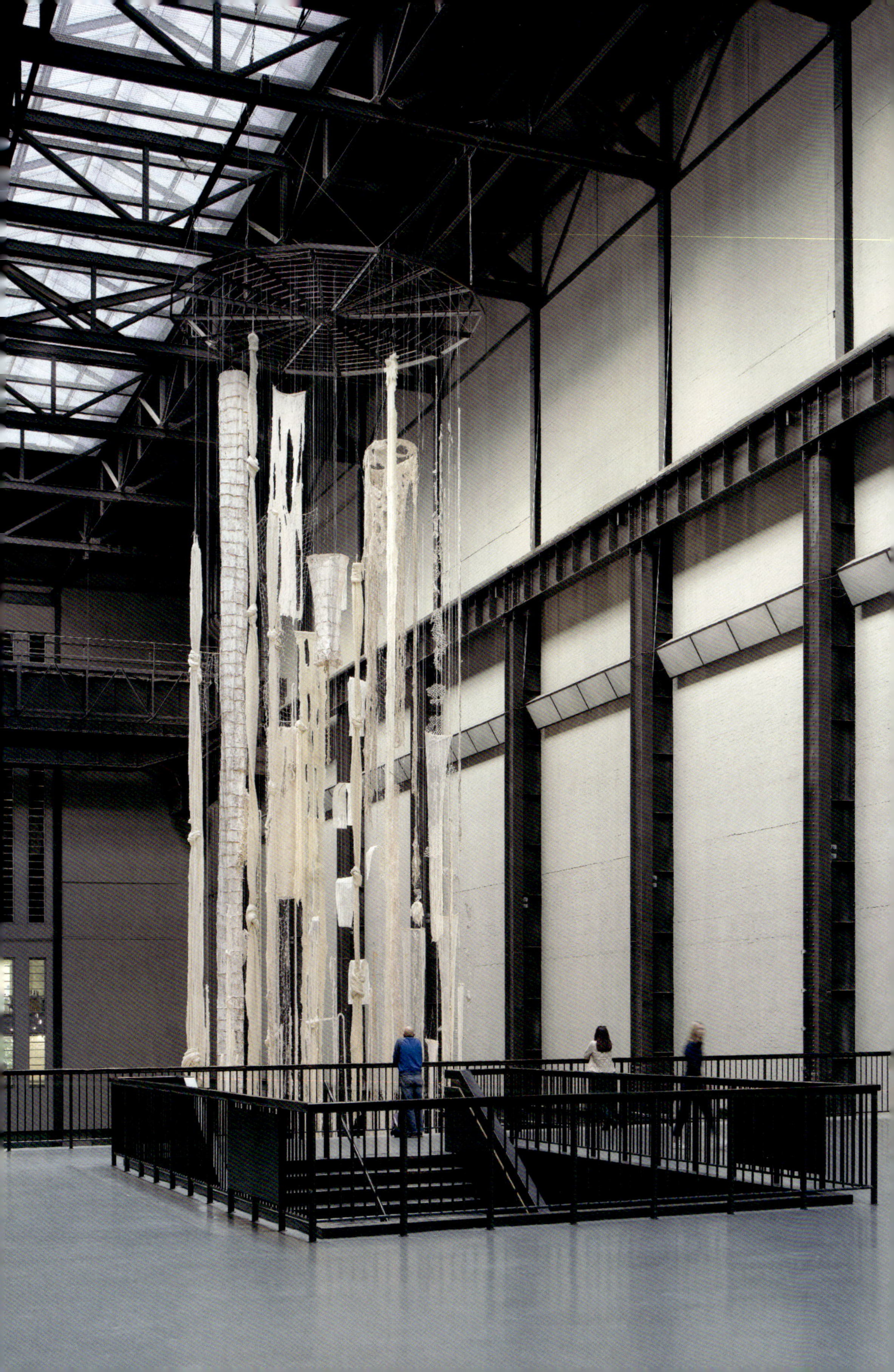

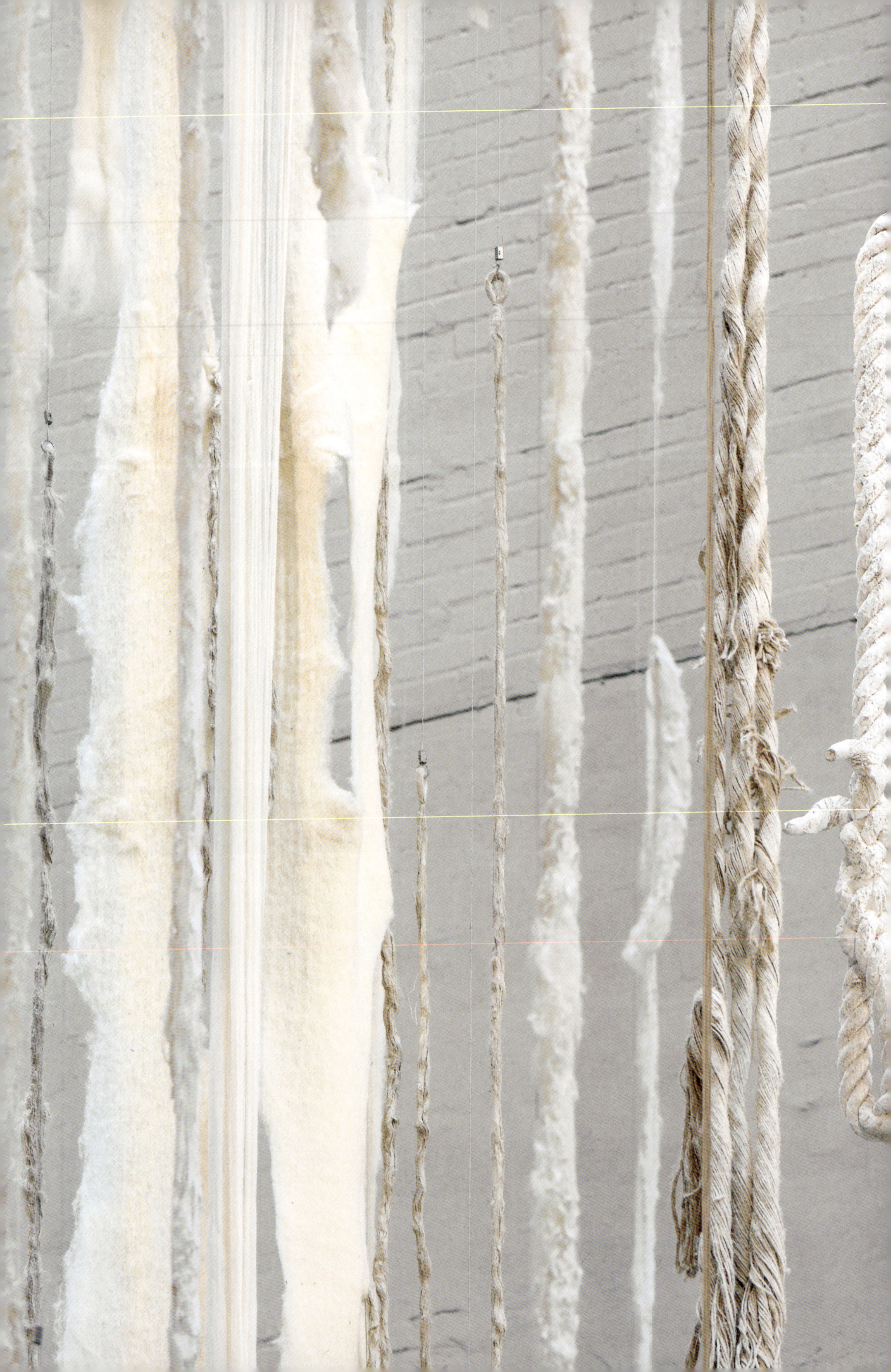

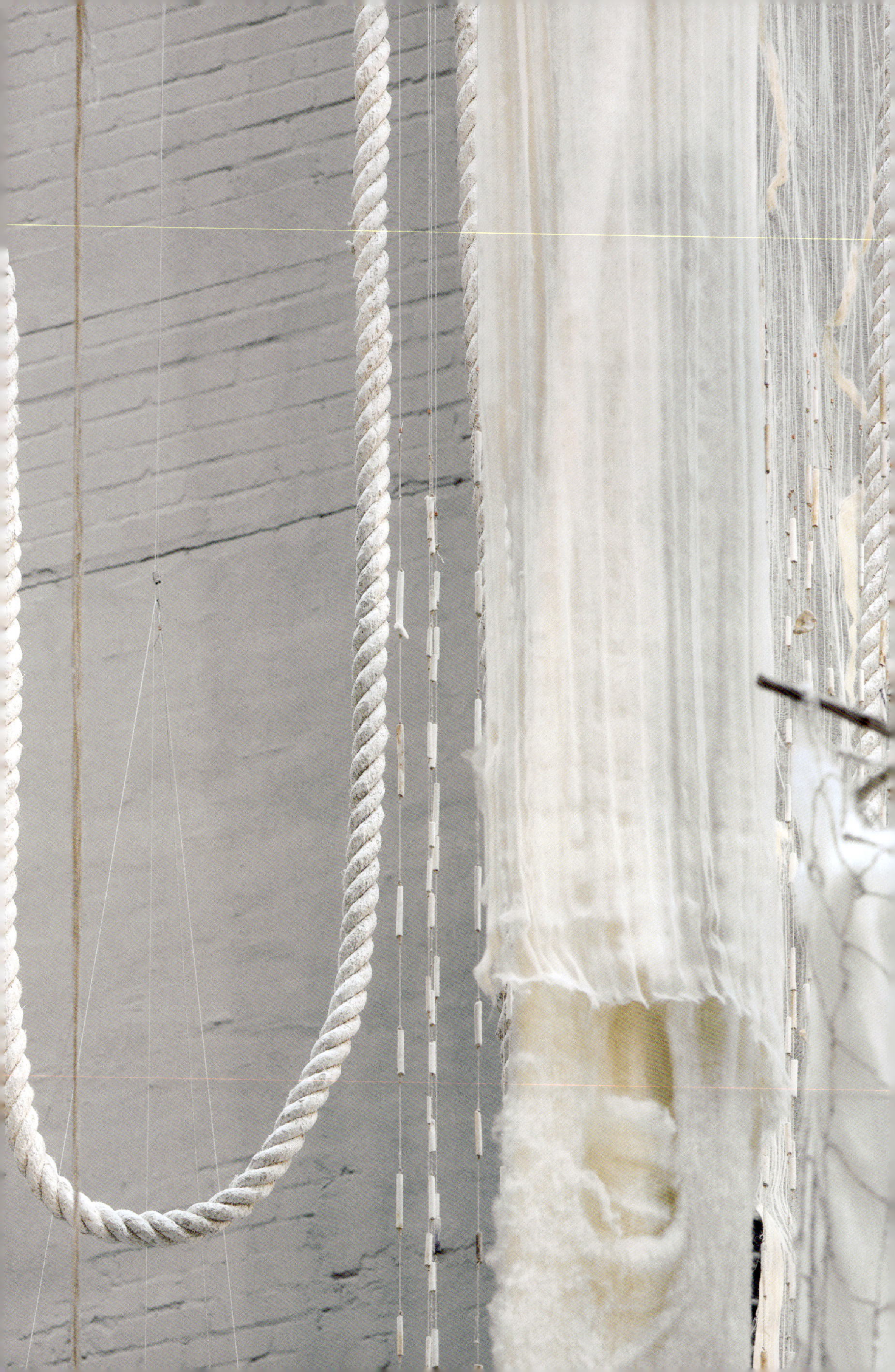

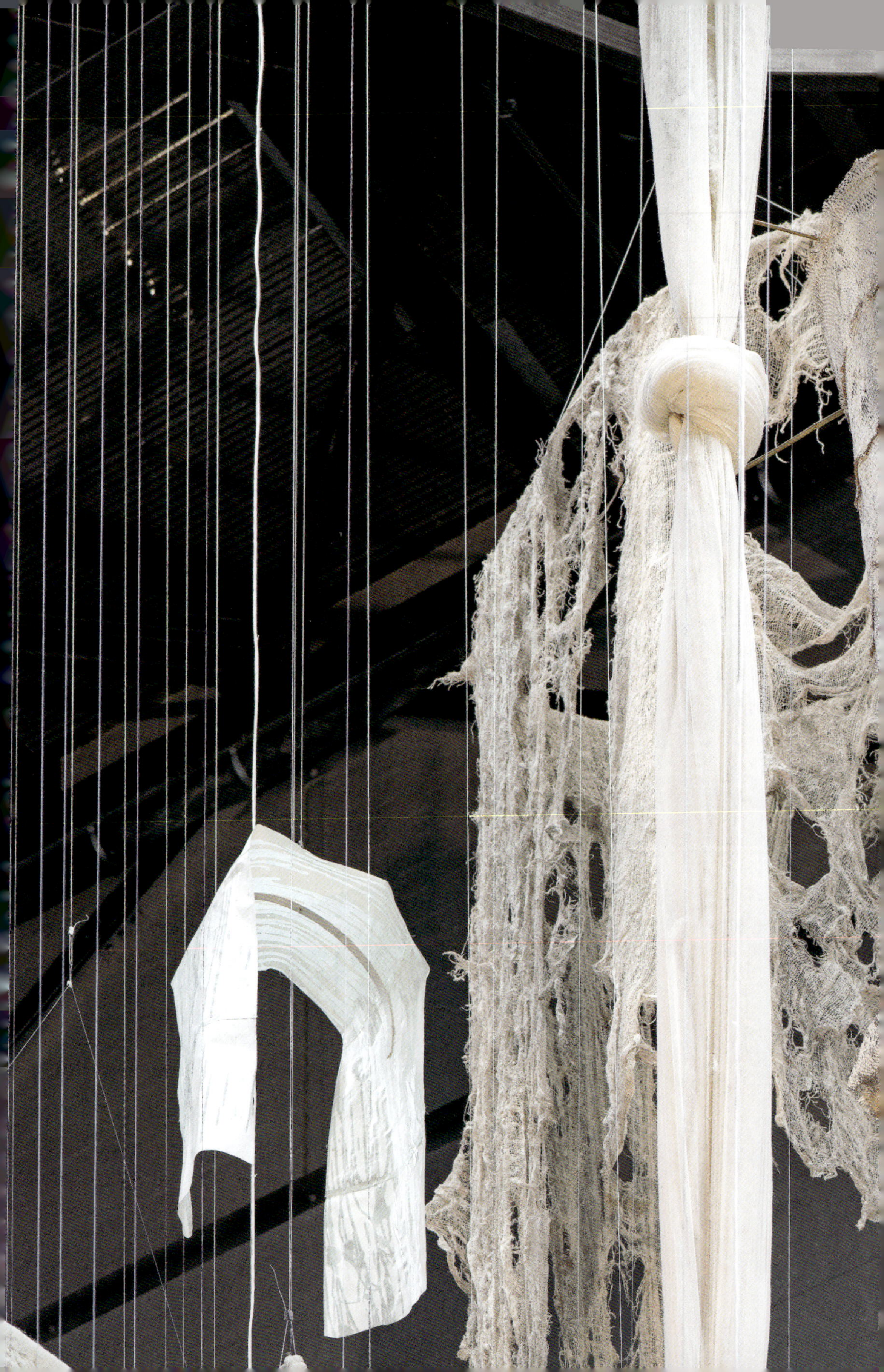

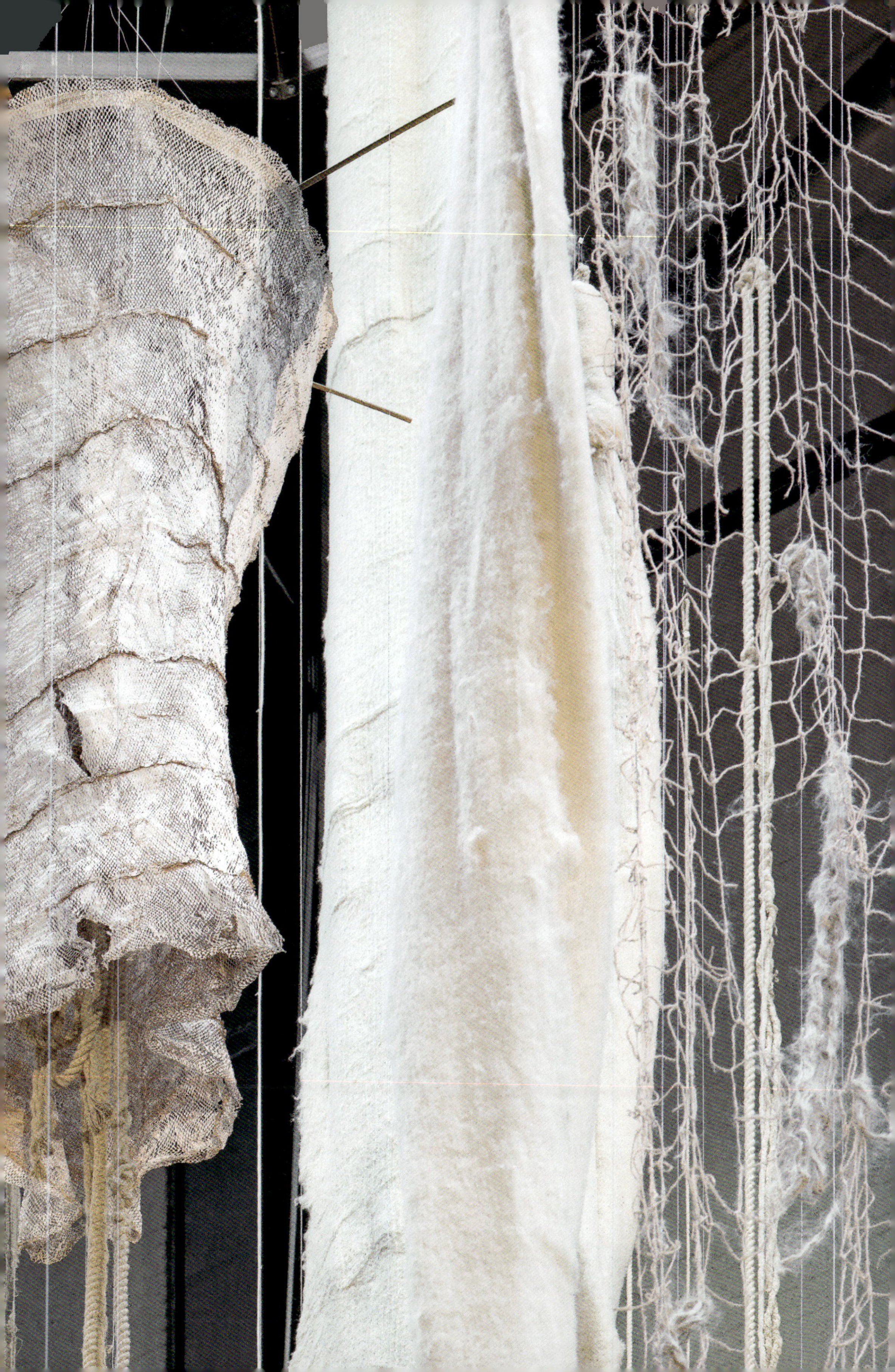

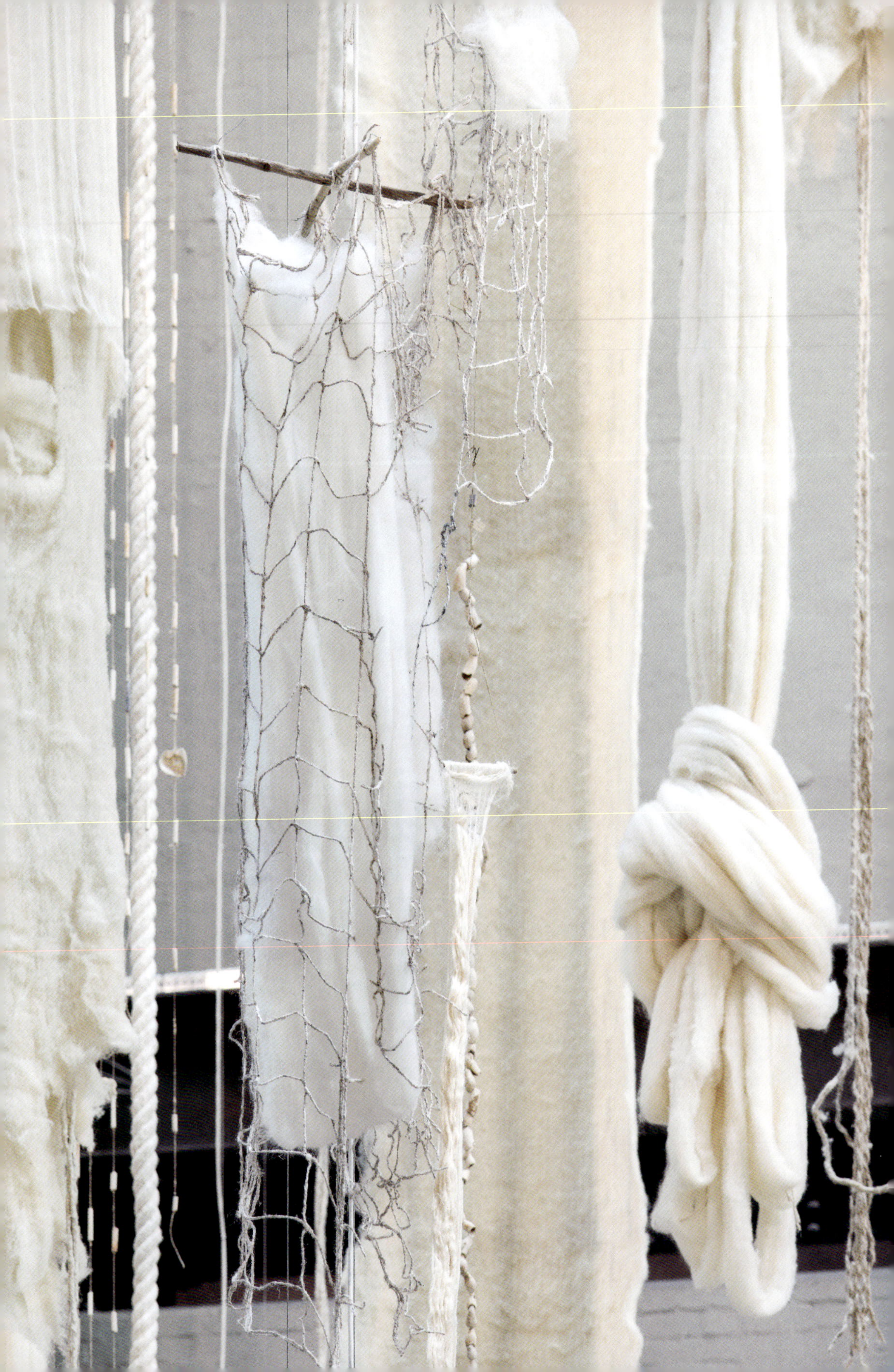

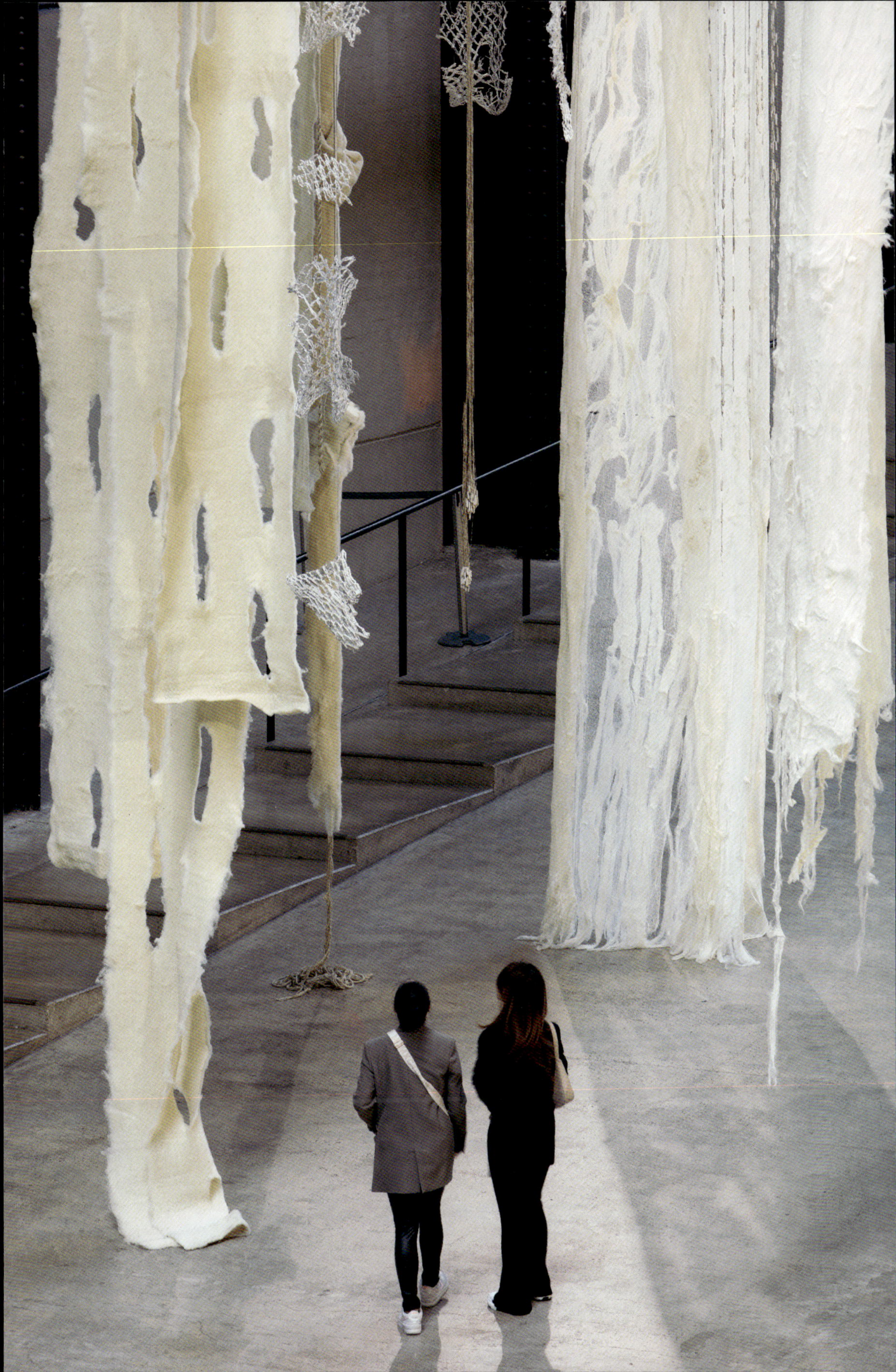

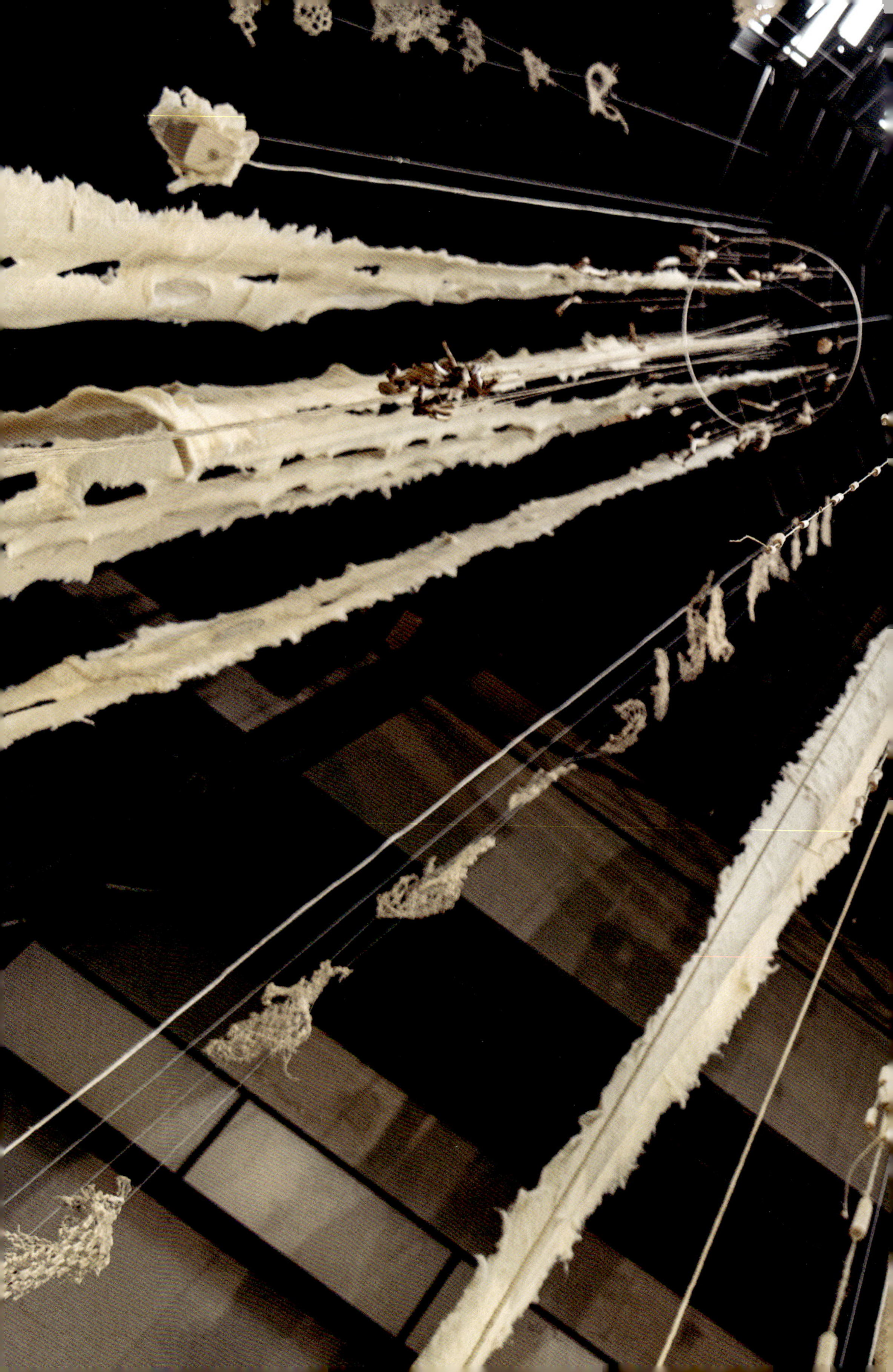

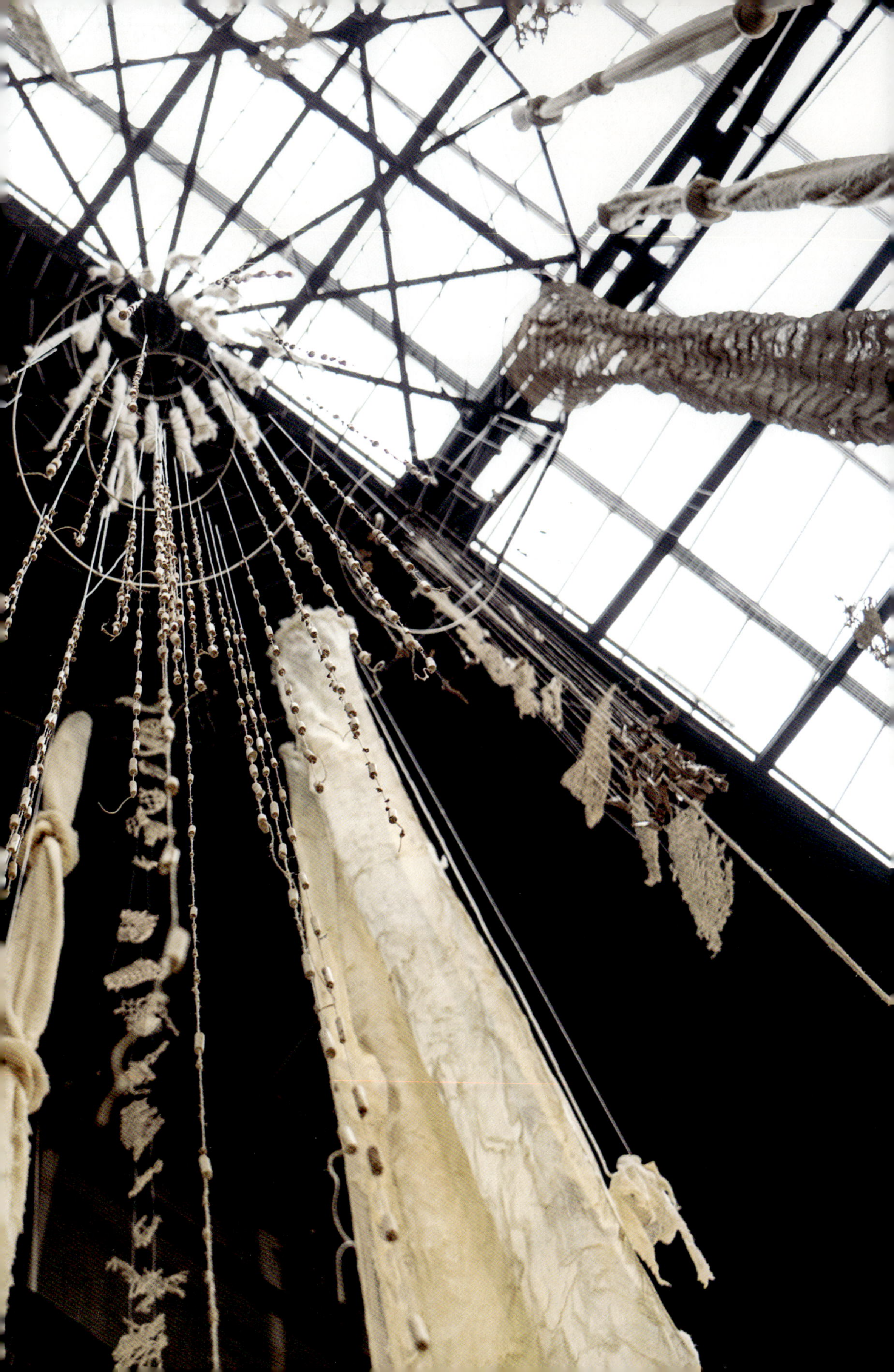

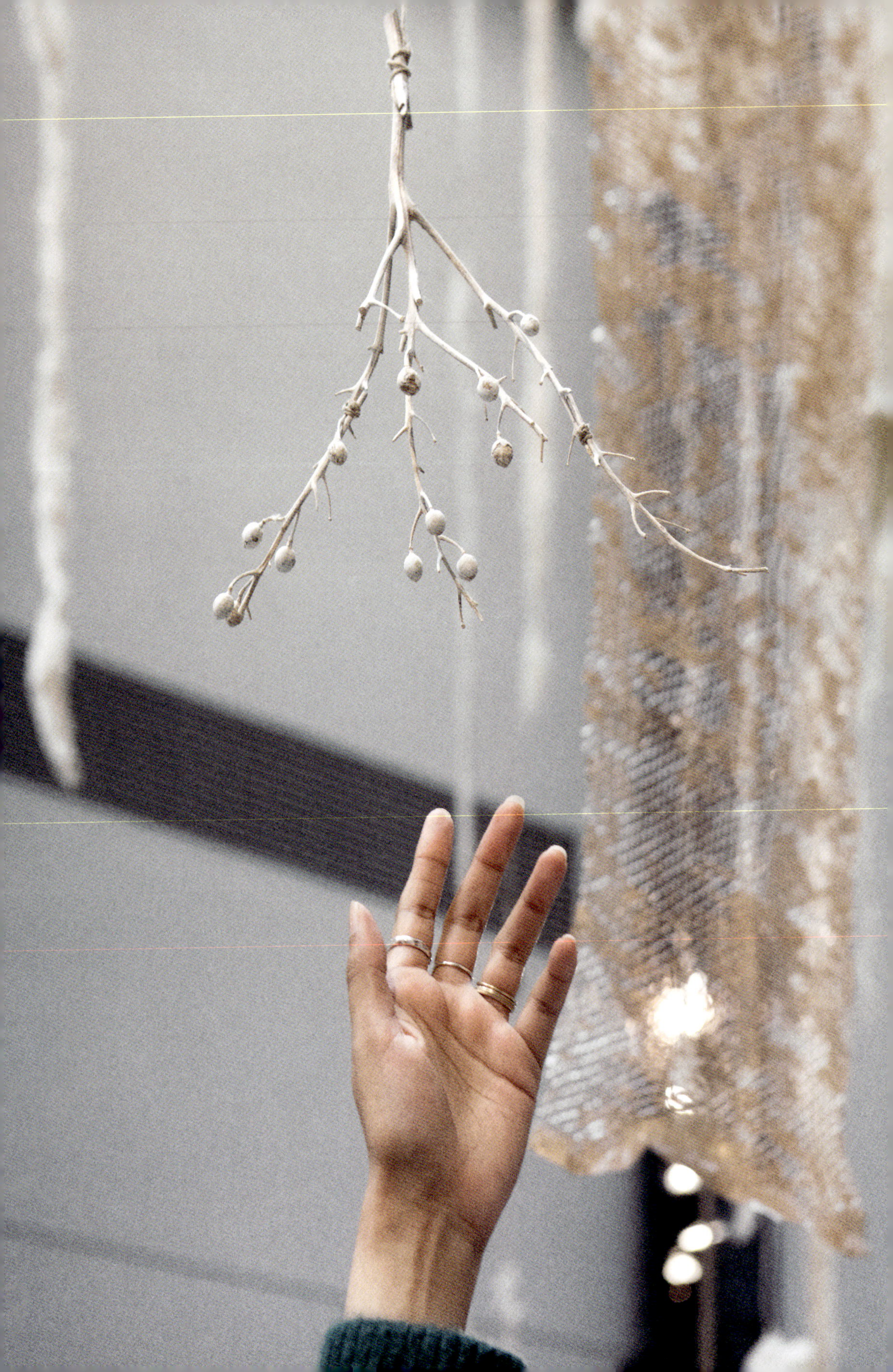

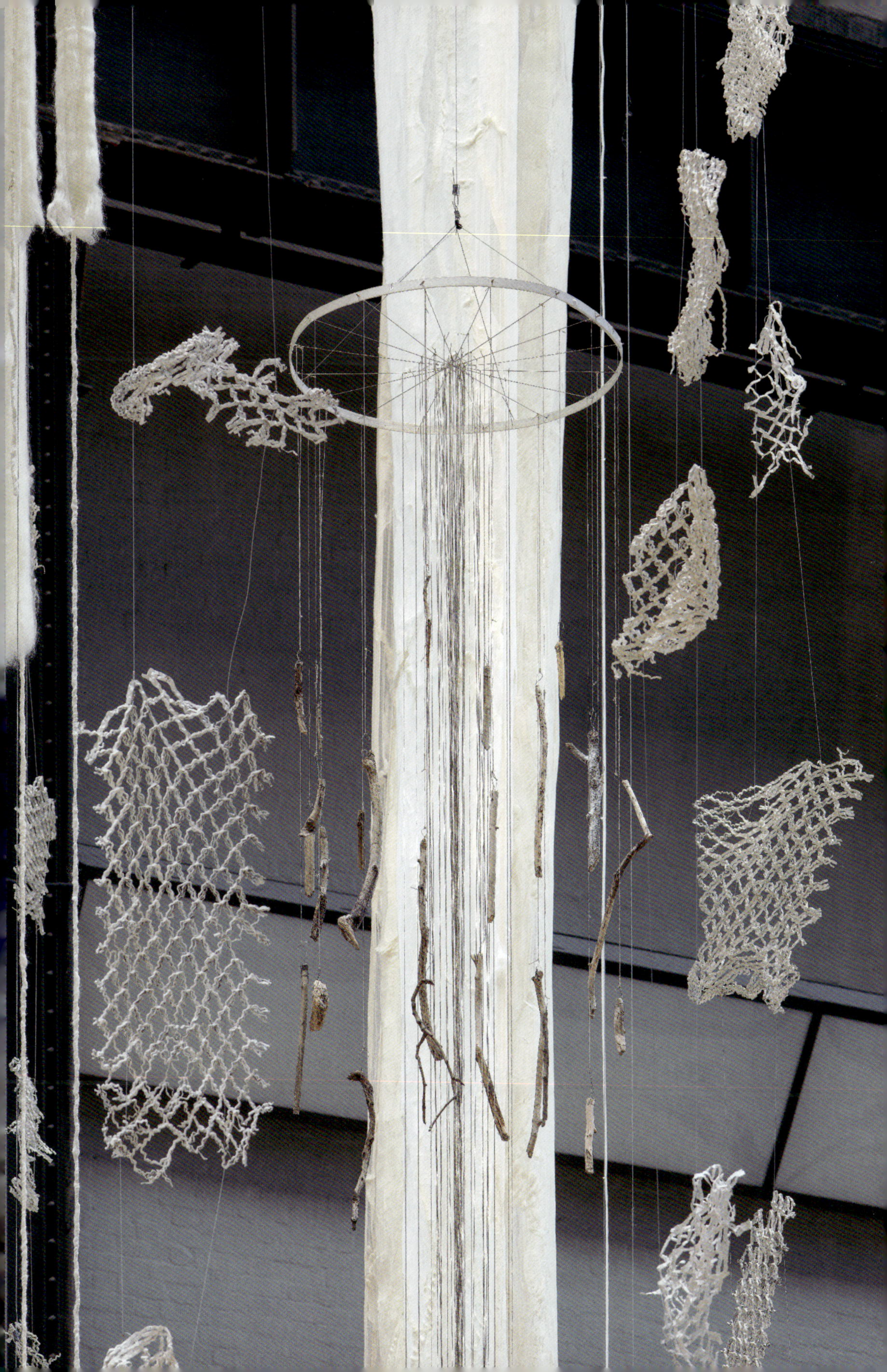

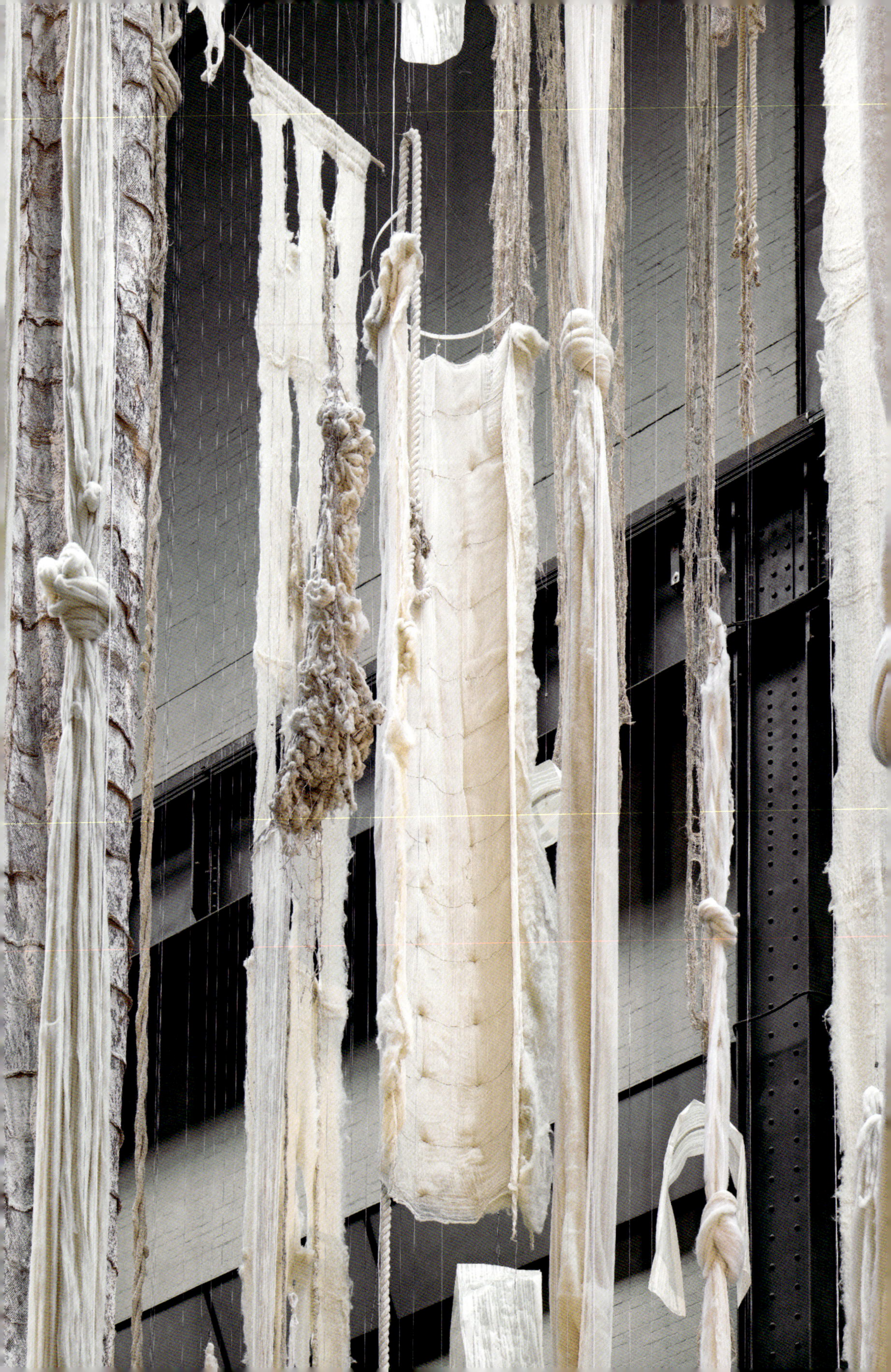

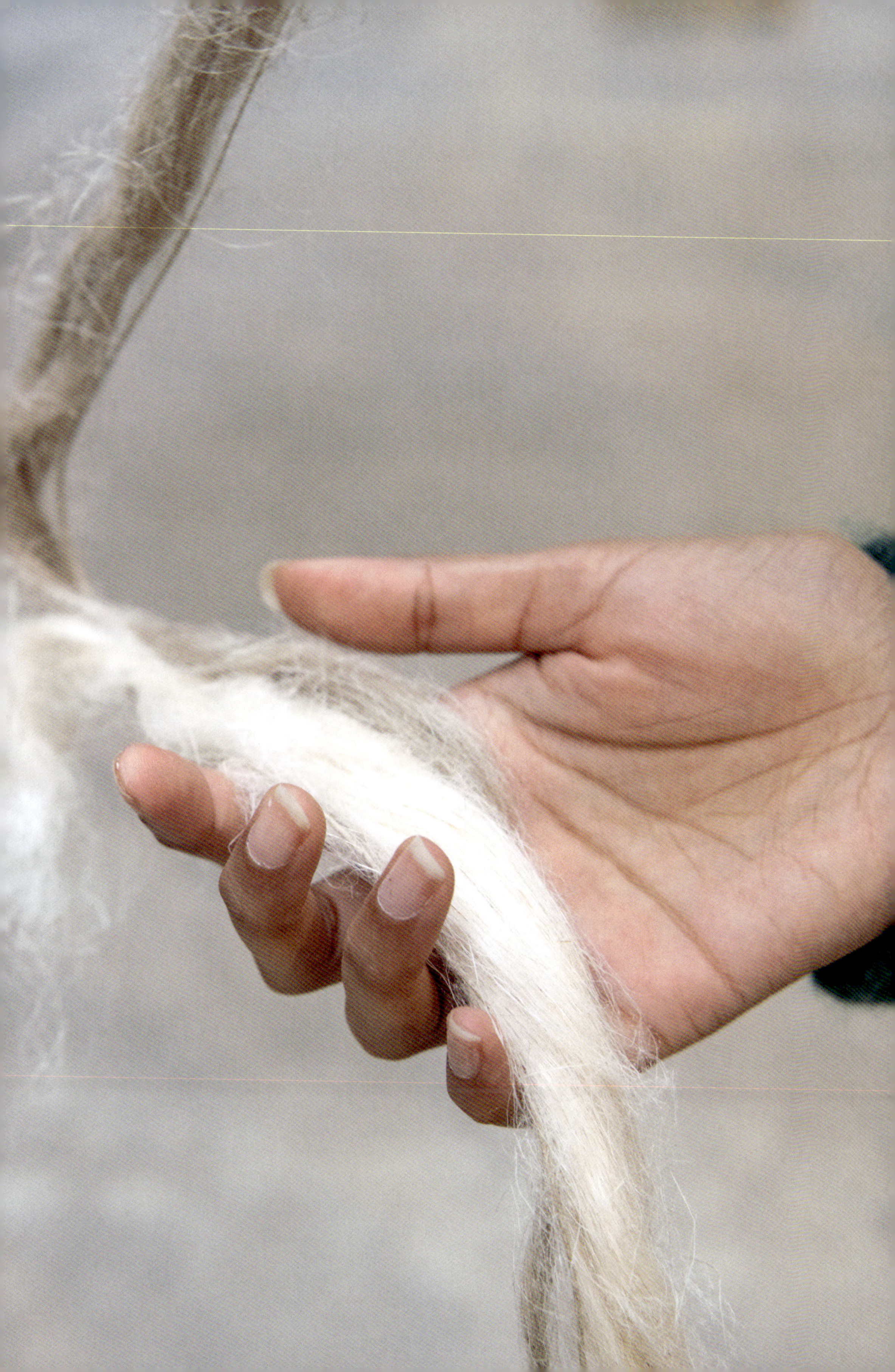

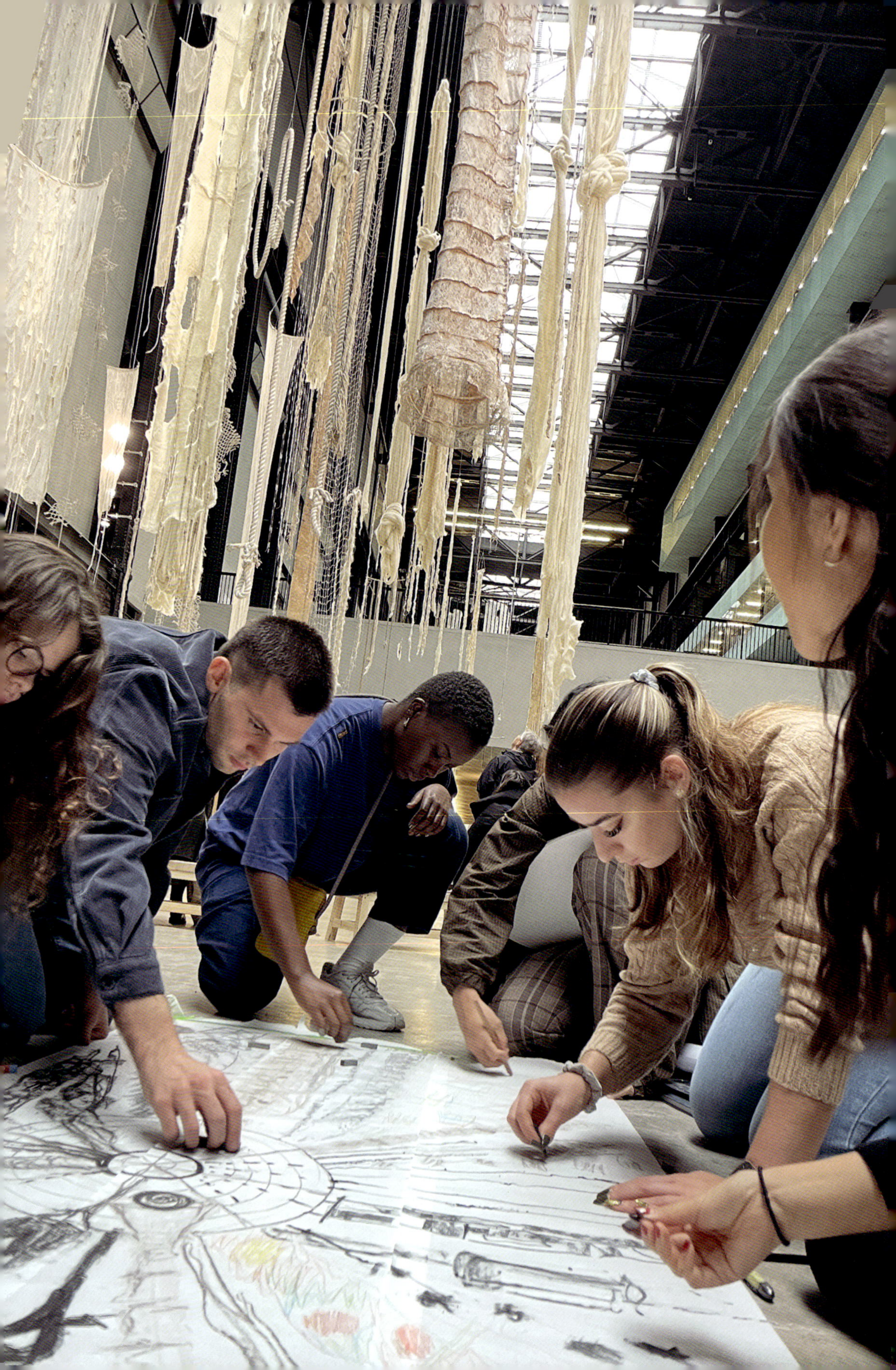

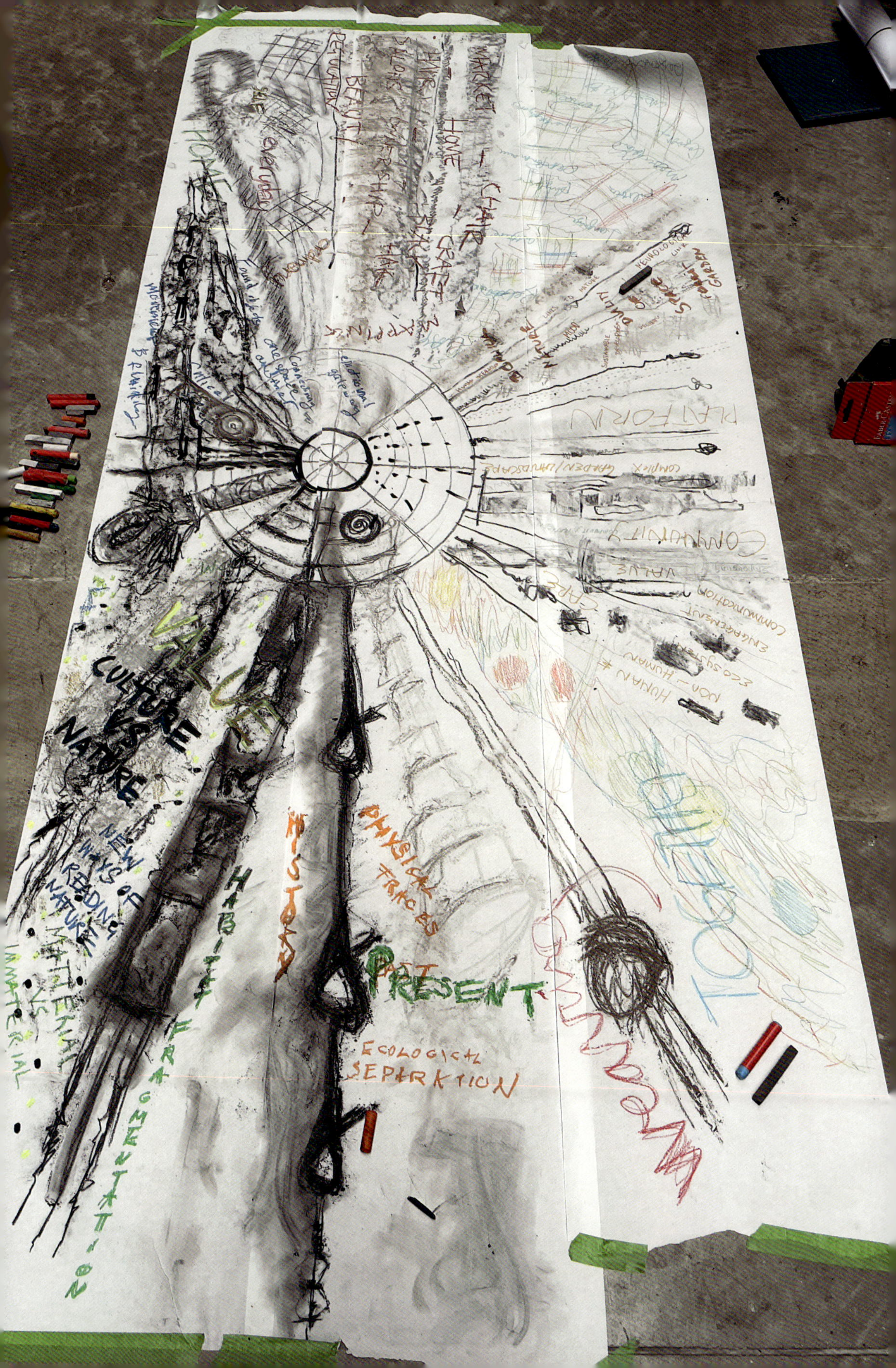
MARKET
HOME
CHAIR
CRAFT
HAIR SALON
TURN
BEAUTY
HOME
RELAXATION
VALUE
CULTURE IS NATURE
NEW WAYS OF READING NATURE
MATERIAL VS IMMATERIAL
FRAGMENT #1 + 02
HABITAT
HISTORY
PHYSICAL TRACES
PRESENT
ECOLOGICAL SEPARATION
PLATFORM
GARDEN
COMPLEX GARDEN / LANDSCAPES
COMMUNITY
VALUE
COMMUNICATION
ENGAGEMENT
ECO-SYSTEM
HUMAN - NON-HUMAN
TOGETHER
COMMON

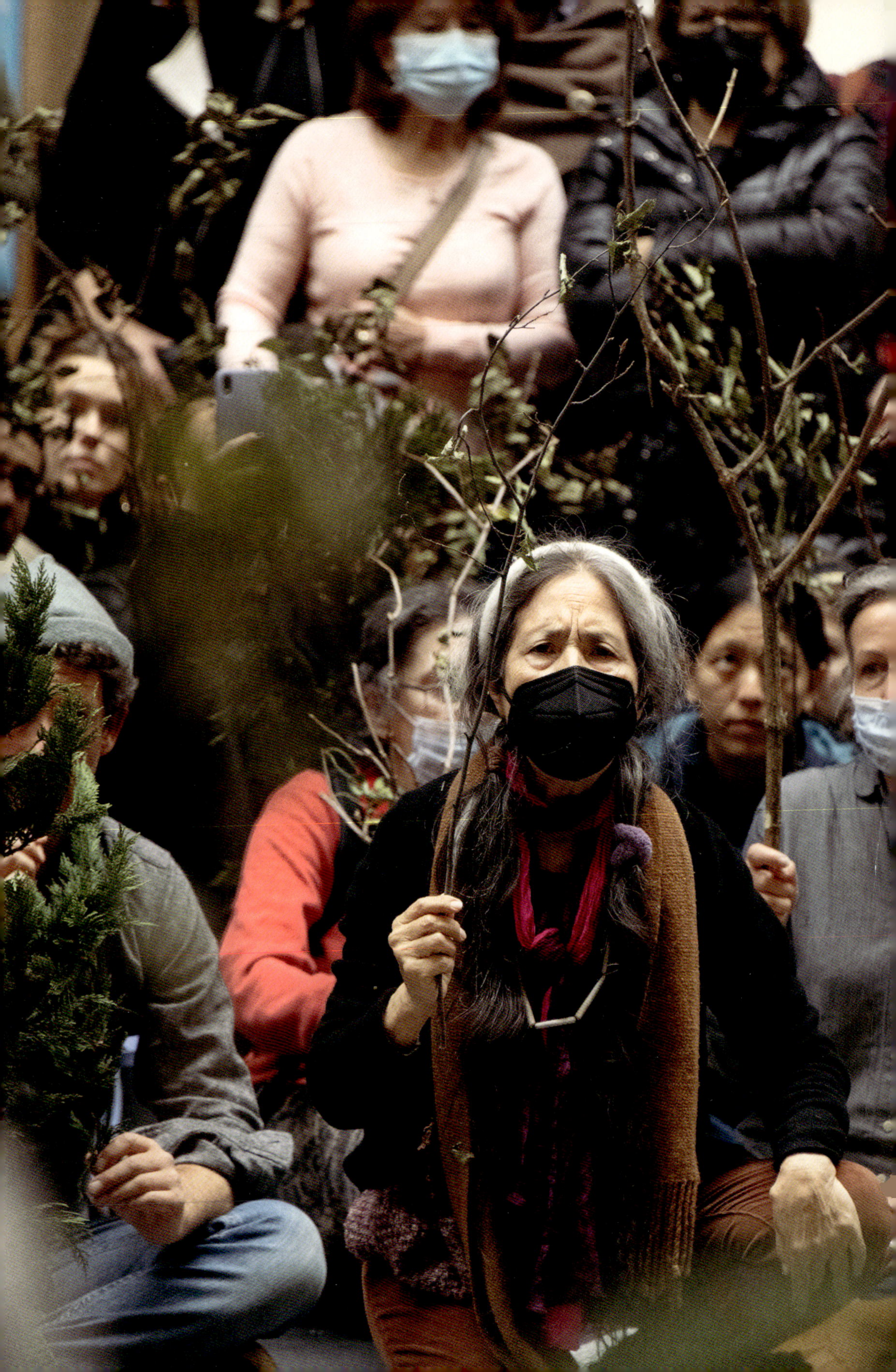